A WORLD OF MY OWN

A WORLD OF MY OWN

The Chipping Campden Diaries
of Christopher Whitfield F.S.A.
1923 – 1941

Edited and annotated by Paul Whitfield

Cover illustration: drawing by Margaret Smith, 1926

Published by Endymion Publications
1, The Manor, Mickleton, Gloucestershire, GL55 6RZ

Printed and bound in Great Britain by MPG Biddles Ltd., King's Lynn

ISBN 978-0-9571531-0-3

*'The only personal survival after death
is in the memory of those who still live.'*

Christopher Whitfield, 1926.

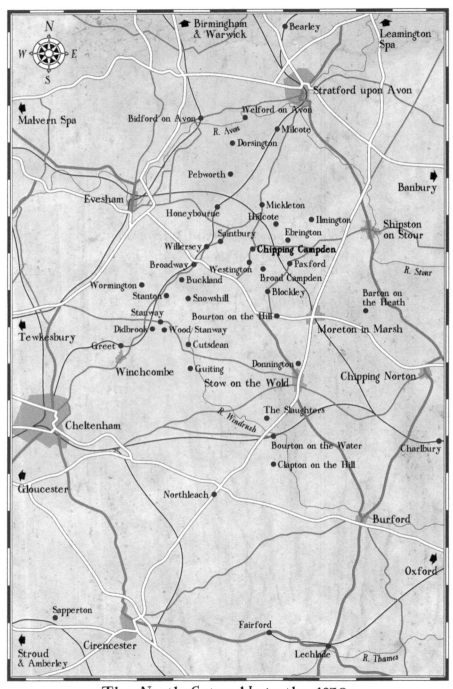

The North Cotswolds in the 1930s

~ Introduction ~

My father Christopher Gilbert Whitfield was born in Birmingham in 1902 and was an only child. His father Gilbert was from a Birmingham manufacturing family, originally arriving from the North Welsh borders in the mid 18th century. They were occupied mostly in metal industries such as safe-making and latterly the manufacture of tubular bedsteads. The family business, founded in 1849, was S.B. Whitfield & Co. in Watery Lane, situated on the border between Digbeth and Bordesley, to the east of the city centre.

His mother was Edith Chatwin and the Birmingham Chamberlain dynasty were distant cousins. The senior branches of the family – including several aunts – lived comfortably at Edgbaston, Leamington and Malvern.

Gilbert and Edith Whitfield were enthusiasts of the 'simple life'. They lived at Hatton, near Shrewley, Warwickshire and then at Fowgay Hall (recently demolished) in what was still-rural Solihull. Finally, after a brief sojourn in Calthorpe Road in Edgbaston, they moved in 1909 to the 'quaint' half-timbered Manor Cottage in the village of Bearley, near Stratford-upon-Avon. They collected old oak furniture, pottery and curios, and ran a small early Rover car, and later a more powerful Vulcan.

A strong formative influence in my father's youth was Barry Jackson's Birmingham Repertory Company, (originally the Pilgrim's Players) of which his aunt Margaret ('Margot') Chatwin was one of the leading players; she had started her stage career with the d'Oyly Carte company. In his youth my father went to the theatre in Birmingham and Stratford several times a month and knew many of the Birmingham Repertory Company. Another important influence was Oliver Baker, the artist, antiquarian and designer for Liberty, who lived in Bearley. My father's *History of Chipping Campden* (1958) was dedicated to him.

My father was sent in his teens to Stanley Wood's school, Dinglewood, at Colwyn Bay, North Wales: his grandparents lived in the town. Stanley Wood was a Quaker scholar and critic, notably in the field of Shakespearian studies. His wife was Winifrid Smith, the youngest daughter of C.H. Smith

---

of Didbrook, Gloucestershire, who was land agent or sub-agent for several landed estates in the area – notably for Lord Wemyss at Stanway, but also for the exiled heir to the French throne the Duc d'Aumale (later d'Orléans) at Wood Norton near Evesham. Winifrid, very attractive and lively despite increasing deafness, was twenty-four years younger than her husband and mother to two sons and four daughters. My father – twelve years her junior – fell in love with her while still a teenager; and this adolescent passion, which in time was reciprocated and consummated, persisted for some eighteen years. This unusual relationship was the driving force in his life in his twenties, amounting at times almost to mania. The evidence suggests that Stanley Wood was complaisant, as his had probably become a *mariage blanc;* yet he must have suffered great pain over the years.

The affair moved into a more serious stage at about the time that my father's mother Edith died in 1923, aged only forty-six, from complications following Graves' Disease. His father (with whom he was already on poor terms) went downhill quickly, abandoning the cottage at Bearley for a woman (a serial bigamist, as it turned out) at Wolverhampton, spending everything that he had and running into debt. Thereafter my father had little contact with him. More and more responsibility for the family business fell on my father's shoulders, although still in his early twenties. The tribe of aunts and cousins in Leamington and Malvern had to be kept in dividends, and the workforce, with whom my father warmly sympathised, in employment.

His response to all this was his liberating retreat into Campden, where he dreamed of living the literary life, although obliged to go to Birmingham to work. His distaste for the city is evident in the diaries; his desire to rid himself of 'The Works' and live independently is a constant theme in the diary. Less obvious is his undoubted competence as a man of business, a side of his character that he tended to conceal.

On the evidence of the diaries, it is difficult to resist the conclusion that Winifrid was more than somewhat manipulative, however vulnerable through her unhappy marriage and her increasing deafness; and that my father found not only love and pleasure through the relationship, but also (by his own admission) a mother-substitute. Yet when the Woods retired to Campden after the War they remained on friendly terms with my father.

A mechanical bent ran in the Whitfield male line. An uncle of my father's, James Whitfield, was a partner of Frederick Lanchester, the pioneer car manufacturer, and an early model conveyed him to his christening. When he was eighteen my father assembled his own car, known as 'The Fluke'. This was succeeded by a machine called Wigan-Barlow (a model produced in Coventry for only a couple of years) which made possible his new life in Chipping Campden. Possession of a car was rare in Campden at the time[1], and gave my father the freedom not only to commute (via Honeybourne) to Birmingham but also to range far and wide over the Cotswolds and beyond, and to give lifts to many friends in Campden on various jaunts and jollities.

In 1939 my father bought the site of the Tithe House from Ben Chandler, a wealthy American immigrant from New Hampshire, who had acquired it to prevent its development. The building of the house, which was designed by Norman Jewson, in the earliest days of war forms a large part of the later years of the diary. Ben Chandler was greatly interested in the Arts and Crafts movement and gave considerable support to the preservation of Chipping Campden, and to Fred Griggs, the artist, whom he quietly helped financially. His (second) wife was Frances Robbins, who came from ancient local stock: her mother was an Izod and her father farmed Top Farm at Weston-sub-Edge.

The Chandlers had restored and lived in fine houses in Broadway and South Littleton and came to live briefly in Campden at Westcote House in the High Street before restoring and settling at Hidcote House three miles north of the town, in the mid-1920s. After 1945 they moved to Pike Cottage, Westington, which they already owned.

My father married the Chandlers' daughter Audrey in January 1942, at which point the diaries cease. I arrived in December that year; my sister Judith in July 1945. In 1947 the family moved to the Malt House, Broad Campden as the Tithe House had become too small for a growing family. My father died there in 1967 and my mother, by then an invalid, returned to the Tithe House five years later under the terms of an informal agreement with the owners, and enlarged it. She died there in December 1993.

---

1   Cutts's Garage in Campden opened in 1921. It flourishes still.

From my father's very copious diaries I have selected these extracts to show how he reacted to life in Chipping Campden: how the town shaped his life and writing, and how he chronicled its wide range of characters from fox-hunting gentry to sprout-pickers; artists to soldiers; farmers, tradesmen, craftsmen and writers and members of the Home Guard. Spanning a period of eighteen years, they end with the approach and grim realities of the Second World War and his completion of the Tithe House opposite St James' Church, his ideal bachelor home: there can be few private houses in England with the date 1940 carved on the keystone.[2]

Much of the incidental detail in these diaries gives a vivid sense of what life was like for a young bachelor of modest means in pre-war England. I have tended to leave this in, for it is from every day details such as the price of things that history can be understood. The diaries also dispel any impression that a busy love-life before marriage is more or less of more recent times, as implied by Philip Larkin's famous lines in 'Annus Mirabilis' (1967). As I have omitted much that is devoted to his relationship with Winifrid Wood, so have I excised nearly everything relating to fox-hunting; this became, from about 1929, a passion of a different kind, occupying much space in the diaries, and forms a valuable and lyrical – and possibly unique – record of the pre-War North Cotswold Hunt. However, in both cases I hope I have left a representative selection.

My father's love of Campden and his shrewd and sympathetic observation of country life show not only in his private diaries and poetry, but in his published works: notably *A World of One's Own* (1938), his *History of Chipping Campden* (1958) and *Robert Dover and the Cotswold Games* (1962). He also left several novellas and volumes of poetry, some such as *Mr Chambers & Persephone* (1937), privately published by his friend Christopher Sandford's Golden Cockerel Press, that attest to his love of the country and passionate observation of nature. (A bibliography is included on pages 261–2 for those who wish to pursue his works.) But he never became the independent writer that as a young man he had dreamed of: his attachment to the lyric style and the experience of war saw to that, as well as the responsibilities of marriage and fatherhood never imagined before the war, but doubly present by its conclusion.

---

2   It was the last complete work by Norman Jewson. The carving was executed by Charles Blakeman.

The diaries were kept in manuscript, and were typed up by my father himself at the end of the War. Although handsomely bound in cloth with calf spines, the five volumes contain cheap and now yellowing paper, flecked with bits of straw and other signs of the austerity of those years. There were later, more fragmentary diaries, which I remember reading after his death, but these have sadly disappeared. I have, where necessary, tidied up occasional spelling mistakes, abbreviations and proper names, but left such period indicators as the use of 'to-day' and 'to-morrow'. In the footnotes I have tried to summarise the many interesting people my father met, referred to or corresponded with. Where possible, facts have been double checked, but I apologise for any inaccuracies or omissions. In a couple of instances I have referred to someone by an initial only, as there may be family still living in or near Campden.

These extracts from my father's diaries conclude when he was only in his fortieth year. Therefore they do not purport to be a complete picture of the man, but rather of a relationship between a young, sensitive, and poetic incomer to a place that became muse, friend and almost parent to him as he matured. This record of his life and feelings, taken as witness to Campden as it was for the two decades before the onset of the Second World War, will add a useful layer to the history of a lovely town. Chipping Campden deserves not only admiration and nostalgia, but the will of those who love it to preserve it through inevitable change, by means of knowledge and sensitivity as has mostly been its good fortune to receive these last hundred years. The diaries also reveal a multi-faceted picture of a town and a way of life that have changed out of almost all but superficial recognition in much less than a century. There will be few alive now who remember my father or the Campden described here; but those who do will find it greatly changed, as indeed I do, having known it all my childhood and youth, and having recently retired nearby.

I wish to record my thanks to Dr. Jerrold Northrop Moore for his invaluable encouragement and much needed editorial skills, without which my task would have been much harder. Judith Ellis of the Campden and District Archaeological and Historical Society (CADHAS) has been particularly generous with her time and help, as have other members of CADHAS. My brother-in-law, David Wyndham Smith, has saved me from several errors of fact and typos, as has Alan Crawford. Arthur Cunynghame has skilfully converted my typescript into book form, and Jeff Edwards created the map. It is my intention that the original volumes should eventually be lodged, together with my father's other papers, at the Bodleian Library, Oxford. His Shakespearean papers are already available at the Birthplace Trust in Stratford upon Avon.

Paul Whitfield
Mickleton, 2012

Christopher Whitfield seems to have been acquainted with Campden by the time his diaries first mention the town in 1922, probably through visits to the Smith family at Didbrook and Wood Stanway.

~ 1922 ~

July 24th   I have been to [Chipping] Campden, staying with the Allcotts[3], whom I met through the Oliver Bakers[4] at Bearley, and who are artists. He paints and she binds books, and I envy them their simple, happy life. Campden was as calm and quiet as ever. Even the rain fell in a peaceful, soft way there.

---

3   Walter H. Allcott, RWA, RBSA, 1880-1951. Artist.
4   Oliver Baker, 1856-1939. Artist, antiquary and designer for Liberty. CW's parents lived at Manor Cottage.

April 9ᵗʰ   Yesterday I went with Margaret Smith[5] to see a Mr Wade[6] at Snowshill. He comes from the West Indies and is very dark, sallowish. He sleeps on a hard Welsh bed with sliding doors and beautifully carved work around it. Lying about, on the stone window sills, on tables, on chairs, are a thousand priceless small things: books, carved skulls, icons, portraits. Everywhere there is an atmosphere of age and antiquity, but the whole effect is one of useless chaos and misdirected energy; his little puppet shows, that work when you open a door into a room; his minutely carved work, villages with people who walk in them; bird cages without birds, used to cover the bread bowl; carvings, paintings; are all wonderful, but after you have looked at them for a time you wonder why on earth he has taken such immense trouble to achieve what really amounts to nothing.

He wears long black hair, tweed breeches, and shoes with copper buckles and red heels. One can imagine him wandering about the house in the dusk, alone, slowly stopping here and there. He has, in the main part of the house, in which he does not live, a wonderful collection of costumes and dresses, hundreds of them, all arranged in glass wardrobes and drawers. The quantity of the work and its quality are stupendous.

---

5   1876-1955. Artist, eldest daughter of C.H. Smith of Didbrook. Her portrait drawing of CW is on the cover of this book.
6   Charles Paget Wade, 1883-1956. Architect, collector and eccentric, he inherited a considerable fortune based on sugar and devoted his life to Snowshill Manor, which he gave to the National Trust in 1951.

February 18th I have spent two nights of supreme discomfort on a small camp bed, the clothes of which came off if one moved, in Allcott's room. Each night he tickled my nose and tucked me up, no more. He is quite innocent, but strange when one is alone with him. We went to the [Alec] Miller's[7] dance at the Town Hall, an odd, fancy dress party, rather than a dance, and the dancing was awful. I went in an Elizabethan costume of Oliver Baker's and with my beard was quite a success. Several people would not believe that it was not part of my costume, stuck on with glue. F.L. Griggs, the etcher[8], to whom Winifrid [Smith] was half engaged when she was a young girl, was not at the dance, and I was sorry, for I had hoped to meet him, and tell him I knew them all at Didbrook. He and his wife were said to be housebound by the two babies having whooping cough. I met a man called Dick Blaker[9], who writes, but who looks as though he will be only moderately successful, and a lot of other nice people; painters and weavers and such folk. The Millers are nice, and he is charming. I am beginning to know quite a lot of people in Campden, and there are many who are interesting, and I am thinking of living there. I shall try it in the summer I think, for a month, and see if I like it. The long train journey puts me off a little, but I could manage it. If I like it I should get two unfurnished rooms there and take my furniture from Bearley. It takes me half the evening to get it out of my mind, and before I have done anything it is time for bed.

February 19th The Campden idea crystallises in my mind and seems to be definitely settled now. It only awaits rooms and those I should get and go there about May. I spend hours planning what my rooms will be like and how they will be furnished; how I shall get marigolds to put in them; and how I shall face living on my own, which I have never done before.

The theatre, with the closing of the [Birmingham] Repertory and my going to Campden, will drop out of my life now. But it has meant a very great deal to me. It has been a sort of little university to me, the Repertory. I have

---

7   Alec Miller, 1879-1961. Woodcarver with the Guild of Handicraft, later specialising in portraits. Emigrated to California in 1939.
8   Frederick Landseer Griggs, A.R.A., 1876-1938. Renowned etcher and illustrator, a link between Samuel Palmer and the twentieth century neo-romantics. See Jerrold Northrop Moore, *F.L. Griggs, The Architecture of Dreams*, Oxford, 1999.
9   Richard Sidney Blaker, 1893-1940, author of thirteen novels.

---

found friends and people I could talk to there, and I have seen plays I should never have seen any other way, except perhaps in London. Apart from all the modern plays and operas and things, I have seen there, and at Stratford and in London, all of Shakespeare acted excepting *Henry VI* and *VIII*, and *Troilus and Cressida*, which not many people have achieved by the age of twenty-two.

March 6th Campden will do a great deal of good for me. I have a definite offer of rooms in the main street, which I shall see about on Sunday, and there are others in view.

March 11th I went to a play at Campden with the Allcotts, written by a man called Blair-Fish[10], a rather fantastic thing of Spirit and Earth that needed a [Walter] de la Mare to write it with mastery and perfect art. As it was the rhymes were awkward and the whole thing seemed to have been written hastily and carelessly. It was a children's play, acted chiefly by children, who, in contrast to their self-conscious mothers and elder sisters, were charming.

March 18th In Campden I have found and decided to take a wooden house which was an Estate Office and is now empty. It is in Father Bilsborrow[11], the Catholic priest's orchard at the back of Campden, and it has three small rooms, one of which is the hall, and is all wood, with a corrugated iron roof. I propose to build on a garage, kitchen and lavatory and it can be made quite charming. I shall arrange about it on Sunday next, when I go over. Bower, the local agent has offered it to me

I feel flat and a little colourless. I want to be on Dover's Hill at Campden, and I am in my office at work. I do know I shall ultimately have to leave all this if I am to do anything more than dabble in literature, but that will all come as it may, and by the time it does come – in five years or so I reckon – I shall probably have enough money to keep me alive in a wooden house like the one I have seen.

March 20th I hear from the Allcotts that they have found me someone to wake me up in the mornings and cook for me and see to my wooden house.

---

10   Wallace Wilfred Blair-Fish, 1889-1968. Amateur poet and socialist, he lived at Broad Campden at Sedgcombe House, converted from a barn for him by Joe Warmington.
11   Father Henry Leeming Bilsborrow, 1873-1948. Priest at St Catharine's Church, Chipping Campden.

They send measurements of it and I have made a plan of the alterations, and estimate the cost to be about £40.

March 25th I have given up the idea of the wooden house at Campden, and have got two rooms and a garage and light and coal and breakfast and dinner for £2 per week in an old house in the street. It belongs to an architect called Woodsend, and he is going to live in part of the house [Peyton House], with Bower, the local agent and his wife, and I am having two rooms at the back. My sitting room is 24ft by 18ft and has a separate flight of stone steps leading up to it from the garden, and a charming porch. It is half-timbered at the back, unusual in a Cotswold house, and has a long stone mullioned window and a carved Tudor fireplace. There is a little bedroom next door, and a bathroom next to that, which will be used also by the others.

A period of serious illness (pneumonia) and convalescence intervenes. By the end of May CW had moved from Bearley to Campden, complete with his mother's two cats, staying initially at the Allcotts while the work at Peyton House was finishing.

May 28th I have been to Stratford to see the doctor, and took with me Kitty and Biddy Slattery, the daughters of the woman who lives at Greville House here, as superficial companions. I am going to be painted by Allcott this afternoon in Huish's[12] *(sic)* studio at the back of the High Street.

May 29th Mrs Allcott tells me that she has had a 'wonderful dream' in which she seems to have been jumping off chests of drawers over and over again, then slowly falling. [Allcott] has started my portrait, and the sketch seems good. We are going to see Gere[13] at Painswick on Sunday. The Woodroffes[14] came in last night and we go to tea there on Saturday. He is an artist and stained glass worker like Payne[15] at Amberley.

May 30th Already I begin to feel the quiet influence of Campden working on me, and feel sure it will be good for the kind of work [poetry] I want to

12   Wentworth Huyshe, 1847-1934, journalist and antiquarian. He was stepfather to the Hart brothers. See T.F.G. Jones, *The Various Lives of Wentworth Huyshe,* CADHAS 1998.
13   Charles March Gere, RA, RWS, 1869-1957. He lived at Painswick from 1904 with his half-sister Margaret, 1878-1965, also a painter.
14   Paul Vincent Woodroffe, 1875-1954. Stained glass artist and illustrator. A devout Catholic, he lived at Westington, just outside Campden, from 1904 to 1935.
15   Henry Albert Payne 1868-1940. He married Gere's sister Edith, a painter.

do. I have another twelve days [convalescence] before I go back to work in Birmingham, and I ought to get a lot done in them. It is an opportunity I shall not get again for some time.

June 1st In my new rooms and very happy there, and to be my own master. The day is dark and overcast with a kind of midwinter gloom, the car, left out all night, and damp with the rain that has poured down, will not start. Allcott is here and I could knife him for his facetious optimism if it were worth while.

June 2nd Yesterday was ghastly and our tempers simmered and bubbled but did not quite boil. We went to Huish's studio and talked; Hudson[16], a painter with a tin leg, whom I rather like, and who was at the Slade with Margaret [Smith] and lost his leg in the war; Allcott; a Mr Cust and his friend; and myself. How the men gossip in a small place like this. Fred Griggs seems to be their chief butt, because they seem to think he keeps himself to himself too much, and has not enough sense of humour about himself; also, I gather, because, having no fundamental dignity, he is forced to maintain an unnatural reserve as a substitute for it, which upsets them. I have not met him yet, and want to badly, because he knew Winifrid as a girl, and all the Smiths at Stanway.

Last night I went to dinner at the Slatterys at Greville House, the two girls full of polite accomplishments; the piano, German, French, Italian and a superficial knowledge of art and literature. Katherine the eldest 20, and Biddy [Bridget] 18. There is another still at a convent school. Mrs S. echoes the last syllable one addresses to her every time one speaks to her. Before I knew they were Catholics I was praising Oliver Cromwell, but carefully changed to a discussion on sonnets when I saw their feelings. They are also Irish – Birmingham Irish – and their uncle is one Sir Martin Melvin. Campden seems to accept me as one of its freaks now, and I begin to be asked to tea parties and dinners. My Father is coming down to see me tomorrow.

June 3rd Last night we went to dinner with the Budgeons, people who came over from Ireland during the 'troubles' and settled at Broad Campden, quite charming, but a little dull. They all played Mah-Jong and I, being useless at games and hating them, looked on. Mrs Budgeon is an 'enlightened woman'

16   William Knowles Hudson, 1895-1940s. Painter who had lost his leg in the Great War.

and lets one see it; very melodramatic; descended from Mrs Siddons[17], and like her. Allcott has done some very good portraits of their children on wood panels with gilded lettering and gold and blue frames, and dark blue backgrounds.

June 4ᵗʰ My God, what a wife to have. Mrs Allcott seems to have turned a slight cold into an inattention neurosis, and retires at odd moments to bed during the day. I had to take her to see the doctor, and now she has asked me to take her out 'to get the air'. He does not see that she is perfectly alright, and gives her all the sympathy she unconsciously seeks by assuming illness. She is full too of pseudo-intellectual chit-chat and a horrid affected indefiniteness, but she is extraordinarily kind and well-meaning. She binds books, and her sister at Broadway weaves.

June 6ᵗʰ I begin to notice the influence of Campden on my writing. It improves it, as also does the long time I have had in which to be free and my own master. In some ways this illness and its aftermath have been the happiest times I have had for years.

June 7ᵗʰ I am taking the Allcotts to Painswick to see Gere today, and tomorrow the fetes and festivities of Whitsun begin here. I am taking the two Slattery girls to Moreton [in Marsh] this morning.

June 12ᵗʰ I am beginning to grow used to the works again, and in a week or two I shall have become settled into the new groove as I was before I was ill, chafing more perhaps, and hating it more, with Campden as a greater contrast, but bearing it and going on with it all.

I have arranged to put my car at Honeybourne station, and by leaving Campden at 8.30 I get here [Birmingham] at 10, and I catch a train at 6 and get home just after 7, so each evening I have four or five hours of freedom. I shall still not come on Saturdays, and my Father has not made any objection to this.

June 13ᵗʰ My Father has let me have £50 to pay my bills with, and I have paid them all and have £10 left over. I feel free and materially secure because I have £20 in the bank, a motor car, some books, and some furniture.

---

17   The renowned eighteenth century actress, painted by Gainsborough.

June 16th I am happier now than I can ever remember being. Last night I went out after dinner, up on the hill above Campden and sat on a grey wall there watching the evening close, and the fields and trees and hedges breathing their gentle breath of sleep. The birds, all singing their last songs, were suddenly stilled, and only the voices of people in the road below came up to me. I felt a huge and peaceful gladness and I gave myself up to the land that I love.

The summer passes without specific reference to Campden. With the anniversary of his mother's death (15th August 1923) and his all-enveloping feelings for Winifrid Wood, CW experiences something approaching a nervous collapse. He finds refuge in writing poetry, but frustration also. In September comes the first contact with the Griggs family:

September 8th Mrs Griggs: I have now met her, but he didn't come to tea at the Aylings and sent her to apologise for him. She wore a dark black sateen dress well made, but home made, and a mauve hat which looked very commonplace. She looked like a well educated shiny faced young governess or nurse out to tea on Sunday. Her hat was awful, small and all wrong with her black dress. She has a good figure, considering the [two] children she has had, but is not pretty. She is rather timid and virginal and her conversation seems to echo the instruction of a larger mind, which knew what it meant, but she didn't. An obedient, chaste wife, I should think.

September 9th I did nothing last night but play around in the social atmosphere of Campden. I went to see the Blakers *(see footnote p. 24)* and we went for a walk in the moonlight and talked about ghosts. There was an American there who is learning to etch from Fred Griggs, and he seems interesting. His name is Komstock[18] *(sic)*.

September 13th Fred Griggs last night. On a first impression I like him very much. He is far and away the most interesting man in Campden. I made him laugh twice and we got on quite well, and he asked me to go and see him any evening I liked and said he wanted to see my poems. All the time at the Slatterys I was conscious of him as the only person who mattered in the room, and several times we caught each other's eyes. I hope he will tolerate me for I feel I shall find him very valuable to me in many ways.

---

18   Francis Adams Comstock, 1897-1981. American artist and architect. He published a *catalogue raisonné* of Griggs, entitled *A Gothic Vision,* Boston Public Library and The Ashmolean Museum, 1966.

A crisis in the management of the family business in Birmingham, S.B. Whitfield & Co, caused by CW's father's effectively abandoning his post, takes up much diary space in the following weeks, and it is not until October that Campden and Griggs feature once again.

October 3rd This diary acts as a sort of midwife to me, bringing to birth the self that is being created by life, and it brings me back to my proper self after my present days of senseless automatism and business.

I called on Fred Griggs last night and liked him very much, and I think he liked me too. We talked of tradition and art, till Father Bilsborrow came in, when the talk became more general and local. Fred and Nina Griggs are coming to see me tomorrow. I like her better. She has more brain and character than I thought at first, and makes good and subtle jokes, at which he chuckles for a long time after everyone else has finished laughing. His house [Old] Dover's House is full of beautiful things and is damp and the distemper is peeling off the walls. There are marvellous Gimson[19] pieces of furniture and perfect pictures and prints, always in the right place, and his books are amazing, such fine editions and so finely bound. He said, 'I am afraid I have not read any of your work, Mr Whitfield.' I told him that he was in no way to blame, because none of it had been published. He said, 'Well, I must confess that I have a great respect for poets who have never tried to publish any work.' We laughed, but he does not know my longing to be accepted and to get something published, so that I can say to myself that I really am a poet, in the world's sense.

A long and interesting letter from Frank Kendon[20], who writes better letters than his first promised. He is 31, older than I thought, and really seems to like my work.

October 4th Griggs has been in and now, 11 o'clock, has gone. Of course, he soon discovered that I knew Margaret [Smith], from her drawing of [her father] C.H. Smith. He asked after Stanley and Winifrid too, and asked me if I knew Dudley, Winifrid's brother, who died in 1916. Knowing that he had once been engaged to Winifrid made him seem an old friend, and I felt that he was a link with the life at Wood Stanway that I did not know and would give my

---

19   Ernest Gimson, 1864-1919. Architect and eminent furniture designer in the Arts & Crafts style.
20   Frank Samuel Herbert Kendon 1893-1959. Writer and illustrator, he later worked at Cambridge University Press.

eyes to have known, in the days before the war. He was very amusing in his talk and has a keen sense of humour. He has asked me for a poem on Campden, or inspired by it, for his book; an anthology of work about the place[21] and he has poems already by Masefield, Squire, Freeman, Shanks and de la Mare[22] so I shall be in good company. But he has not yet seen any of my poems, only myself. Talking of Allcott and his [drawing] tricks with knives and sandpaper, Hudson, who had come in, said. 'He actually puts them under the tap.' 'Yes,' said Griggs, 'and doesn't leave them there long enough.'

I am so happy here [Campden] when I am clear of business. I must work my way out during the next five years. All day I go about with a sense of autumn richness; the sun on the treetops, as it went down, and lighting up the whole side of the church tower; the peace of the evening; the rooks going overhead, back to Northwick Park; the silence and wordless beauty of the stone houses; the hills; the coloured woods.

October 21st Last night Griggs and Dick Blaker[23] came in. Griggs brought back my poems and stammered some criticism, but would not say that some of them showed great promise[24]. He objected to their occasional obscurity, and suggested that it would be remedied by closer craftsmanship. Which I suppose is true.

Work is dull and tiring. I would give anything for a month at Campden. I love [it] as I have never loved any place; its peace and its simplicity, and its abstraction from this awful tin-can civilisation in which we live.

Over the next few weeks, the obsession with Winifrid Wood seems to calm somewhat, and there is increasing attention to the writing of poetry. Problems in the family business continue, but are gradually resolved, resulting in CW's hoped-for financial security coming closer in prospect.

---

21   Planned over many years, but published posthumously in 1940 (on hand made paper, a remarkable achievement, given the date), Oxford, Shakespeare Head Press. There was to have been a text by Griggs's great friend, the journalist and poet Russell Alexander (1877-1951) while the wood engravings, from Griggs's drawings, were executed by eminent practitioners (B. Sleigh, W.M.R. Quick, C. Housman, A. Buckels). The work was incomplete at his death and was published with an Introduction only by Alexander. For CW's poem, see p. 259
22   Poets writing in the 'Georgian' tradition: the conservative style between the Victorians and Modernism.
23   Richard Sidney Blaker, 1893-1940.
24   In fact, Griggs sent his poems to Percy Withers, and relayed the latter's helpful comments, see Moore, *op. cit.*, p. 165

November 11th I cannot get to sleep at nights now. At one moment it is a poem that keeps me awake, at another Winifrid, at another the works; all teem in my head and clatter about in my brain and will not let me rest.

As winter comes on, Campden takes centre stage.

November 24th Yesterday I returned feeling full and eager and fresh. I wrote till four and then walked to Broad Campden to Blair-Fish's for tea, returned at seven and ate and went to Griggs's where the Bakers[25] were, and Comstock and Hudson. We played novel writing consequences till 11.30, then I walked back down the dark empty street with Hudson, our footsteps waking the sounds of a thousand bygone footsteps of other ages. Hudson came in and stayed till 12.30. I had gone away so precipitately that he had been quite worried about me, thinking as he does that I am a little mad, and when he heard that someone had been found dead on the hills near Snowshill, he had gone white, really thinking it might have been me.

November 27th To-night I go unwillingly to a Cricket Club dance, only willing because I have not worn evening dress for a long time, and want to.

November 29th Last night I spent in social gadding as a stranger from another planet into a world that was unreal because it contained no index of reality – no sign of Winifrid. I went to the dance at 8.30 and danced twelve duty dances with twelve sylphs, ogres, sirens, vixens, witches, virgins, bromides, children, hags, onanists, cows. Then with Hudson's sister Mary who was the best dancer there. We all talked a great deal of nonsense, all round sex, and at about twelve I brought Mary up here to my room and read Keats and Wordsworth and Shelley to her and some poems of my own. Later, back at the dance everyone looked at us and Mrs Slattery and seemed pained by my attentions to anyone not one of her daughters. Comstock started by cutting me, but later began talking to me a lot. I took little notice of him lest I should insult him again. All went on with the restrained silliness of a country dance until 2. Griggs looked on with a worried expression and said 'You know, Whitfield, it all seems the same, and the conversation too seems to be forced down to a monotonous

---

25   Eileen and Leo Baker ran Kingsley Weavers from Westcote House, High Street, 1926-31. Their looms were in Calf Lane behind Dover's House, now The Long House.

---

level by the beastly music'. At two, Hudson, the two Ayling girls[26] and Mary and I came up here to my room and I made tea for them in the kitchen. When I came up with it I found Hudson and Joan kissing behind a curtain set on two tall candlesticks, and Mary and Grace on the settee, Grace one end and Mary full length with her head on Grace's lap.

I gave them their tea and stood by the fireplace watching them all. Then Mary asked me to sit by her and scratch her back, which I did. Then Grace came and sat by us and I scratched her back with my other hand, while Joan and Hudson groaned and sighed and made the chair creak. Later I read them all Shelley's 'West Wind', and at three they all went. Hudson stayed and discussed his sensations until four, and then I went to bed. All the time I felt like a father, cold and detached from those children, but I enjoyed the feeling of being free from all social restrictions, and I enjoyed sitting on the floor and reading to them all.

They have all been in again this morning, and I am going to another dance tonight, still against my will. Now I am going to walk with sandwiches, to let the wind blow away the remains of last night. I have been ten miles, through an enchanted wood, to Blockley and back through Broad Campden. I called at the Allcotts, chiefly because I wanted to sit down, and talked to him a bit. Then to tea at Hudson's rooms, then with him to attend a meeting of the Arts and Crafts Society in Huyshe's rooms, a meeting of twelve incompetent people which, in an hour, did the work of ten minutes and adjourned itself. I went home and slept in front of the fire, and now, after dinner, am going to Mrs New's[27] to a sort of social evening. But it is all cold to one's heart, to be among all these people who make one realise more and more that one is alone. Only Winifrid can ever make me feel not alone.

December 4th Poor Hudson has been here, raving about the war. He met some man who was at Arras with him and it seems to have driven him back into the mental torture of war. He sat and talked for three hours about it and kept going off into a sort of daze and muttering about trenches and nerves and

---

26   Joan and Grace. Joan (1904-93) was a painter in miniatures who took lessons from Griggs. She (or possibly both sisters?) served as model for the figures in his etching *Owlpen Manor*, 1931. See J.N. Moore, op.cit, pp. 228-9.

27   Wife of Oliver New, solicitor, of New & Saunders, Evesham. They lived at Ivy House in the High Street. New had been a protagonist in the 1919 War Memorial dispute. For an account, see J.N. Moore, *op cit,* pp 130-31. Henry Saunders was Griggs's solicitor.

shell fire. It is horrible; a creature, a man born sane and shattered utterly as he is. Drink he says is the only thing that takes his mind off it. Before the war he scarcely drank at all.

December 10th I have been out, round by the Church and Court House, watching the moon trying to break through great masses of white cloud. It was perfectly silent. A moorhen called down by the stream and a cow coughed, and all the trees were frozen by the diffused moonlight. Now my lamp has gone out and moonlight comes in mistily to my room. In the fireplace the dead coals crack and move idly, and a small blue flame flickers about.

December 15th Hudson and I went to Griggs's on Saturday night and we discussed the Arts and Crafts meeting and the gossip of Campden. Dick Blaker was there and was elated by the success of his new novel, *Geoffrey Castleton, Passenger*. He will never do much more than tell a story well though, with rather self conscious wittiness.

A wonderful evening tonight at Griggs's, playing consequences and talking. At 10 o'clock the others went and left Hudson and me drinking whiskies with Griggs in his library upstairs, and talking a mixture of sense and nonsense for an hour. Griggs has started a visitor's book, which we both signed. It is of hand-made paper and bound in vellum. Nina is very clever and amusing and draws caricatures well.

December 21st Yesterday I went [to Birmingham] in the car and took Hudson with me, bought the jade earrings for Winifrid, went to the Art Gallery, had lunch, and went and sat all afternoon at the old Palais de Danse where I used to go so much. We left at six and drove to Stratford, prowled the streets for half an hour, and then went to the Shakespeare for a drink, came home, called at the Aylings', sat there and ate apples and talked, went to Hudson's rooms and ate bread and cheese and drank cocoa, and went and watched the village dance till we could stand the smell no longer.

December 23rd Last night when I was getting out of my bath at 11 a voice called and I looked out of my window. It was Charlie Blakeman[28], the son of

---

28   Charles Francis Blakeman, 1907-1987. Stained glass artist, he trained with Paul Woodroffe and worked for five years as assistant to F.L. Griggs.

Mrs Blakeman Hudson lodges with, who works at Woodroffe's on stained glass work. He said: 'Hudson wants to see you to say goodbye. It's too late isn't it?' I told them to come up and went to my room and opened the door and found Hudson there drunk. He had been sick and stank of beer and sick, and had got to that morbid state when he felt utterly depressed and worthless. The war kept coming back to him and his talk was confused, now repentant, now aggressively defiant against everyone, He cursed Joan Ayling because he said she had made him [get drunk] by being cold to him and not letting him love her lately. He would not come in. At last he went away with Blakeman and I went to bed. The night before I left him quite cheerful, after visiting the Orpens[29] at Broad Campden. What can one do to help him and to save him from the remorse and degradation of it all?

December 31st Now back at Campden, as I crossed the Square after putting the car away, in the biting cold wind, I was glad that I was going to be quite alone in my room and looked forward to it with intense pleasure.

---

29   Richard Caulfield Orpen R.H.A., 1863-1938. Architect, painter in watercolours and caricaturist; brother of Sir William Orpen, the renowned war artist and portraitist.

~ 1925 ~

January 3rd I got up late, about 10.30 and at eleven went out and walked about the street, talking to people and going into different houses at random. I met nearly everyone in Campden except the Griggses, all in the main street, which anyone passing through would have thought dull and deserted. I thus lounged about talking to people till lunch time, had my lunch, and came up here to my room, which seemed restful and quiet, and sat down to write. Everything round me gave me a smug sense of rightness and pleasure, which the grey sky and still bare trees outside increased. I wrote a poem called Winter Landscape and it pleased me. Then I wrote to Winifrid, then went on reading Renan [*The Life of Christ*]. I read for an hour by the crackling wood fire with my cat in its basket in the hearth, then had tea brought up, and went on reading, gave the cat some milk, took it on my knee and talked to it, and read again.

I have lived to-day the life I want to live, a quiet, restful life, with creative idleness as its key. Ah, how much I want it. To-night a dance at the Orpens at Broad Campden; to-morrow another day like this, maybe; then work and the drowning of my spirit in the vast city-machine. But I shall have had at least one perfect, solitary, domestic day such as I dream of.

January 4th A very trying night last night and a queer day to-day. Hudson, when I went to fetch him for the Orpen's dance, was drunk, but he insisted on coming. I would not take him, and at last compromised by arranging to go back and fetch him in an hour. I did so in two hours, having made excuses for him, and found him more sober, but not fit to go out. However, he insisted on coming and threatened to walk there if I did not take him, so I took him, making him apologise for being so late, and to sit quietly until the dance was over. Instead of that, he went about the room shouting that he was drunk and that he had been out celebrating the cricket score against Australia. After a time Mrs Orpen asked me if I could take him home. I got the Aylings to say they must go, and he came too. The two Ayling girls got in the front of the car and I told Hudson to get in the dickey, and he lost his temper and slammed the door and began swearing and hitting the car with his stick. At last he got in someone else's car and I drove the Aylings home. When I got here I found him by the door waiting for me in a state of remorse and tears and had to sit up until half past one, talking to him and listening to him and alternately cursing him and sympathising with him. At last he went home and I went to bed, tired out.

January 5th   Hudson seems to have no sense of the right thing to do, and treats a respectable party like a Slade [Art School] Dance if he feels inclined to, just as he did last night, yet he is perfectly all right and no one could be more charming when he is sober.

It is strange how I am attracted to such people. They seem to need me, while others seem able to go alone. I do not care for Hudson more than many others here, except that he is younger, but I feel drawn to him by a strange bond of pity, and I know that if it meant giving up others or him I should stick to him. One is bound by invisible bonds to those who suffer or who are miserable or who degrade themselves to escape solitude. Yet one's means and one's power are feeble, for when one comes to the final question one stands at a loss for an answer. One can only try to understand and give something, living without an answer oneself.

January 6th   I have eaten too much, or eaten something that has upset me. I am ill and my stomach is cold and feels as though several frozen white mice are chasing each other round it. I have drunk quinine and only eaten toast for lunch.

Last night I could not write, so went for a walk with Hudson. Everyone is tearing about trying to save him; in fact his escapade has made him more popular, specially with women. But I am beginning to dislike the Aylings; they have not behaved well over this affair.

My motto for writing must be: Let no word ever force you to say what you would not, but make your words say what they are unwilling to say, if need be; avoid inversion; write as nearly in the order of speech as you can.

January 10th   Two dances, each ending at three in the morning, and bed until twelve this morning as a result. Then I took Hudson up to the top of Westington Hill in the car and left him there to paint, had lunch, and went for a walk for two hours. Later I went and fetched Hudson, had tea with him, and have since written a sonnet. He has done as good a picture as I have seen of his and it seems to have made him happier.

The Roberts'[30] dance at Dorsington Manor last night was amusing, the people country, farming, hunting people. The women couldn't dance, and the men talked cows and sheep and Brussels Sprouts.

Hudson, who can be quite amusing sometimes: 'I feel like a hare that has been run off its track and got lost.' 'Grace Ayling is the sort of girl who laughs if you eat two sandwiches at once.'

January 11ᵗʰ A perfect January morning, and a feeling that spring has already come. There is no wind, the sky is cloudless, and the birds singing in the garden seem to call out to warm, waking buds and fresh grass and blue sky and larks high above. I cannot believe that it is still winter, and that snow will probably fall soon and whiten the earth. Only the hour lives, and the hour is of spring, and I am happy. I feel clear and decided and I have sloughed off the film of late nights and dances. I am in my own soul again now. This year I feel is the year in which I shall either succeed or fail; either write the best I shall ever write, or go on sluggishly and drift into being a permanent mixture of writing, business, good taste and love of money.

A wonderful day on the hills. Hudson has done another good picture. Tea at Griggs' and the children brought down. Coy lovemaking with Margery, aged one and a half, who kissed me, and long conversations with Griggs and Hudson about painting and writing. It is strange how, after not seeing people for a time, one suddenly becomes at ease with them. It has happened today with Griggs.

January 12ᵗʰ I hate Birmingham to-day with a fierce, ineffective hatred. By the end of this year I should have about £250 saved towards my £3000[31]. I shall have to do better than that or I shall be at it too long. I <u>will</u> escape in

---

30   The Roberts family of Dorsington Manor, Warwickshire, also Birmingham business people, were an important part of CW's business and social life. They were: Reginald Hugh and Margaret Roberts, and their sons Roger and Hugh.

31   The capital sum CW had calculated would give him enough to live independently, worth roughly £400,000 nowadays in terms of average earnings.

five years, whatever happens[32]. Griggs has been trying to make Hudson work more seriously, by encouraging him and advising him. He wants him to get a studio and work for good exhibitions, and to work generally with more object than painting for its own sake, which isn't enough for Hudson, not enough to keep him at it.

January 13th To-day I have made my first investment – £60 worth of Yorkshire Insurance shares. When shall I take the last step to freedom? I dreamt that I had £2000 left me and already possessed £1000 and was free. In my dream I got up and looked out of the window, and the world was incomprehensibly beautiful, a new world, and my gladness was great and wonderful.

January 14th The organ in the Baptist Chapel next door is practising songs of praise with a dreary monotony; it does not rain, but a thick mist makes everything drip, and I feel I cannot breathe. And only on Sunday the air was warm and spring seemed almost here.

January 16th Sleigh[33] is coming down this afternoon and is coming to Campden for the week-end.

January 19th Sleigh has much improved and has become more mature and has lost his Oxford affectation of accentuating every difference between himself and others. I like him better. He seems surprised at the growth of my poetry and says I am either a genius or a bloody fool.

I am going to move to Mrs Blakeman's[34], where Hudson is; two rooms that will be 2/- a week cheaper and more pleasant to live in; lighter and smaller sitting room, and a larger bedroom, but both get more sun. No bathroom though, but that does not matter, as I can always get a bath at the works.

January 20th I have told Mr and Mrs Bower that I am leaving, and they said that they are glad because Woodsend, the architect, whose house this is, is going to sell it, and they have been worried as to where I should go to.

---

32   It was to be almost exactly thirty years.
33   Bernard Sleigh, 1872-1954. Mural painter, stained-glass artist, illustrator and wood engraver. Like his mentor Arthur Gaskin, Sleigh was one of a group of talented decorative artists in Birmingham at the turn of the century, and he was specially skilled in the art of wood engraving.
34   Next to the Catholic School, on the Lower High Street.

January 22nd I am going to move in two or three weeks and start my homo-spiritual housekeeping *chez* Hudson, at Mrs Blakeman's. It is strange how we get on together and, though I have no great opinion of him or his work, I like him. I seem to have stopped his drinking at least for a time and made him paint more. There is no homo-sexuality about our relationship, but I imagine that our reputation in Campden is otherwise, for we are together a lot now. I am glad I am going to move. This room is too big and depressing, and Mrs Blakeman is a woman in a thousand. She is about 60 and one of those simple people who have found wisdom without education, whose heart has great and simple and forgiving under the guidance of her faith — she is a Catholic — in her religion. She reminds me of the nurse in [Proust's] *Within a Budding Grove*.

January 24th The sun shines and I am happy and careless about the inevitable return to Birmingham on Monday. We are going to a dance at the Brampton's at the Norman Chapel [Broad Campden], not with any great enthusiasm.

January 25th The dance last night was quite good, and I met at it a girl called Vere Knox from Springhill House [near Snowshill]. A hard, partly beautiful, partly ugly, but very attractive girl with gold shingled hair who danced with me not only tummy to tummy, but body to body, most engagingly. Utterly selfish, I should think, and hard, taking everything of life in a desperate effort not to give.

January 26th I have stolen a day. When I was called this morning I thought I'd sleep on a bit and catch the late train. I slept and decided when I awoke that I would stay in bed till one and would not go to business at all. I got up at one, slowly dressed and had lunch, and have just been out and bought, with great care, and holiday laziness: a 4d bar of soap; a 2/- wick for my lamp; a 1/- packet of notepaper; and 1/2d worth of blotting paper. Now I have a nice warm fire and a whole free afternoon; no noise; quiet grey roofs; nothing unpleasant to do of necessity; and I feel like a schoolboy who has overstayed his holidays because he has been to a party where there was someone infectious, yet who is not ill himself.

February 2nd Yesterday I spent carrying furniture down the street under the gaze of twenty yokels and a stream of Catholic church goers. Hudson and I sat on a settee in the sun on the grass bank outside the Blakeman's and held a reception. My sitting room is done and looks very nice. The bedroom will be finished next weekend.

I have realised that the Orpens at Broad Campden are more charming than I thought and call for more attention. He is nice and Irish and clumsily kind hearted and she is subtle, fat and refined, with a delightful voice like a soft mist laden wind, and a face which, though not beautiful, has the beauty in it of tender feeling and imagination. Hudson has sobered down well during the last month and they have both been charming to him, though it was there that he appeared drunk last. More removal to-night and to-morrow.

February 3rd I took Hudson into Birmingham to-day. He told me that [Paul] Konody, the Observer critic, who ignored his show in London completely, has now recommended him to Hutchinson's as being very suitable to illustrate high class guide books, and that Hutchinson's have written to him to ask him to do a book on France and Spain. Allcott takes it all as a compliment. He tells me that he is better off now than he has been ever since he had to leave Birmingham, and come into the country on account of his consumptive tendency, in 1916.

February 6th After two days in London I found myself at the works swamped in a mass of accumulated detail work, and have only now got free and home to write. The New English [Art Club] show, Margaret [Smith]'s ceaseless and amusing talking, her studio, a whirl of taxis, a new hat from Hilhouse's, and good-bye to civilisation running after its own tail, once more. Back here there is peace, and I am busy moving books and erecting shelves. I am now penniless, but London has been invigorating. The picture shows; the consciousness of beautiful things all around one; the atmosphere of prosperity; the change, have given me a new life. But it is strange how, each time I go to London, or merge myself in what I call 'civilisation' too much, I feel more and more apart. I feel separate from the flood of life that goes on round me, as though I were a heavier liquid sunk in a lighter. And as I leave, life grows clearer, more purposeful, more whole, the further I get away. I may print a Rhyme Sheet for the Campden Show this summer, but I shall not try to get a book published yet.

February 8th My removal is accomplished and my rooms are charming and I already like them better than the others. I have just carried the slop pail, the towel rail, and my two cats in, been back and had a bath, and received an invitation to go for one any time. And here I am, settled as though I had been here for years. Whenever I move, or arrange furniture I remember my Mother very vividly, for all these things were chosen by her, and I see once more what good taste she had, reminded of it by the way in which all the curtains, cushions, carpets, chairs, tables, go together and settle into a room. I look at the things in my rooms now and recall a thousand soft pictures and scenes of my childhood, with her in them all. Somehow now I do not feel sad that she died so young, for it was time for her to rest. As I think of her the sense of peace and quiet that I find in Campden and its country; the ever changing softness of the sky; the grey roofs; the mellowness outside; the self contained unassertive vitality of the little town; seem to be part of my sense of her. And because I live here and know that she always wanted to, I feel I am nearer to her than I am anywhere else.

February 13th I feel that I have lived for a long time in a semi-darkness, a mass of details, all means to an end, yet so crowded that the end is lost sight of. Now slowly I emerge, for a time at least. Business is better and there is a system growing round me of my own creation there; our overdraft is half what it was a year ago; I feel that at last I have got this ugly dragon under my hand; the work is easier for me because I know it well; 100 men and 50 staff do what I say they shall do; I dare almost say that I have succeeded, or at least begun to; and I feel that this time of striving has done me good and made me stronger. Besides that my rooms are nice, and I get hot buttered toast for breakfast and everything is clean and brightly polished.

February 16th Griggs' criticism of my poems rather patronising, and depressing to me, but after a first depression I have rebelled and now feel gloriously independent. Sleigh has been to tea at the works and is coming down to Campden again soon.

February 21st This afternoon I went to Campden Wood and was amazed to find a blaze of primroses on a sheltered bank there, and filled my hat with them, remembering my Mother and her love for them with a strange sense of beauty, came home and had tea, tied them all up in nine bunches, and went out and left them for Nina Griggs.

February 24th Hudson does not like solitude; I do. It is a luxury some of us demand of life, and cannot live without. Some dare not live with it and will do anything to escape being alone. He is one of those, and it is trying at first, accommodating oneself to new conditions. I am beginning to impress on him that I really do need solitude, and am not just being odd, as much as he needs company. But I have to give way partly, for it is better that he should have company than too much of a promiscuous beer-drinking crowd of Campden working people, excellent though they are. I am beginning to be able to be alone, to slip unnoticed into myself, when I am with others, which is good. Yet when people have been worrying me with their presence and then go, and leave me alone, it is wonderful, for all my secret thoughts, timid as wild things, come close to me and whisper to me.

February 25th I am afraid, almost, of greatness. Shakespeare makes me feel afraid; Milton, Hardy, Dostoyevski, Chaucer; they are all too great, those great ones, and I fear them because they make me feel so minute. Rather I love the lesser great: Wordsworth, Keats, Shelley, Thomson, Blake, Coleridge. I feel more at home with them. With the others I am like a bank clerk staying for a week-end at Buckingham Palace.

February 28th A journey to Gloucester over roads which I last went through with Winifrid. Wet and grey lowland through Evesham and Tewkesbury, then on to Gloucester. A visit to the hospital there on business, and after lunch there on to Cheltenham and tea at George's, where Hudson got excited over girls from the school, who whispered and giggled at us.

March 2nd The Orpens to tea and a quiet, mellow day. There is a satisfaction in seeing Hudson paint better. He seems altogether changed and has not been drunk for two months, chiefly because he now has me to talk to, which stops him growing depressed and seeking company for company's sake in the pubs.

I have met Brian Aherne[35] to-day after a long time. It is sad how people change. We could scarcely find anything to talk about and he did nothing but make over civilised remarks and I felt both insignificant and independent. Brian is on the stratum of civilisation that can think of nothing but its

---

35   William Brian de Lacy Aherne, 1902-86. A teenage friend, met through the Birmingham Repertory Theatre. By 1925 he had made his mark as an actor, and went to Hollywood in the 1930s. Married the actress Joan Fontaine.

---

immediate living surroundings; clean, well fed, well clothed, worldly and full of superficial knowledge. I would rather talk to a ploughman, sweaty and dirty and ignorant and crude, for he would have something in him that these other people do not; emotions that are not disguised or tired; health; enthusiasm; and an unconscious love of beauty; and no grey devil mediocrity, despite artificial silk in Evesham shops, and tins of food, and cheap cars and motorcycles.

March 5th   A charming morning of wandering about and talking to people. [Alec] Miller seems to like my poems. I am better (*CW had been ill for two days*) and though I hate the idea of going to the works again I feel I can face it now. But when I have enough cash to live on for eight or ten years I must get away and write, in the hope that at the end of ten years I shall be able to earn enough to live on by writing. But I must get the job done that I have begun; get the business straight, before I do anything like that. Soon I shall start taking a day off a week I hope, and that will be better.

March 6th   Griggs came last night and was in a mood I have not seen him in before; depressed with his own work and humanly and unpatronisingly sympathetic. He is going to send some of my poems to Grant Richards[36].

March 8th   Last night to the pictures at Evesham with the Aylings and Hudson. On the return journey, a Rabelasian adventure. But it is strange how cold I am with them, cold in my heart, though physically warmer. But that is only because they are female. My hair with its new treatment, sprouts like young wheat. (*Three weeks earlier CW had bought some lotion for three guineas.*)

March 10th   I have now got together a collection of my poems, the best of them out of the last nine months. All before that I put aside as experimental, and these 20 or so I am going to try with Country Life, The [London] Mercury, and The Adelphi. I am going to write poetry now with the object of getting it published in magazines, and ultimately in a volume. Another year and I should have a volume ready, and after all, 24 will not be too late for that. I must be more objective, and clear and cut out mystical obscurity.

---

36   Grant Richards, 1872-1948. Literary agent, publisher (of A.E. Housman) and founder of the 'World's Classics'.

March 11th A director's meeting. I see a row coming with my uncle Harry. He said I ought to live nearer the works because the journey was too tiring for me, meaning so that I could get there at 9 and leave at 7. I told him that I shouldn't think of it, and that was all. But I feel freer and freer every day, less and less bound to money. And yet the place haunts me, the fact of being bound in slavery to it, to a system I hate, in order to gain a thing I increasingly despise. I feel inclined to cut away with my few hundred pounds and live on it till it has gone, and trust to luck for the future. Why should I waste my life, a thing so short and precious, doing what a thousand fools can do as well; fools who cannot even write a paragraph of decent English? Thank God that, even after six years of the works I still have my hatred of it left, of it and of the vile machine life of cities, and of the eternal labour to obtain nothing but money, the god that dominates city people's lives. With my hatred left I can go on a little.

March 14th Everyone regards me as a young man who has nice but rather depressing thoughts. People regard my work as that pastime of an eccentric young man who, but for his eccentricity, would be much nicer. And this that they call eccentricity is the part of myself that I value highest, and love most.

March 15th Hudson and an old school friend of mine from Oxford called Wade, who married a shop-girl there and ruined a brilliant career, and who is staying here this week-end, got drunk last night, and Hudson is morbid this morning. They went out and I, feeling rather priggish, would not, but wrote a poem about a kingfisher.

March 18th I sat up till twelve last night reading 'St Agnes' Eve' to Hudson and found when I was halfway through that he was still thinking of the first two verses. God, what power Keats had. I feel weak and frail before it. I have been told that the Inland Revenue authorities sent an assessment form for tax on the Beggar's Opera[37] to Mr John Gay, addressed to the theatre where it has been revived, the Lyric Hammersmith. I see no reason to doubt it.

March 19th Dinner at Griggs's last night and long discussions on tradition in art, which so excited me that I said it would do the Cotswold Group good if

---

37   Composed 1728, and revived by Frederick Austin.

---

they had a few Paul Nashes[38] dropped down amongst them. Griggs is terribly fatherly and patronising sometimes. I don't like him any more than I did, if as much. He is not an open artist, a broad man; he is full of side trackings and the pedantic stressing of points that are not fundamental. I should think he is selfish and absorbing in a slow way. I often feel quite sorry for Nina, entombed there.

March 21st   A calf in the cold winterly air last night, when I put my car away, bleated, and I am writing a poem about it. This morning Hudson and I followed hounds till we lost them in Campden Wood. We have eaten pork pie and water cress and spring onions and lettuce and bread and cheese, and now to write. It is trying to snow now, and yet the hedges are almost out and the days are nearly those of spring.

March 22nd   A walk over Dover's Hill this morning. Writing this afternoon. To tea now at the Aylings. It is nice to be free of this town and its fields and woods, as though they were part of my own estate, for so, with my familiarity with them and love for them, do I feel.

March 25th   I seem to live at ten times my normal rate in London, like a mouse in a jar of oxygen; my brain becomes a whirlpool in which my thoughts whirl around; my will goes; I live by a sort of groping process that carries me from event to event, till at last, like a hunted creature, I find myself back in the train once more.

Following a description of a lively 24 hours in London and Essex for his cousin's wedding, terminating at the Ham Bone Club in the West End in the early hours, CW continues:

Now I am back in silent Campden, where I find two rejection slips, one from Country Life and one from The Mercury. But the peace is wonderful; like going out of a roomful of people who are all talking at once, into a still cool church. I hate London, yet it fascinates me. I am weary now. Bed.

March 27th   All my poems have been rejected. I will go on sending them out till I have used them all up, or got three published. It depresses me. And now I have not even been elected to the Council of the new Campden Society,

---

38   Paul Nash, 1889-1946. War artist and modernist painter.

though Hudson has, and a lot of local dullards. I am furious in a smouldering way about it. It would have been an act of courtesy and a decent thing to have done.

Over the next two weeks the entries mostly concern CW's thoughts about his poetry, his difficulties with it, and his lack of recognition.

April 7th Last night [Hudson] and I sat in the moonlight and talked to old Bob Guthrie[39] the blacksmith, who knew Winifrid's father, C.H. Smith, and his father, and told us many tales of Campden years ago.

April 18th Hudson and I are steadily growing more away from these people *(a reference to the Slattery girls, who had begun to irritate CW)* and more concerned with our work. The petty social buzz of Campden, charming at first, is exasperating after a time. We feel that our chief friends will tend to be Miller, Griggs and Arthur Gaskin[40]. The others will fade into the distance, having ceased to be interesting.

April 25th Hudson is on the line at the R.A. and the picture is his first to be hung, one of Snowshill, which he did in January, when Sleigh was here. He has been celebrating his success by drinking 15 bottles of stout and eating chitterlings with Ladbrooks[41] the butchers opposite. He came in quite steady and said he felt like a chicken that had broken out of its shell, all wet and bleary eyed and floppy, and saying, 'So this is where I've got to, is it?'

April 26th I am going to print 'The Church Clock' *(a recent poem)* and two or three other poems for the exhibition this summer: 500 copies for £4. If I can sell 150 at 1/- I shall make money on my first venture, and that should be possible.

April 27th A long letter from Kendon, an appreciative letter, which gives me courage and pleasure. Griggs and Hudson are the only two Campden people

---

39   George Robert Guthrie, blacksmith at Leasbourne, b. 1854 and took over the forge before1891.
40   Arthur Joseph Gaskin R.B.S.A., 1862-1926. Painter, illustrator, teacher and designer of jewellery. He married one of his students, Georgie Cave France in 1894. The Gaskins retired from Birmingham to Campden in 1924. Georgie Gaskin was herself a fine designer of jewellery, and died in 1936.
41   Lawrence and Charlie, butchers and brothers. Their shop was on the Lower High Street, now called Butcher's House. See *Campden Characters*, CADHAS 2011, pp. 39-44.

to get in to the R.A. this year. Allcott, Miller, and Woodroffe are out; 10,000 pictures were rejected.

May 4th Yesterday I was morose and, as Sleigh said, more anti-social than usual. We messed about all day doing nothing worth doing. Sleigh seems to be getting the job of tutoring Woodroffe's son till August. It will be good if he does, for he will live in Campden.

After we had been to the Slattery's where Sleigh crowned the evening with a Sermon on Sentiment at the end of a charade, we took him to his rooms at Keens, and I began kissing Nora Keen in a passage. We wriggled and kissed a lot. She has a large mouth like Winifrid's and all the time I imagined she was Winifrid.

May 9th Yesterday Sleigh and I went to *King John* at Stratford. It is amazing how the parts written by Shakespeare stand out in beauty and strength from the dead words of what is merely the old play. That was worth seeing. Sleigh has got his job with Woodroffe. A dance to-night at Greville House.

May 16th Hudson and I got up at 6.30 this morning and decided to go off and see Eve Kirk[42], with whom he was at the Slade, in Hertfordshire, where her parents live. Hudson had a letter from her and she is going off to Paris with [Henry] Rushbury[43] the etcher.

There was trouble at the Slattery's dance last Saturday and since then Hudson has been drinking a lot and this letter suddenly pulled him up and made him realise what a narrow life he leads. So we have wired and we are going off. Sleigh and I had a fight half an hour ago, after breakfast and I won. It was jealousy I suppose. I like him alone but with Hudson it doesn't always work. I have a genuine affection for Hudson, and Sleigh with his homosexuality is as jealous as a woman.

May 19th A charming week-end in a charming house with a garden of wild grasses and tall elms and plane trees. The Kirks are very nice and Eve a delight,

---

42   Painter, 1900-1969. Painted (and loved) by Augustus John. She ceased painting and moved to Italy after the War.
43   Sir Henry Rushbury R.A. 1889-1968. War artist in both world wars, renowned for his etchings. An early student of Henry Payne.

---

not beautiful but lovely, soft and tinged with the hand of pain. Her drawing and sketching are wonderful, and I felt I knew her at once, and we were talking about our souls and our lives by dinner time. She has had many loves, and seems a poor, torn creature who has loved too much. Hudson has returned with a more balanced outlook on this place and his own work, and we both enjoyed ourselves very much.

But Eve – it is strange how all the symptoms of being in love accompany my thoughts of her. She is lovely, and has fair hair and wears long tight waisted dresses and goes about with bare feet and has a delightful smell and a large soft mouth and a gentle voice. She won't live anywhere except London or Paris, so there won't be much opportunity for it to go much further.

The rest of May is taken up with a period of feverish illness followed by a visit by Winifrid Wood and the diary here is occupied solely with this.

June 1st The town is full of fetes and busy self important people today, and there is a dance tonight.

The following lyrical passage, while not about Campden, sums up well CW's feelings about the Cotswolds, and was to form the subject matter of a poem called 'The Village', begun a few days later.

June 2nd I am writing this in the car at Cutsdean, where I have brought Hudson to paint, under the threat of being abandoned if he falls asleep. It is a lazy hot day. I did not get to sleep till 2 last night. At 12.30 we were at the Slattery's and we all went off in three cars to hear the nightingales by Nineveh Bridge[44]. Of course, they were not singing, or there weren't any, but no one seem to mind that. As I went to sleep later, I felt it had been a day wasted in doing things that there was no need to do, and I was annoyed with myself for not having resisted them all, so that I should have done some writing.

As I sit here, the fields and hedges still in the heat; the sound of birds coming from every direction, like the sound of a distant sea; and the buzzing of flies and bees near me. Across the fields, gold with buttercups, lies Cutsdean, asleep under its elms, utterly at peace and still; three cows lie chewing the cud near a

---

44   Near the railway tunnel at Mickleton.

barn there, and two children are playing on the white roadway where it leads into the village. A cock crows, his cry rising far off and penetrating the buzz of flies that is near me; and in front of me the white road to Snowshill stretches away walled each side, its banks covered with swaying cow parsley; even the clouds are still, like becalmed ships on the horizon.

In the village there is a school, a church, a post office. What huge ungainly fabrics of organisation these conjure up in one's mind: Boards of Education; Postmasters General; Parliaments; the Church of England; Rome; Greece; factories; machines; foundries. A sea of chaotic reflections engulfs one, each one more confusing than the last. But no, the wind, the swaying grasses, the buttercups, the trees, flies, birds, flowers, earth; the quiet village, its soul untouched; draw one's soul back to peaceful meandering in the home meadows of quieter beauty. Some day I shall live in a place like this, gardening, writing, thinking, visiting friends, and dreaming of love that has been.

June 6th I have been out to the [Scuttlebrook] Wake[45] up the street, and I went on the swing boats as a measure of self discipline, and stood watching it all for about half an hour. On one of the roundabouts there was a little old dog that had got on the revolving platform by accident. It lay there, ears back, and looked as lost as I felt.

June 16th [In Campden] the houses seem to grow out of the land. There is a serenity one finds nowhere else; the whole land is like a man who speaks seldom, unless he has something to say. Last night I leant out of my window and looked up the street. There was a film of light still hanging in the sky above the roofs, and one could see the street, the grass verge, the trees and the black roofs outlined against the dim light. All was silent. A few windows still had lights in them. The air was warm, heavy like a sweet syrup with its summer warmth, though sometimes a breath of cool air met one's cheek as one gazed. From a window opposite someone spoke. In the house a voice answered. Down the street the crickets were chirruping, and far away on the hills I could hear a horse's hoofs as some farmer's trap took him home through the night, and – so still it was – the faint crunching of the wheels on the road. All was still, warm, becalmed in rest. The door of the Priest's house down the street

---

45 A traditional Whitsuntide fair named after the Cattlebrook at Leasbourne, covered over in 1831, where it takes place to this day.

---

opened and footsteps came down the path and he went by, muttering prayers. He must have felt me looking, for he looked up and waved good-night with a white hand. I drew my head in, and went to bed, and as I lay half asleep, I heard the priest come back from the church, open his door, close it and lock it. Then all was utterly still, and I slept, strangely part of the peace of this place.

June 30th   Last night I wrote a little, then read, then slept out in Father Bilsborrow's orchard with Charlie Blakeman. Alone there, for he went to sleep before me, I lay under a small pear tree gazing at the red moon as it sank behind thin clouds. I awoke at four and got up and watched the sun rise in a cloudless sky over the roofs of Campden, and the birds sang so loud that, when I lay down, I could not go to sleep again.

July 1st   Last night I found writing tedious and dull, so I went to see the Allcotts and read *Nunc Dimittis* to them, and they seemed to think it the best poem I have written. Hudson returns to-day. Sleigh read Chaucer to me and the Blakemans last night. We have something every night now. Either he or I read and we have read Drayton's *Nymphidia*, [Keats's] *Hyperion*, [Byron's] *Prometheus*, some Coleridge, and have had good talk over them.

July 11th   The whole of Campden is in a whirl over the Exhibition, framing, labelling, talking, rushing about, quarrelling, knocking in nails, tearing hair, cutting sacking; for the Exhibition is now taking in work and is opening next Saturday. The Poetry Bookshop [in Bloomsbury, London] is taking a dozen of my *Five Poems*.

July 12th   The Exhibition is taking all attention and energy. The things are beginning to look in order. We spent six hours hanging yesterday. Looking at it all, I feel that Hudson's work is far the best in the room except Griggs'. It has life and flesh and blood, and the rest is pallid and bloodless and afraid of life.

There follows a period spent mostly away from Campden, on holiday and on a business trip to Rouen, during which CW seems to have developed glandular fever.

August 17th   I have not been to Birmingham to-day because I am still deaf and full of cold. On Saturday night a party at the Gaskins at which were

Bache Matthews[46] and the [A.E.] Filmers who used to be at the Repertory, and Gwen Ffrangcon-Davies[47] and Margot [Chatwin][48] and myself. Gwen wore a huge panniered dress with an enormous trail, which looked ridiculous in the Gaskins' small room.

There is no further reference to Campden life for the rest of August and most of September, during which the diary is given over to CW's emotional and inner life, business and the lowering effect of the lingering illness, which had left him temporarily deaf. By late September autumn is heralded by a shooting party with Reginald Roberts of Dorsington.

September 19th Till four o'clock in the pouring rain with the desolate beauty of those hills between Bourton [on the Water] and Northleach I walked and walked. It rained all day and still rains. I shot a brace of partridges, a pigeon and a hare; Roberts shot another hare, and that was our bag. It was awful weather, but despite, or even because of it, it was beautiful to walk those fields under the cold sky and, rounding a corner, to come upon a grey stone barn with its stone roof, sleeping in a hollow of the land, part of the earth and yet the work of man.

September 26th I met Griggs this morning and he said: 'Who are you?' for I have not been to see them lately. I explained that I had not been out at all, and that I had been working. I am going to-night.

September 29th Last night I walked for two hours over the fields searching for mushrooms in the misty moonlight with young Blakeman. He understands the trees and the ways of wild creatures and loathes the spirit of the towns. He is an interesting young man. His father was a keeper, and he went from the Catholic school straight to Woodroffe's to learn stained glass work. Hudson gave him a few lessons in painting and he now paints better than Hudson does. I like him and am helping him with his reading. He has the soundest taste possible. We walked miles among great shadowy hills and beneath tall trees; pools of mist lay in the hollows; the moon was veiled in thin cloud; in corners

---

46   Assistant Director at the Birmingham Repertory Theatre, and author of a history of it, published in 1924.
47   Gwen Ffrangcon-Davies, 1891-1992. Renowned Shakespearian actress, appointed DBE at the age of 101, while still working.
48   Margaret Chatwin was CW's aunt and a member of Barry Jackson's Birmingham Repertory Company.

---

of fields we would come upon cows, their white faces queer in the half-light, munching as they lay; and owls cried up in trees. As we walked through a stubble field a lark suddenly put up, and a hare rushed away. We came back and I was tired and we drank tea in Mrs Blakeman's kitchen and talked to Mrs Blakeman, a woman with a being complete and full of earthy peace, and Cathy, a creature who also is imaginative and full of the fields and earth. Later we went up to bed with our candles and lamps, and I slept like a log, and dreamt that I was proving to the other directors at the works that it was 'legally impossible' for me to catch my train. They agreed and I woke up and it was morning, and I got up and caught it.

October 7th   On Tuesday night Griggs came in to see us and we had a long talk, and, pressing Freud, whom he hates, I got him to admit that what he seems to find it necessary to call 'the old Adam' has a lot to do with art.

October 11th   To-day at Cutsdean at Arkell's farm, where I have brought Hudson and young Blakeman to paint. I am sitting in the car, and pigs are grunting and grovelling and snorting and sneezing and jumping about with little squeaks near me; there are great, delicate ash trees; solid stone barns with soft coloured roofs; geese, sows, calves and dogs; and there is a clear blue sky above with white clouds. The wind strokes the leaves of the ash trees, but the farmyard is so still that one can hear the faint rustle of the hens peck among the grasses. There is no time here to disturb one. Thought seems to flow easily and steadily like a wide river.

It is evening and we have got back and had tea: buttered toast and strawberry jam and rich fruit cake, and eggs. The fire is hot and glowing and outside it is a cold October night. On such nights it is good to feel a house around one and a fire close beside. We are going to the Slattery's after dinner; talk there, then a walk back under the stars down the silent street, saying good night to everyone who passes.

The next few weeks are filled with thoughts of possibly going to live in London, following a notably adventurous weekend in Fitzrovia with Hudson, Eve Kirk and Oriana Woodyatt[49], known as 'Stripes', with whom CW began a passionate affair.

---

49   CW describes her as 'great-granddaughter of Tennyson's'. She married Francis A. Helps, a painter, at Marylebone in 1926.

This is played out under the continuing spell cast by the absent Winifrid Wood, and an intense reading of Dostoievsky and Tolstoy. He finished a long poem entitled 'Adonis', but his gradual recognition of the lack of a future in both his relationship with Winifrid and as a poet, left him depressed. In early December, he calculated that within two years he would have put together savings of £1100, enough to start on a life in London, however precariously. Meanwhile, in Campden, Hudson had got in to trouble again. Following a drunken row and a slap delivered at a dance at the Town Hall, the girl involved had issued a summons for assault.

December 10th Hudson's summons has come and the whole town is talking about the affair. I am afraid it will be bad for him, because it is making him popular with the wrong types. Joan Ayling, poor child, seems to be very much in love with him, and writes a delightfully innocent letter, asking him to marry her sometime.

December 14th Hudson's case shows signs of being settled out of court, owing to a second apology, which I wrote for him. Griggs began on it last night, and was very nice about it.

December 16th Our Annual Meeting over, all the aunts satisfied and sentimental after a lunch at the Queen's Hotel [Birmingham]. Hudson's case has been settled out of court, he to pay costs, five pounds, which I have lent him.

December 19th A broken day in which nothing has happened. We have been drinking gin and Italian with Griggs and have just had dinner. Winifrid still haunts me all day.

December 20th Fog, snow, vile weather out, and I am miserable.

December 22nd I hate Christmas. It creates more disturbance than any other holiday and seems to make a gap in the year during which the weather is vile and everything prevents one from doing the things one wants to do. Last night Hudson and I sat up until 12 discussing the Griggs attitude to life, the Campden Society[50], the preservation of buildings and revival of crafts and

---

50   The Campden Society was established in 1924, primarily to promote the artistic activities of the town. It lapsed before 1940, but was revived in 1970 as an amenity society. The Campden Trust was formed in 1929 to perform a conservation and protection role. Trustees included Griggs, William Cadbury, Benjamin Chandler, and Henry Saunders, the solicitor. CW became chairman after the war.

so on. I argue that however pleasant the past may have been the only thing to do is to take stock of the present and, instead of weeping over or trying to recover the past, to use all our energy in trying to create a better future. To weep over the past is to admit failure with the present. The very fact that Griggs has become a Catholic is enough to show that he has resigned from life as it is. Our weeping and sentimentalising over the past gives us imitation period furniture, period houses, etchings of ruins and delightfully clean and impossibly sanitary 12th century towns. Men have got to be given or find new life at the roots of their souls. The problem is not a material one and it can only be got over by material means in so far as material beauty can create spiritual beauty. Our problem in this century will probably be solved only by our civilisation becoming top heavy and falling. Then, out of the wreckage there may grow a new world, but even that depends on whether man can once more find his soul, can create in fact a new religion, which is of the future, not the past. Christianity was raw and new when it was greatest and strongest as a spiritual power.

December 23rd Stripes is coming to-night. The snow is deep and beautiful in the sharp sunlight. The hills are smooth and wonderfully virgin with it. I have had a toboggan made. No more business until January, I am free for a week.

December 27th Four days of eating, sleeping, making love, talking, drinking and fooling about. Stripes is here, Winifrid is here, a ghost; Hudson is here, a parasite, and I am sick of him. He has suddenly become stupidly jealous of me and Stripes. We have tobogganed; we have walked, Stripes and I, five miles in the snow; we have drunk and danced; we have made love and argued. I feel a mild affection for Stripes and I have an idea of marrying her when I get free from Birmingham, to which she hypocritically agrees.

December 29th Stripes went back this morning. Hudson and I have had a long and rather amusing quarrel, in which we neither of us really wanted to quarrel at all. I gained the victory by the only means that affects him, material means; by taking Stripes out in the car and leaving him in the car; by then taking him at home; by then taking him out to paint and leaving him under a wall in the snow; and by various other ways and we have slowly got back to out normal friendship again. Stripes told me that Kramer[51] told her that he would get some of my new poems in a new London Quarterly and in Yorkshire Poetry, but I have heard nothing yet. Stripes gave me the *Sailor's Return*[52] and the [Aldington] *Golden Asse of Apuleius* and I have bought [Charles] Doughty's *Arabia Deserta* with the money two aunts gave me. Yesterday I went out shooting, and the day out in the wind and rain at Clapton, walking miles over the hills, did me good. Now the dullest darkest month of the year must be faced and sometime beyond that there lives spring.

The last entry for 1925 sums up CW's confused and febrile state of mind.

December 30th   Winifrid's letter and those extraordinary moments of sorrow that she speaks of; that terrible momentary sense of desolation of the artificiality of one's life. I can no longer describe those moments and I do not any longer want to try, because they are worse now than they used to be. She is part of everything I do, or see, or feel, or think; she is in every scene of beauty I look on; in every book I read; in every poem I write; in every thought or near it; she is like the spirit of life which is in all things. That is how I love her. It comes to me when I am laughing, smiling, talking, stroking, making love even, to someone else, and my soul weeps until it cannot weep again, and I have to live and go on, laughing, stroking, sleeping with Stripes, while it eats away the hope in my soul. So ends this strange year.

---

51   Jacob Kramer, 1892-1962. Ukranian-born painter who worked in London and Leeds.
52   Newly published by David Garnett.

Sleeping Out
Woodcut by Geoffrey Miller
for 'A World of One's Own', 1938

~ 1926 ~

January 10th Hudson and I went to see Griggs last night and found him in a black suit, a black bow tie, and a butterfly collar, scratching his head and very worried about Nina, for the baby was due to be born, and the nurse had not arrived. We sat and looked at Turner prints till ten, then Hudson and I went off to Birmingham to fetch the nurse, and got back at 2.30. When we got back the District Nurse was there and the baby was coming[53]. We got to bed at four after drinking whisky with Griggs and airing beds by the library fire.

January 11th I have stayed away from Birmingham to-day and am in the car by the church at Snowshill and Hudson is painting in a cottage garden nearby. It is an almost spring like day, one of those soft gentle days in January when the earth seems to have grown tired of winter and to smile sadly for a few hours.

Griggs came in last night and found me very depressed reading [Thomas Hardy's] *The Mayor of Casterbridge* alone. I told him all my woes and he tried to make me promise to give up writing for a month. His advice is largely right and I shall probably take it. I like Griggs the more I see of him.

January 18th Griggs has been in. He was very grateful for our fetching the nurse and asked me to choose a book from his library. I told him I would much rather have an etching of his, and, though he still pressed the book, he said I should. I am growing to like him very much, though I find intimacy difficult because of our differences in outlook and religion, and his greater age[54]. He said that all my poems reminded him of one particular bit of country – the little valley up by Campden House, Tilbury Hollow.

January 28th Last night there was a marvellous moon and a clear sky and a strong wind. It was so clear that one could see the hedges on Dover's Hill from Allcott's house at Catbrook.

February 1st Yesterday I took Hudson over to lunch at Leamington, and we came back and had tea at the Oliver Bakers at Bearley. Bearley seemed strange.

---

53   The baby was Millicent Elizabeth ('Mia').
54   More than twenty-five years difference.

I do not think I have been there in daylight since I came here. The whole of my childhood and all my Mother's and Father's lives there; all the years; all the live things; all the passing faces of visitors, friends, dogs, cats; the flowers, birds, trees; rose up and called me, saying 'Come back to us, come back to us,' and my heart leapt back but my reason said 'You cannot. None may return whence he has come.' Those two voices struggled in me till my eyes filled with tears. We can never retrace our steps. We can never change or correct what we have been and done. I knew that there as I have never known it before.

February 2nd My heart feels like a heap of cider apples after they have been through the press and my brain won't work.

February 18th I have framed the etching that Griggs gave me, a small part of 'The Almonry', and it looks very nice in my room.

February 28th A most perfect day. Spring; sound and colour and air of spring; sun and warmth. A fox ran into the town on Thursday escaping from the hounds and was killed in Coldicutt's wood yard[55]. The whole town was in turmoil for an hour. It is afternoon and the children are playing in the street, and my black cat watches them from my window while I write. All afternoon an extraordinary stillness and peace. No breath of wind, buds pouting on every twig, and in the fields the soft happy voices of people with nothing to do but enjoy the day; such is a real Sunday. And this evening on Dover's Hill perfect peace. The sun went down; there was no train smoke in the vale; and the sound of cars on the main road was softened. As I sat watching I knew that [it was] such a scene untouched had Shakespeare watched. There was nothing that I could see that could have changed; all was as it must have been for centuries.

March 3rd Last night Griggs came in again. When he came on Monday I gave him 'Idleness' to read and he took it home. He went at 12 and took it out of his pocket, very tired, he said, when he got in and looked at it. He read a bit, then went on and read it all, then read it again and again. Then he sat down and wrote a letter telling me how he liked it and that it made him happy to think I was doing such good work. He is going to send it to Squire[56] for me.

---

55 Behind the former butcher's, subsequently Bragg's, now the site of Grafton Mews.
56 Sir J.C. Squire, 1882-1958, then editor of the London Mercury, showcase for the Georgian poets.

March 8th   Yesterday I spent rather ineffectively doing nothing more than win a toss for a drink, and a game of golf, and pursue half heartedly a twice married woman in the evening, without success.   On Saturday night I read the Blakemans another book of *Paradise Lost*. The theatre at Stratford has been burnt down, thank God. May they put up a better one, preferably in concrete, by a modern architect, all curves.

The following dialogue takes place in one of the Campden pubs:

> Tommy Knott (manager of jam factory, in the Red Lion billiard room as Griggs entered): Good evening Mr Griggs. A terrible thing this burning of the theatre at Stratford.
>
> Griggs: Well ..I....dislike the building so much that I can hardly call it a disaster, Tom. I...er.... hope it may give them a chance to put up a better building, and that would be a good thing.
>
> Tommy Knott: Yes...Yes...perhaps so, perhaps so Mr Griggs. It <u>was</u> an ugly building.
>
> Half an hour later enter Mr Ellis, a Town Councillor, tall red-faced, a fishmonger and china dealer and basket maker and drinker of cider and a reader of The Times daily.
>
> Ellis: Good evening gentlemen. A terrible disastrous thing, the Memorial Theatre being burnt.
>
> Tommy Knott: Oh no, Mr Ellis, a very good thing. A very ugly building. A very good thing I think. They may put up a decent building now.

March 9th   As I came out of the Noel [Arms] Yard with Hudson after putting my car away to-night, we saw a marvellous purple-pink glow in an arc over the houses opposite and stood looking at it. At first we thought it was a fire, then we supposed it must be the Aurora Borealis and we got the car out again and drove up to Dover's Hill to watch. The purple had spread out over the sky, merging imperceptibly into the black night, and within it was a slowly diffusing warm red, and then pale mauve, then green, the palest, most delicate green, and finally white. All round the trees bent and swayed in the wind. After a time the light seemed to fade, so we came back. But when we got in, and told the Blakemans, and went out into the garden with them to look a marvellous change had come; great gentle arms of light reached up into the remotest sky, all tinged with soft pink and red and gold, all of which were so diffused so that one could not see where one began and where the other ended; and behind, at each side of the arc of light, was a deep, reddish purple glow, while in the centre there was green light, far away.

Cathy Blakeman and Hudson and Charles and I stood in the garden watching. Mrs Blakeman put her head out of the door and looked once and went in with a grunt. All was still, the wind having fallen, and there was no sound but our voices. The light moved from place to place in the great arc, and the stillness and the strangeness made the very garden we stood in seem eerie. The nuns next door came out into their garden and chattered loudly, seeming to think it was a fire. Then one said with a dogmatic wit that 'It must be some phenomenon' and they all went in, except the old Mother Superior and one sister, who stayed on, saying that it was a fire, they were sure. Then they too went in, saying that they would see it again in the morning, and we were left in the silence again, watching. I have never seen an Aurora Borealis before, and never have I seen anything of such purity and such weirdness at the same time.

At this period, CW managed to compartmentalise his love-life between intense longing for the largely absent Winifrid whom at one point he describes as his 'spiritual foster-mother', and others more available and closer to hand. The diaries mention many an amorous escapade with local girls, as well as occasional visits to Fitzroy Square to visit Stripes. I have omitted most of these, but the following summarises the local situation.

March 16th M was nice last night. Nothing happened but we walked and talked for a long time and she became quite sentimental which touched me. I find five women in Campden of her sort are fond of me: a barmaid, a nurse, a bootmaker's daughter, and the daughter of the man who keeps the Red Lion. In a way I like them better than the Slatterys and Aylings and those who are of my own class. They have a downright sincerity, which I like, and it gives me an extraordinary pleasure when they express, as they do, any appreciation of nature. They have a clarity of seeing which is not spoilt by semi-education, and they do not, as the semi-educated of one's own class do, imagine themselves as more than very subject human beings, with an intensive awareness of fate and the inevitability of suffering. But there is a gap, and it is harder for me to bridge than for them. I sometimes curse this 'civilisation' which has made it so, and with that they may, the country mind and may, withstand it and grow out of its ruin.

March 17th Squire sends back 'Idleness' and writes that parts of it are very good but that it is loose and vagrant and too decorative, but asks to see some more later. He tells me to submit to the discipline of stanzas before trying any more blank verse. That is all. It has failed and I am terribly depressed. I can't convince myself that poetry is as much a question of craftsmanship as Griggs and Squire and Shanks make out. I realise that my own is not good enough yet, though. The only thing I see in this misery is a command to myself to go on and on till I do succeed, but it is a ceaseless and unrewarding struggle that I seem to be waging.

March 20th To Griggs to dinner and amusing talk and good food and wine. One comes away from him always feeling that one must persevere, and that in the end one will create something beautiful if only one does.

March 22nd Griggs' new etching for the Academy, 'Sarras', is very fine, but he has made it a fortified city and I feel that the city of a dream should grow out of the earth like a wood. I am reading the Bible straight through and have got to Numbers so far.

March 23rd To the North Cotswold point-to-point at Dumbleton, and we have returned penniless. It was a poor course and one could see little of the racing.

Prompted perhaps by his betting losses, CW summarises his financial situation, a regular diary habit.

March 24th I have got to save £50 between now and August to keep to my plan and it is going to be very difficult. I shall than have £300 saved, something at least. My present plan is, when this three years is up, to arrange to go to Birmingham only four days a week, so that I can give more time to writing, for another three years, after which I should have enough. I ought to be free by the time I am thirty, but I fear now not before.

March 27th I have just read Book VII of *Paradise Lost* to the Blakemans. I helped to carry Allcott downstairs this afternoon. The doctor says that there is a chance of his getting better, but is very doubtful. In any case he will not be able to work for a long time, and will have to winter abroad.

To-night to a circus and after I took M for a walk. She attracts me as a character, with her country sense and her rough humour. I might live one day with a country girl, and wander the hills in a caravan. There is such freshness and freedom from sophistication in them, and a natural understanding of out of door beauty. I really believe that unless such people can like one's art there is little good in it.

April 2nd Last night Hudson and I got a little drunk and went and carried two box bushes in pots from The Noel Arms to Mrs Blakeman's and put them solemnly outside her door, one on each side. This morning the boots and the yard man have been in a lorry to fetch them. A crowd gathered and everyone was talking, and we were very amused because no one can tell who did it, though they suspect us.

April 9th The dance at the Town Hall last night was smelly but very enjoyable. I like them and am wearied of conventional society. The native people of this place, with their rough sincerity now attract me more than the people 'of one's own class' in their drawing rooms and their conventions, their powdered faces and evening dresses and empty hearts. I finished up with M in my room here, on the settee, where I have made love to such an oddly diverse number of people.

April 10th Charles Blakeman and I have been on Weston Hill and towards Saintbury all afternoon, looking at orchards. It is a perfect spring day. I grow ever more certain that I shall always live here, or near here now. I realise that London or any other town would be suicide for me. The only thing for any artist to do now is to keep as far away as he possibly can from contemporary influences, even newspapers and books and magazines.

April 12th Yesterday I was 24, but it does not seem to matter as much as being 22 did when I reached that age. There is not the same awful feeling that one must get everything done at once that there was then. I am reading Gilchrist's *Life of Blake*[57], lent me by Arthur Gaskin, and a wonderful fire runs through me and I see that I shall never say what I am struggling to say while I stick firmly to solid earth. I have read half the Bible now. Last night Book II of *Paradise Lost* to the Blakemans.

April 19th I have been out with Griggs to see a man called Fieldhouse at Wooton Wawen near Bearley, the object being to raise money to buy Dover's Hill for the National Trust, and prevent it being built on. We also went to see Wills[58] at Batsford who gave rather grudgingly. We got home at eight, having run out of petrol on the way from Moreton. I had dinner with him and we began talking of England as it was before 1914, and so to Stanway and Margaret and Viva and Winifrid [the Smith sisters]; how he first met Viva at a tennis party at Woodroffe's; how he spent months at Wood Stanway; how he cherished the memory of those days; how impossible it was to go back. He said that sometimes he spent hours at night reading old letters and looking up old drawings to recapture a moment of those days, and that he always gave up defeated in the end.

I am growing very fond of Griggs and feel that I understand him and that he too understands something of me. We sat and talked till late. He read me poems by Russell Alexander[59] and extracts from books and it was all about the England which is going, has gone, almost; which has gone in the last fifteen years as suddenly as though it had been cut off with a knife. At last I said, 'What are we to do?' 'What?' he asked. 'We can only live on and create the utmost beauty in our power, then die.'

April 25th Yesterday was a day of moving, and now Dorothy and my [Chatwin] Grandmother are more or less settled in the cottage [at Broad Campden]. Last night I went to see the Gaskins and asked him if he would do a woodcut for my 'Idleness' poem for this year's exhibition, for a rhyme sheet, which he agreed to do. (See p.70).

---

57   Alexander Gilchrist, *The Life of William Blake*, 1863, was of seminal importance in the establishment of Blake's reputation.
58   Gilbert Alan Hamilton Wills, O.B.E., 1st Baron Dulverton. He had bought Batsford Park in 1919.
59   Russell George Alexander, 1877-1951. Writer, poet and close friend of Griggs.

When I left them I went for a walk and at about ten was sitting under the big chestnut tree in Leasbourne, and old Bob Guthrie the blacksmith came and sat with me and talked for a long time about old Campden and his wife's illness and C.H. Smith, Winifrid's father, and <u>his</u> father, and I was very happy sitting there in the diffused moonlight, watching the slow life of Campden move past. At about eleven Bob got up and went into the house, saying he would come back, and soon he returned with a bottle of cheap red wine called Ruby Red, and knocked the top off the bottle and would insist on my sharing it with him. So we sat there talking in the warm night, drinking by turns and laughing sometimes loud, so that the little town echoed with our laughter. I came home feeling a little drunk and a little sick, drank a glass of hot water, and went to bed.

April 27th A village dance last night, which I enjoyed. Noise, laughter and loud, bad music, the smell and presence of human beings, all give me a sense of my own reality as no polite gathering of cultured people does, where hearts are hidden under acquired knowledge, and brittle egotism is disguised as refinement. There is something steadfast about these country people, which I do not find elsewhere. They have a contact with the daily realities of life, which others do not.

April 28th Here in the fields and small towns and villages is true life, and love, and natural beauty of soul and breadth of spirit and character, and of course there are as well meanness, vicious gossip, weakness. It is the fact that here there is an individual strength and steadfastness to balance those that counts.

April 30th When we write of reality and soul and God, speak of nature as though she were a timid virgin, who would be shocked by an open speech, and of love as though it were an eternal sorrow of the soul, how are we able to relate our art to the mass, the crowd; all the labourers, butchers, cowmen, stonemasons, blacksmiths, harness makers, boot makers, farmers and shopkeepers? Our books are of no use unless they can be taken to the hearts of the people. How is it to be done? I would give years of my life to be loved by the people of Campden for the sake of what I have written, and I should believe in anything I had written which was liked by them far more than in any piece that was liked only by the sophisticated and intelligent. Yet what have I done? I have written a few egotistical, weak poems that may one day exist in limited editions. My writing has done nothing to bring me nearer to the people, and although I realise the need, I have a mind trained so that it can hardly reach them. I don't know what they want, and I often feel that they don't want anything. How can I, a weak, pale faced, bearded aesthetic son of generations of manufacturers get near them or be understood by them, or enter their minds and hearts with my work. When M told me that she had bought and read my *Five Poems* and had read them over and over again I was so pleased that I could scarcely answer.

May 3rd   This [General] strike, if it happens, will be a nuisance, for I may have to go and live in Birmingham. Politically it does not interest me. Our revolution is taking place in the slow, English way and this is just part of it. Campden ignores it completely.

May 4th   This strike is stimulating because of the uncertainty it creates in the mind. The fixed things are no longer quite so fixed; our orientation shifts slightly, delicately but noticeably. I have been to Birmingham by car and have got back early. I am going for a walk, and then I shall go and see Gaskin about 'Idleness'.

May 6th   This strike goes on. I am not going to Birmingham to-day. They can't get a lorry driver to take some beds to London. I shall take them myself if they don't succeed.

I had tea with the Oliver Bakers yesterday. As I grow older, I find myself able to appreciate and know people more deeply; and to hate and despise more strongly too. Oliver Baker is one of the most loveable men I know and it was he who introduced me to the great Elizabethans, through whom I first really discovered literature; and who made many long dark evenings of depression at Bearley full of gentle wisdom for me, by talking to me in his slow, soft voice and imparting to me some fragment of his wisdom.

Hudson and I have been fishing at Donnington Brewery and he caught one small trout. I have since been out shooting young rabbits and got eight with eight cartridges. A marvellous evening, Campden gilded by sinking sun like a place in a dream.

May 7th I have had all the people at the works up in the big room and have addressed them, and they all cheered and clapped and I felt very nervous, but tried not to show it. I have seen the driver who refused and he is going now.

Yesterday I spent taking Griggs round after subscriptions for Dover's Hill. We saw Oliver Baker, Finberg[60], Bernard Newdigate[61], and had tea with his brother and sister-in-law. Then we went through Broadway to see Russell[62], and back over Broadway Hill. In the evening I took young Blakeman to see *Coriolanus* at Stratford, very poor.

I have just sworn in as a special constable, with Griggs, Woodroffe, Woodsend[63], the two Harts[64], Cresswell[65], Kidd, Haydon, and a lot of others, sixteen in all.

May 10th Griggs showed us a print of Graham Sutherland's, an artist of only 24. Very fine work, full of wisdom and feeling, such as few artists have, or at least dare show now.

May 12th The strike is called off. The cause of Labour will be set back by it a great deal, and I shall not be surprised if the miners now get worse terms than they would have got before.

May 14th This strike seems to be going on in bits all over the country. I feel that, although the employees are legally right in their demands, they have been indiscreet. I hope [Stanley] Baldwin [the Prime Minister] with his excellent common sense will balance matters between the two parties. My sympathy is with the miners and always has been, but they have been made the victims of the folly of a few in this business.

Last night to the Town Hall dance. The Campden Band, consisting of about fifteen wind instruments, a drum and other things, plays at one end of the

---

60   Herbert Finberg, 1900 - 1974, son of A.J. Finberg the Turner scholar. Started the Alcuin Press 1928.

61   Bernard Newdigate, 1869-1944, typographer, then at the Shakespeare Head Press.

62   (Sir) (Sidney) Gordon Russell, M.C., 1892 - 1960. Distinguished furniture designer, craftsman and manufacturer at Broadway.

63   E.G. Woodsend, architect, owner of Peyton House.

64   Probably George, the silversmith, and Fred, the antiquarian retired Royal Navy Commander. See p.135.

65   Captain Herbert Pinkney Cresswell of Campden and Charingworth Manor, 1881-1962.

room, and the noise is deafening, but it is what I like, a real row that gets inside your head. Whippets and men straight from their allotments stand at the other end in a group, while the more self conscious shop assistants, and adolescents sit in rows down each side, the girls mostly on one side and the men on the other, a few sentimental couples among them, holding hands and not intending to dance. The band strikes up, and everyone begins to dance, and the dust rises so that it nearly chokes one. On they go, ramming each other, shouting, laughing, whistling, singing, squeezings, leering, teasing and jostling the self conscious ones, who pride themselves in a kind of suburban dignity. In and out among it all Hudson and I with our girls go, really living with all the others as one is seldom able to do with those with whom one has no more than a kind of socio-intellectual bond. It is exhilarating and fills one with love for England such as no formal affair could do. Someone tied a dead baby rabbit to Hudson's coat and he brought it home with him with great pride, stroking it.

May 15th   Last night Hudson and I sat in Jack Bridge's at the Red Lion till twelve, talking to him of all his experience among local people, of hunting, of strange bargains, curious ways with horses, people almost epic in their local fame, of sport and money and the old days before 1914.

For the next two weeks, CW is away on holiday and on business. He returns in time for Scuttlebrook Wake, and the entry is transcribed in full. Not a lot has changed in eighty five years.

May 30th   We did go to the Wake last night after all. It is an amazing gathering. All Leasbourne down to the Chestnut tree is crowded with every sort of merry-go-round and sideshow. They begin setting up the stands at midday on Saturday and must go by Sunday morning. Swing boats, horse merry-go-rounds, shooting booths, monkey shows, badgers, throwing booths, cocoanut shies, sweet stalls, gingerbread stalls, and every conceivable sort of side show is there. Every pub is full and it is an hour's work to get a pint of beer. All the pub yards are crowded, and there is a constant irregular stream of people from the densely packed street to the various doors. There one can scarcely move. Everyone is there, old men and women who have not been seen since the last wake, tramps and wanderers, youths and girls, children with their mothers, from outlying villages and farms. The girls rush about the street, even the most respectable a little abandoned, shouting and squirting water down people's necks, and throwing confetti. The youths chase them with shouts and yells. Even the older people seem to grow young again, vying with the young in their shouting and joking. The great steam organ of the largest merry-go-round blares out a continuous accompaniment. Lurchers and curs slink about in the light of the flares. Drunken folk shout and wobble and try to shoot the dancing celluloid balls for more drinks, and go away still arguing about who has won. The swing boats form great arcs of movement on the sky, and the flaring lights shine brightly on the trees and houses near. Among all the people those 'of one's own class' walk with an appearance of dignity and return home early. The great humming merrymaking goes on. The pub yards before closing time are fuller than ever, and the beer is staler. Then the pubs empty and a fresh crowd of excited people is added to the main body, and the excitement spreads like a fire from one to the other till it matters not who knows who in the great whirl of communal action and eager coarse pleasure. At twelve the wake begins to close down and the people disperse. A few are left waiting, watching the taking down of the booths, which begins at once. Youths and girls wander off into the fields and make love in the summer night, and all down the street there is a stream of older and more settled folk, who go back to their homes, there to sit up for another hour or two, talking and drinking tea, or cocoa or beer. In the morning everyone is weary, and no one works, but it does not matter, for it is Sunday, Trinity Sunday, the Sunday after Scuttlebrook.

May 31st Last night at eleven I suggested to young Blakeman that we should sleep out. We took my small tent, a sleeping bag for me, and a heap of rugs and things for him, and went up on Doe Bank at the side of Dyer's Lane opposite Campden Wood. By one we were settled on the rather lumpy ground and soon went to sleep, a nightingale singing in Campden Wood beneath us. At half past four we woke, surrounded by the great chorus of bird song, the sky growing light and the earth all clean and fresh. At five we went out with our rifles after rabbits and walked round the wood. At six we went home and made tea and washed. As the sun rose out there the fields were like lakes of gold, for it is a fine buttercup year, and the dawn was one of the purest I have ever seen; a virgin silver light, a pale gold sun; and those lakes of golden buttercups, and dew on every blade of grass.

June 1st I have ordered two new suits at 11 guineas each, as I feel poor and have no money. The Campden Society have bought Dover's Hill at a cost of

£4400, of which they find half and the National Trust the other half. I am very glad.

June 2nd   Last night I spent with Griggs, taking him to Willersey deliciously pleased about Dover's Hill and quite heedless about where the money is to come from, though he has guaranteed a lot if it.

During the next few weeks little is recorded of the external life of Campden: a visit by Winifrid Wood and the passionate introspection it engendered fill most entries. The habit of sleeping out continues from time to time.

June 20th   Charles Blakeman and I have bathed this evening at Northwick Park in the lake, and Hudson and I have been a walk, to watch the trout rising in the old bathing pool, here. It has been a hot day with a warm wind, and Campden has spent a real Gloucestershire summer Sunday, standing in groups outside its doors, talking and watching the people go by, shouting remarks across the street, walking out with girls and mothers and husbands in best clothes, and intimately occupying the whole street as if it were its garden. Now as I look out of my window old Mrs Ladbrook the butcher's wife, Mrs Dyde, two girls and some children and dogs are grouped round the postman's door opposite, talking in low voices. And I think how, behind them are their houses, where they have lived for years, and behind those the gardens and the fields, then miles and miles of more fields and woods. This is England, the England I love.

Griggs and Russell Alexander and Norman Jewson[66] have just been in to see me and have gone. Now to sleep out on Doe Bank, to wake to hear the birds sing and to see the dawn.

June 29th   Yesterday, missing the train I rang up and said I was not going to Birmingham, came home and found Blakeman free too, and we took our lunch and bathing things, and walked to Northwick Park[67], bathed, ate, and walked on through Blockley and Longborough, climbed up the church tower, looked about the village, and went on to Moreton, had tea there, then walked

---

66   Norman Jewson 1884 - 1975. Architect in the Arts and Crafts tradition. Arrived in the Cotswolds in 1907. He married Ernest Barnsley's daughter, Mary, and at this time was engaged at Owlpen Manor, his most successful work.

67   Seat of the Rushout family until 1912, when inherited by George Spencer-Churchill. Now divided into multiple residences.

---

over the fields, dropping down to Blockley again and on to Northwick where we bathed again. We then called at my Grandmother's cottage at Broad Campden for a drink, and came on home. We walked just 20 miles and talked of everything, religion, art, nature, the past, the future, the procreation of pigs (having watched it), clouds, Ruskin, shade, trees, economics, architecture, a whole day spent in the air with feet on the earth and the sky above us.

In the evening I went to see Griggs and we walked up and down the cooling street talking of poetry and Campden and art, and I went to bed feeling full of joy and knowing that a certain sense of happiness was before me in which all things will be accepted and beauty will still live. Charles is a very good companion and I grow to like him more and more. We love the same things, and walk the same pace.

To night a Welsh miners' choir came and sang with marvellous beauty in the warm street. Every stone, every face became a thousand times more beautiful. I gave them my last pound. The Bakers, weaving people who live opposite me now, gave them tea, and Mrs Blakeman gladly bustled about boiling kettles.

July 9th   Last evening I brought home from Honeybourne an old half mad man who lives at Broad Campden, and whose name is Seitz[68]. All that is known of him is that he was a medical student, half Indian, and went queer and came to live here years ago on a small allowance from his family. Now he goes about in rags and drives cattle on market days, and his cottage is said to be lousy and without furniture, and he will not allow anyone in it. He talks incessantly of Bombay and Colombo, but very seldom coherently now. Sometimes he will quote long passages from the Bible, interspersed with bits of Shakespeare and medical knowledge. But his eyes. God, his eyes! They seem to know everything and still to hope brilliantly. As I got out to help him get in the car he fell down on the roadside, though he was not drunk, probably from fatigue and hunger, and he looked up at me as I helped him get up again. His eyes looked through me, and we seemed to know each other on some other level. I got him in the car but he would not talk. But those eyes and his gratitude for the lift have made me happy ever since.

---

68   Charlie Francis Seitz, 1858-1933. From an educated Anglo-Indian background; in Campden from about 1890. He lapsed into wild eccentricity verging on madness, and died in abject poverty at Broad Campden. See CADHAS, *Campden Characters* pp 47-48.

July 11th All yesterday and to-day working at the Campden Exhibition. It is too hot to think or read or write. I just sit now and do nothing, get up, look out of the window, go into Hudson's room, go upstairs, come down again; the awful restlessness of hot days that make one long for autumn. Griggs's father has died, and he has come back very tired and has gone to bed with a cold.

July 14th I went to the Gaskins last night and saw Griggs. He was teasing Gaskin about some of his woodcuts. 'How long does it take you to do one of these?' he asked, about a small rather modern thing of two walls and acres of black field and a figure drooping. 'Oh, a day and a half.' 'Really. How very amazing. No longer?' Mrs Gaskin. 'Oh, yes, Arthur's been working very hard lately, haven't you dear? He's done lots of these.' 'Really, you surprise me.' Then, 'Wouldn't a Martian think us an odd lot here if he came in? There's Gaskin with a moustache and no beard, and Mr ... with a different moustache, and Whitfield here with a beard and no moustache.'

July 16th Samuel Palmer. I can never express how grateful I am to Griggs for introducing me to his work. He has given me new eyes to see with, eyes which have not yet made my mind speak. I look with a new sense of brotherhood on every tree and field and hill, on every wild creature, every light and shade and touch of colour. I admire and respect him too because he has the first thing I look for in a man; that fixity of purpose and indomitable determination which is the Englishman's greatest possession, and he has too that quiet steady courage which seems almost to be indifference, and the deep emotional sensitiveness of the rarest beings. Those things I admire wherever I see them. I talk of these things, I a mere half business man, half poet, falling at every hour between poetry and material comfort; I talk of these things and my pen does not turn round and bite me.

July 28th I did not work last night but went out with a gun on a farm by Weston Park with Blakeman, rabbiting. It is a delightful and almost Virgilian place, consisting of and old house sunk below the top of the hill, surrounded by great ash, fir and oak trees, and with its barns and yard in front. It looks over Weston Park and is almost in it. The garden is half vegetable, half flower, mingled in a careless way, not too trim and yet not too neglected, with every kind of vegetable and country flower in it, and a small pool made by a spring, and a watercress bed. There are only four fields, all grass. The farm belongs to a charming old woman, a Miss Sansome, who lives alone there and runs it herself with a man. Her father had it before her and she carried on with it when he died. She keeps a few cows, pigs, poultry, and churns herself, working all day from early morning to dusk, when the fowl are shut up. It is a romantic place, pastoral in the best sense, and one only has to see her simple, red cheeked virgin face to realise how perfectly one can live in such a world. Such a life is the foothold on earth of the ideal wisdom of man. When he has passed through the pain of seeking in reason and intellect what is not there, he will find wisdom in such ways.

July 29th Dorothy [Chatwin, CW's aunt] and Dorothy Massingham[69] called last night and took Hudson and me to the Noel Arms, and we sat and talked. Dick Blaker was there. I walked up with them to Broad Campden afterwards and then walked back with Dorothy Massingham. She is an interesting and intelligent woman to whom one can talk. Words mean the same to her as they do to me, and that is a thing one seldom finds.

Man has tried to explain himself and all the world of matter and spirit in and about him, for thousands of years. Now he must begin to see that this is not for him to do. For him is to accept all, including the fact that there is no explanation.

August 9th Griggs and I got back last night [after staying with the Jewsons at Sapperton] at seven and I had dinner there. At first, so completely had I taken myself away from Campden and lived at Sapperton, that Campden seemed almost a new town, very beautiful and noble, the houses very dignified. We both felt pleased to be in it again, for we both love it so much.

August 11th Charles and I went to Clapton last night. We slept by the old stone bridge over the Windrush and got up at half past five and ate some sandwiches, then went out with our guns. We got only one duck, which he shot. I only had one shot and that was an impossible one. But it was delightful despite the rain, which began at six, to see early day in a countryside we did not know as we know Campden, and to walk beside the river, where moorhens and herons were feeding, and where water voles rushed off the banks and dived with a great plop into the water. There were trout rising too, and we saw rooks and pigeons and partridges, and heard them calling in the cattle for milking, far off, up on the hill by the village.

---

69   Actress daughter of H.J. Massingham, writer on rural issues.

Last winter I came back from London determined to give up this life and go there and try to earn my living by writing. How utterly impossible that seems now. I have completely given up the idea of ever trying to earn my living by writing, but I intend now to earn it at the works, and save enough as soon as I can to live on. It seems possible to me now. With the comparative freedom that I have at the works, where I am my own master, I can find quite a lot of time for writing.

August 16th After dinner Griggs got on to old England. He and I differ entirely about poetry. He cannot distinguish between verse of a kind he happens to like and poetry itself. He looks for craftsmanship first and allows emotional quality, the soul of the poet, to slip in after as an embellishment. I don't believe for a moment that he <u>understands</u> Shakespeare. When he speaks of him he quotes about the old England from the *Merry Wives*. If one says that one thinks *Antony and Cleopatra* the greatest play he just looks as though one had said that Methodism was the noblest religion. He has deceived himself, to shield his soul from life. It is a miracle that his art is as wonderful as it is.

August 17th I have just been in to see the Gaskins and he was out, so I had to sit and listen to her anecdotes of how she taught William Morris to ride a bicycle etc.

There is little of Campden interest during September, during which CW's grandmother's illness, Winifrid's absence staying with a sister in Surrey and thoughts on the nature of poetry occupy many entries. Mrs Blakeman, CW's landlady, was also ill.

September 28th Hudson is leaving Campden. The Blakemans have asked him to go, making Mrs Blakeman's illness the excuse, though they have wanted to be free of him for some time. He talks of going to Stow to paint and not trying to get other rooms here. Now that it comes to his going, I begin to recall the pleasant times we have had together and to forget the thousands of times I have longed for him to go. On the whole though, although I shan't go off on painting jaunts with him, or to the Point-to-Points, or to odd dances and places, for which I am really sorry, I am glad he is going.

September 29th I am writing by candlelight for we have had a gas explosion in the street and there is no light. All the town stands at its doors, or out in the roadway, or in groups on the pavements talking about it, making a droning sound in the still night.

September ends on a bleak, reflective note after some time reading Oswald Spengler, the German historian and philosopher who enjoyed a high reputation in the 1920s. CW was probably reading The Decline of the West.

September 30th The question that comes up naked before me is this: I write poetry. I shall probably write poetry for years. It may be good or bad, but whatever it is, what is the meaning of a poet now? Is not the time of poetry over? Was not Keats the last of the great poets? Therefore how dare I imagine that I have any place or purpose as a poet? And it seems to me now that one must accept the fact that it is no use, no vital use, writing poetry, and that if one does so it is as an accomplishment, and not a mission. Poetry is no use and I have given my soul to it. Love is impossible and cannot be fulfilled, is as it is for me a stupid self-deception, and I have given my soul to it. So do I feel to-day. That sums up all I have been feeling this month, and that is why I have done nothing and have felt scarcely depressed at doing nothing.

October 24th It is cold to-day. The wind howls through the air and whines thinly in the chimneys and the grey roofs stand out against the sky stern and utterly self-sufficient, while rain falls as though each drop were forced out of the clouds by the wind. The street is empty. The mountain ash by my window is half naked and its last leaves are brown and shrivelled. I feel very human sitting here by my fire, in my little room, looking out on the street, watching the tree shiver and the few people who go by in their Sunday clothes bend themselves against the wind.

I like the Bakers. They are not obsessed by an ostrich like conservatism as Griggs is, nor are they second rate artists hiding their littleness in the country, but people whose brains are alive and accept the fact that they are just craftsmen doing their job. They have both been at the Old Vic. He is now reading my Spengler and we discuss it. They have a sense of humour and something like the same kind of thought that I have. I see great possibilities in them.

October 30th Last night I went to see Griggs and found the Bakers and Jewson there and they all sang songs to a creaking harpsichord and a great deal of it annoyed me, but some of it amused me, and I came away pleased with the visit.

In rebarbative mood after a business trade lunch and a board meeting in Birmingham, CW growls at the Campden culture.

November 9th My temper is turned against those fools who dote on the past because they are afraid of the present; the fools who sit and stare at the past with bleary eyes like dogs staring at their own retchings; folk-dance idiots; hand woven whimperers; idolisers of hand-woven, hand-carved, hand-baked things; jackasses who, because they are afraid of being engulfed in the present, bury their heads in the past and imagine the smell of its excrement to be rose leaves and dried herbs.

November 12th Yesterday we went to the meet at Mickleton. The [Armistice] silence at eleven was very impressive; the sounds of the horses shifting about, the clink of a bit or stirrup, the hounds' soft padded movements, were all one could hear. One old man stood with his hand to his ear listening intently all the time.

CW's maternal grandmother Mary Chatwin (b. 1854), whom he greatly admired, had died at Leamington on November 10th.

November 19th I've been over to Leamington all afternoon choosing things to keep, and have driven Dorothy's car back to use while mine is being repaired. This evening Charles and I have walked down to Honeybourne to fetch mine back, a lovely walk, the moon continually looking out from thin clouds on the pale land.

November 21st I went to see Griggs last night. The Chandlers[70] were there to dinner. Fanny made one of her unconsciously amusing remarks about 'G.K's Weekly'[71]. 'Is it a weekly paper Fred, or does it come out every month?' Griggs has been offered £1000 for 'Fen Monastery' by Finberg and now does not know what to do about Colnaghi's[72], to whom he is engaged by a sort of moral agreement.

---

70   Benjamin Martin Chandler and Frances Izod Chandler, née Robbins. See Introduction, p.9.
71   Founded by G.K. Chesterton in 1925.
72   P&D Colnaghi, the distinguished Bond Street art dealers, established in 1760.

December 6th   Yesterday I messed about at home and went to the Bakers to tea, where I met a nice young man from near Winchcombe called Cardew[73], who has a pottery there, which I should think he runs at a loss.

CW spent Christmas at Colwyn Bay with the Woods, and before leaving Campden records a seasonal sight in the town.

December 21st   The butchers' shows in the shops down the street are a fine sight, great carcasses of meat, joints, sucking pigs, all sorts of things in the windows, decorated with holly and mistletoe and brightly lit up, with a small crowd at each door talking and gazing at the sight and comparing it with those of other years.

*Woodcut illustration to the poem sheet 'Idleness'
by Arthur Gaskin, 1926.*

---

73   Michael Cardew, 1901-1983. A pupil of Bernard Leach, he worked at Greet near Winchcombe and at Wenford Bridge, Cornwall. He later worked in post-colonial Africa (Ghana 1942 - 48 and Nigeria 1951 - 65). He was appointed OBE in 1981. In his memoir *Pioneer Pottery*, 1969, he refers to CW as: 'a poet who on week days made iron beds in Birmingham and at weekends used to tell me about the inexorable experiments recently made by a certain Russian scientist called Pavlov.'

December 1926

~ 1927 ~

January 1st I went to the New Year dance with Charles Blakeman last night, drank some beer and felt very fit, then drank some cider and felt rather ill. This morning I have a heavy head.

This afternoon Charles and I spent shooting at Evenlode with Collett the baker, a small, empty shoot, but a change and there was a glorious red sky behind the Blockley hills as we left, and a solitary hunting man riding down the lane in the dusk, through the deep toned brownness of the land. Birds were singing as though it were almost April, thrushes and little brown finches and hedge sparrows, and there were minute wrens moving silently in the hedges. We came home for tea and I slept after.

I have just finished Keats' letters again. Those last four or five, how terrible they are. Keats is in a way my brother. I am conscious of him all the time, the greatest spirit of us all after Shakespeare. Those last letters always make me cry involuntarily, so terribly close is the soul that is in them to mine in its nature, in respect of suffering. I hear Griggs is very pleased with the little poem I sent him for Christmas.

January 2nd A happy evening yesterday. First I got my thoughts about Persephone[74] cleared up, then wrote a little poem about a bird, and after that spent my time half dreaming, in a drowsy state, with Winifrid and nature as the guardians of my drowsiness. At ten thirty I went and read 'The Ancient Mariner' to the Blakemans, and I think I read it well, and they liked it. Griggs called and said how much he liked the poem. He said it is the first modern carol he has seen and that he did not believe a modern thing could have the spirit it has. Baker too says it is a real poem, and I trust his judgement more.

Earth's little deception that it is spring goes on to-day; a clear blue sky and it is so warm and there is such hope in the air that one almost believes the deception oneself.

---

74   CW spent much thought and effort on this theme. No poem emerged, but *Mr Chambers and Persephone*, a novella, was published by the Golden Cockerel Press in 1937.

January 3rd   Yesterday morning Charles and I wandered about Campden Wood and the fields in the warm sun, and it was strangely beautiful. Earth was like a being who has grown used to sorrow and has accepted it, and who therefore does not fear happiness when it comes.

After lunch I suddenly decided to walk to Stanway on a pilgrimage, for Winifrid's voice seemed to call me there. I took Charles and we went across country all the way, through Campden Wood, up Tilbury Hollow, past Happylands, the [Broadway] Tower, down over the fields, through woods of great beeches and oaks and red bracken, over stubble fields and pale grass, to Snowshill. From there we went up the old lane, over the plough and down through Lidcombe Wood and out to Stanway at 4.30. Mrs Wyniatt came to our knock, opened the Bakehouse door eight inches, let us in unwillingly, and then was quite pleasant and gave us a good tea. At a quarter past five we set off back, past Stanway House, through Stanton and Broadway and up over the fields, stumbling and falling in the dark, to Campden Hole, on to Campden Wood, and home along the edge of it. At home a warm kitchen and Sunday supper; cold duck, sausage, toast, and a Welsh Rarebit and clear cold water, glass after glass. It was a wonderful walk. Going there the sky changed continually over the lowering sun, and there was a rich mist over the nearer distance that made the whole world seem aware of the fact that its day of warmth and sun was only a dream in a broken sleep. In the evening I went to see the Bakers. Griggs and Bill Simmonds[75] were there, and Cardew. I went to bed early, feeling that I had spent two of the most real days I have spent for a long time.

January 4th   The Millers' party last night was very dull. I stayed till two, and Griggs went just before me. He looked the picture of misery almost all the time. When, at one moment, when he went by laughing at himself, I said 'You look very cheerful'. He pulled a long face and said 'Oooh?' and went on. I teased him about it all evening.   Griggs took me by the hand with an air of great pleasure and led me across the room and introduced me to one of the plainest girls there, who turned out to be the daughter of Percy Withers, who once read some of my poems and is a publisher's reader. He had often talked of her and had said what a sweet girl she was, and he looked as though

---

75   William Simmonds, 1876-1968. Artist craftsman who had trained as an architect, settled at Far Oakridge near Stroud in 1919. He specialised in making puppets.

---

he expected me to produce a priest out of my pocket and marry her on the spot, but I disappointed him, for after a little polite talk I sidled off. I went in Oliver Baker's Elizabethan costume and someone took me for a parody on Shakespeare as I entered, with that and my beard, and it stuck to me all evening. I won the first prize, a box of chocolates.

January 6th The play the Bakers have done in the Town Hall was a success, and there was a full house afternoon and evening, and much applause. We worked hard, from 1.30 till night on Wednesday, and yesterday from ten till 11.30 at night. After the matinee the Wrights (he is tutor to Philip Chandler[76]) came to tea with me and we talked about poetry. I enjoyed yesterday, and I like the Bakers and their friends, and the atmosphere reminded me of my youth behind the stage at the Repertory. I like Cardew. Bill Simmonds acted well, and [Philip] Mairet[77], who was at the Old Vic also, and is now editor of the New Age, was good. The words of those mysteries have an extraordinary translucent beauty, like that of an old ballad.

January 9th The play is over; and the Town Hall is left waiting the next meeting of the Women's Institute, or the next dance. It has been a success and the expenses were covered. Leo Baker proposes to do another in May. Charles and I had lunch there to-day, and I took Cardew and the Bakers to Winchcombe this afternoon. Cardew is a strange and delightful person. He is 25, was at Oxford with Sleigh and knew him, and with a few hundred pounds has taken over the pottery at Greet. His father is a retired civil servant, and they come from Devonshire. He spent three years in Cornwall with Leach, learning to pot, and now hopes to make a living out of the place at Greet. He has only been there six months yet, and hopes to have his first firing this week, to which I hope to go. He lives in the pottery and has his bed among the pots and kilns, and a kind of living room among more pots. He lives quite happily in the greatest discomfort, with a damp floor, poor lighting and either cold or great stuffiness, and usually gets his own food, and seems very happy. I shall go and see him often, for he is one of the most possible people I have met here; my own age; determined to do something that he is fond of; charming, intelligent, and quite literary. Jewson and his wife Mary called in this morning before they went back to Sapperton. My God she is dull.

---

76   Only son of Ben and Fanny Chandler, 1909-1955.
77   Philip Mairet, 1886-1975. A designer, journalist and writer, he followed Ashbee to Chipping Campden and married (as her second husband) Ethel Coomaraswamy, the influential weaver.

I went shooting at Welford [on Avon] yesterday and after to tea at the Gaskins, where all the people connected with the play had been asked. I loathe the thought of going back to Birmingham again, and once more long to get free soon. As things are going on here, with the Finbergs' printing, Cardew's pottery, the Bakers' weaving, I feel I may well find a niche for myself which will help to supplement what I have saved[78], or shall have when I do anything about it all and really leave.

January 10th Cardew yesterday, having sacrificed everything for the work he loves made me feel depressed, for I have not done that. I have compromised, and there is something commonplace about the means I have chosen. But I am in the middle of it all and there is no choice now but to see it out for a time, five years at the most.

January 13th In the evening I went over to the Bakers. He has bronchitis. He has given me some of his poems to read, those he wrote at Oxford and in the Air Force in the war. He has written none since. It is strangely depressing how many people paint or draw or write up to the first stage of their adulthood, and then cease at about 25. Baker's poems are in an odd way similar to mine when I first came to Campden, with the same rhythm, the same mystical sense, the same kind of obscurity, but they are not bad, though they promise little more from him. His poems may be what Winifrid described him as – myself rolled out flat, and then blown up again. I read the opening chapters of Haydon's *Autobiography* at tea yesterday and wept for sheer pity, knowing his fate[79] and reading of all his youthful ardour. It was terrible.

January 15th I have enjoyed shooting. We got 20 rabbits, a duck, a pheasant and a hare. Baker has been to see me and brought 'Adonis' back. He says I have it in me to be a real poet, but says I must improve my technique. Chandler's tutor Wright has been too and we talked of his poems, which I have read and not much liked.

January 17th Yesterday afternoon Cardew came, after I had written all morning. We sat and talked all afternoon, about everything, poetry, pottery, sex, weaving, Spengler, politics, on and on with scarcely a pause till tea time.

---

78 Which, as was CW's habit, he had calculated at the New Year, was £656.
79 Benjamin Robert Haydon R.A., 1786-1846. Historical painter and writer. Overwhelmed by financial problems and lack of critical recognition, he committed suicide in a messy way at the age of 61.

We had tea, and Griggs came in pleased as a boy with a design for a garage sign he had done. When he had gone Cardew and I went on talking, then went over to the Bakers who had been out, and had supper and more talk. Eileen has asked me to call her Eileen. All our talk was very delightful and stimulating, and my mind was so full of it afterwards that I couldn't go to sleep for a long time.

Poor Cardew has had his first firing and fears it was very unsuccessful, but he is amazing in his faith in his work. He likes the classical in art, particularly in literature and architecture, and prefers the head to landscape in painting. I find him a very pleasant and stimulating acquaintance.

January 18th   A board meeting and uncles all day. Griggs came in last night for a few minutes. There seems to be a fine sort of quarrel in the Campden style breeding; he thinks the Bakers are offended with him, and they think he is offended with them. Something about the play. I am watching with interest, but am trying not to get involved.

January 23rd   Yesterday afternoon I took the Bakers over to see Cardew and we inspected the pots from his firing, and I bought two. The Bakers brought a lot back to put in their showroom. Charles came. The firing has been more successful than he thought at first and there are a fine lot of pots, dishes, bowls, cups, preserving pans, everything. We came back after tea and brought Cardew and he stayed with me, sleeping on my sofa, and we went to the dance at the Town Hall in the evening, and it was empty and dull. This morning he and I got talking again and have done nothing but talk – to me most stimulatingly – all day, on every subject from book-keeping to psycho-analysis, God, poetry, sex. These week-ends are what I have lacked for so long; people of my own generation and interests to talk to. Cardew as Griggs in his own manner said is 'a rather possible <u>chum</u>' for me. His ideas about everything are totally opposed to mine, but they start off from the same premises. He has written poetry and believed in it, and has taken up pottery as a logical development of his discovery that he could never succeed as a poet. He longs to marry and to have house and children. He is a virgin. I can talk to him all day and not be bored.

It is an extraordinary thing how many people there are who lack the courage to cut adrift from ideals that have failed them, or that they have failed. The awful irritant in a man like Russell Alexander is that he clings to ideals that are no longer valid for him in life; Jewson is the same. They are the wrecks of an idealism that has not been able to reconcile itself with reality. At some time in their lives they have failed to say 'This will not do; it does not fit the truth', but have gone on saying, 'This must be true; the truth must be made to fit it.' And so they live out lives of self-deception and are only half alive. Cardew, the Bakers, many genuine craftsmen have tried to be creative artists and have realised that as such they cannot succeed, and have accepted that and become craftsmen and are therefore still alive, not walking self-deceptions cloaked in bolstered mediocrity. I have not yet admitted to myself that I have failed as a creative artist. I still feel that I can be a poet and a good one, so I can still look life in the eyes. The day may come when I have to face the fact that I am not, and take to weaving or pig-breeding, but it hasn't yet. When it does I feel I shall know it and accept it.

January 27th To the Bakers last night and we argued about war and imperialism. I was surprised to find a strong vein of imperialism coming to light in me. But I feel that these things, war and conquest, and victory and defeat, just happen and are there simply to be watched and experienced; they argue and discuss and talk, saying, 'This ought not to be. It ought to be like this,' and so on. I do not criticise life now, but I try to interpret it to myself and to express my interpretation of it.

January 28th The dance last night was amusing and I enjoyed it thoroughly. The Bakers came too and they really seem to appreciate the spirit of a Campden dance. It is strange how my old mistresses seem to produce families and how gossip attributes them to me, though I have nothing to do with them. N now has a baby coming in September, and she is going to marry the man, a sort of relation of M's who has just come back from Canada

January 30th Alexander has come into a little money and is going to print his poems. We discussed the shapes and clothing of books, and he seemed amused by my remark that books, like people, have manners and are ill bred or well bred, coarse or fine. Even if he has failed as a man, failed to accept life and sought refuge in Catholicism, Griggs has succeeded as an artist through that faithfulness alone. He is a man who interprets his ideals very narrowly though, and they have become embalmed through an over close devotion.

In early February CW was in London, meeting Frank Kendon and the poet John Drinkwater for advice on his own work; visiting his aunt Margot in Kensington but enjoying amorous adventures in Fitzrovia, despite finding 'Stripes' married and Eve absent in Cannes. He returned to find a flu epidemic in Campden.

February 12th   To-day a walk with the Bakers and Cardew has made me better. The thick hoar frost on the trees has melted and it is still a gentle day. The children in the street have started marbles, the first outdoor game of the year here; next comes hoops, then tops and hopscotch.

CW was himself ill during the next few days.

February 18th   This morning I went to watch the Bakers dyeing their wool blue. It is a strangely calm day, the earth moist, the lambs in their folds looking surprised to be born, lying by their mothers.

February 20th   To Painswick [with the Bakers], and back through Cheltenham and Winchcombe and past Stanway, and after dinner to the pictures at Stratford, where we saw quite an amusing skit on the old cowboy film and enjoyed ourselves very much. The Bakers went to look at a house at Painswick, for they are thinking of moving soon, which makes me sad.

February 25th   Back at the works to-day, and full of a new loathing for the place after having been away.

A meeting of the Campden Society to-night, which Griggs is going to attend. Jewson seems to be here too. Apart from my jealousy of him over Winifrid I feel such a contempt for them all in their apologetic mourning over the past that I can hardly bear to meet them. Griggs is above it and Simmonds, but God what a set of sentimentalists they are. The Bakers, appreciating their good qualities as I do, share my loathing, and we rave in the evenings together.

February 26th   The meeting last night, at which Griggs looked like a white lobster sitting on the edge of the pot into which he might have to jump and get boiled. The society has done a lot of good work and is getting stronger. I saw Brampton who is chairman, and he tells me we shall not be able to get the shoot at Clapton again. I heard from the Allcotts to-day, from Palma.

February 27ᵗʰ Yesterday afternoon I went for a walk with Leo Baker and went back to tea with them, home for dinner, slept for an hour, and went back again and talked till nearly 12. Cardew came after tea and we talked hard, like a lot of parrots, about Weininger[80] and women's freedom. Baker read the beginning of *Hamlet* to us, very well and I enjoyed it. This afternoon I have been for a long walk with Cardew and Charles Blakeman, tea at the Bakers and long discussions on Marx, pottery, Shakespeare and ourselves.

February 28ᵗʰ How I have loathed the works again after my two weeks nearly all away from it. When I think of the age I shall have to wait before I shall be free it almost drives me wild with despair. To have possibility dangled in front of me, with impossibility staring at me from its very face seems to be my fate in life; in writing, in living, in loving, in all things. I am slowly getting used to it, but I dread dying in spirit before I am free.

In my room now my two candles are lit and the fire glows red. I have just framed and hung up the little Palmer that I bought in London. The wind howls outside and it has been wet all day. I sit here, snug and happy in a sense of fellowship with Keats, Leigh Hunt, Coleridge, Southey, Lamb and Wordsworth, and I dedicate myself once more to the pleasure of solitary evenings of writing and reading.

March 2ⁿᵈ Griggs has resigned from the Campden Society in a white, livery huff. He is a silly man when he cannot have his own way, unable to fight resistance by giving way to it.

March 3ʳᵈ The printing of Adonis seems to be further off than ever. I shall probably do only another rhyme sheet this summer and wait until I am 30, then, if I have no publisher, print a volume very well, a volume of 100 pages with a vellum back, tallish, an inch or so thick, costing sixty pounds or more, a farewell to my first 30 years of life, then leave the works and start afresh with it

---

80   Otto Weininger, 1880-1903, Austrian author of the misogynist *Sex and Character*, published posthumously.

under my arm at tea parties and write Nature Notes for the Evesham Journal, or marry and grow potatoes or breed pigs. I read *The Merry Wives* yesterday, and shall *The Rape of Lucrece* to-day.

March 9th Father Bilsborrow came in last night while I was writing and said, 'I've got a poet in my house. Come and look at him.' It turned out to be Wilfred Childe[81], the Catholic mystic poet, whose work Griggs has shown me. He is something at Leeds University and knows Kramer and Abercrombie. A white faced, very womanish man but with a good head and far more in it than the Alexander type.

March 13th Griggs came in when I was having breakfast. He has gone to print his 'Duntisbourne Rouse' etching, which I love.

Shortly before his 25th birthday, CW devotes a long entry to self-analysis and criticism, mainly in the context of his poetic abilities. The following is an extract.

March 15th I shall be twenty-five in a month and my youth, the years between eighteen and twenty-five will have gone, and as yet no real maturity has taken its place. I have been looking at my early diaries and I see how I was a youth then, and how I have been stunned and at the same time stimulated by my experience of life. I have learnt to write more or less decent verse; I have got to know people I never dreamed of then; I have got my fingers on the edge of the literary shelf; and I am nearer to being free of the works. I begin to see myself merely as a potential minor poet, and my faith in myself as a great one (and it was firm till only a few months ago) is fading. That is terribly hard to accept at once, and consequently I find myself utterly miserable when I try to face it. I have come full circle, round to accept the fact that I have denied so hotly for so long. Technique is of vital importance. If one has not greatness in an art technique is the only resource.

In all this I depend on Winifrid as I have done ever since I loved her. Without her I am, as I have written to her, a lark without a sky. I shall need her during the next five years probably more than I have ever done, need her to stay beside

---

81   Wilfred Rowland Childe, 1890-1952, a convert to Catholicism and author of *Dream English: a Fantastical Romance* (1917). Perhaps coincidentally, there is a watercolour by Griggs of the previous year, entitled 'Dream Cotswold', which shows an *avant la lettre* view of Dover's Court in relation to St James's church.

me and be the centre of my spiritual life. Now to go on into the wilderness of those years, with faith in the fact that however small one's gift to the language that Shakespeare wrote, if it is one's best it will be worth something.

March 17th I have begun to read *Ulysses*[82], which Sleigh sent me in payment of a debt of £2 that he owed me. He got it in Holland and brought it back with him. It is a great book, whatever its obscurity and formlessness. Charles and I are going to Cardew's firing to-night.

March 18th The firing was very amusing. We sat and talked, the whole pottery lit up by the glow of the four fireholes in the kiln, and every half hour or so we stoked up again. At about two we toasted bloaters and cheese at the red glow of the fire and ate them and drank cider. I was very tired, but to sit by a great fire and talk sleepily about fine things to the man whose work is there inside the huge kiln waiting its fate, was delightful.

March 20th I went to the pictures at Evesham with the Bakers last night and I am going ratting with the two Ladbrooks from the butcher's opposite here this morning.

March 21st A drowsy day doing nothing yesterday. Tea with the Blakemans in Charles' new work room in the orchard of old Campden House, dinner at the Bakers, and the evening at Griggs'. Marjorie Lindsay, one of their pupils, began squeezing my hand as we all walked back down the street from Griggs', and told me that she would love to walk on Dover's Hill with me one night.

During the latter part of March, the presence of Winifrid, staying at Stanway, dominates CW's thoughts. Eileen Baker had made heavily flirtatious approaches to CW, apparently with the knowledge of Leo.

April 4th At tea time I took the Bakers to Birmingham to see [Chekhov's] *Uncle Vanya*. Just before I had a visit from Eileen, who was very affectionate, and who is more like a child that has been chidden by its parents and seeks consolation in a friendship that she cannot find with her brother-husband than anything. We enjoyed *Uncle Vanya* and the acting was good, and we brought

---

82   By James Joyce, published 1922 and still banned in England at the time.

Margot [Chatwin] home to Broad Campden, glad because she has another part: the Countess in *All's Well*.

April 8ᵗʰ   The Point-to-Point at Buckland, to which I took the Bakers. A poorer course than Dumbleton and one could see very little of the racing, but the sun shone and the hills lay sleepily along the skyline, and spring was there, and I won 15/- and enjoyed it. Afterwards we went to tea at the Old Bakehouse at Stanway and then on to the daffodil field at Toddington and picked wild daffodils.

April 12ᵗʰ   A walk with Eileen Baker this afternoon, then Roberts to tea and to see the new shoot at Charingworth. In the evening I took Dorothy [Chatwin] and my old governess Phyllis Gearey[83] out to dinner at the Lygon at Broadway. All night I seemed to dream of my childhood and of Mother and Phyllis and Bearley.

April 17ᵗʰ   A marvellous warm day, all the plum and cherry blossom out in the vale, and the green trees and bushes in the woods making them look as though they had been showered with tears of bright joy. This morning, I went to see the Oliver Bakers at Bearley and this afternoon took Cathy and Mrs Blakeman to see some old friends of theirs at Besford near Pershore. A wonderful 'Farmer's Wife' sort of household and tea party and a delightful afternoon. Those people all have roots firm in the earth and eyes and mouths like ancient sculptures. A charming little 16ᵗʰ century half-timbered church there, with a little triptych memorial with a child's portrait in it, dated 1564.

In the evening Eileen Baker came over and asked me to go across as Leo was in bed with flu. I went and we talked and kissed a little, and she became more charming as we did so, and her pale face became quite coloured and lit up, and her lips full. Poor Eileen.

April 19ᵗʰ   Yesterday badger digging all day with old Jeffries and a number of others, after the meet at the Fish. We found badgers at one at Attlepin Farm[84] and dug till six but did no good. Their earths are huge there and centuries old, and go right under the roots of an old elm tree. I saw one for a moment, as it

83   Who was to become my nanny in turn, in 1943!
84   Part of the Burnt Norton estate near Campden.

dashed from one hole to another and so escaped us, and that repaid me for all the digging and waiting. I nearly quarrelled with the Bakers before I went, over blood sports. They make me furious with their sentimental nonsense about poor little foxes. I am afraid we shall quarrel about it one day, or something like it.

Old Jefferies is six foot high, three foot broad, has two great sticks as tall as himself to get about with, breeds greyhounds, and lives in an ugly little bungalow near Bledington [near Stow-on-the Wold]. Of C.H. Smith he said: 'He was a fine bloody sportsman, mister.' I like him, and he seems to like me, though I must seem an odd bearded creature to him with my pale face and poetical ways.

In the evening I went to a dance at the Town Hall and took Cathy Blakeman out for a walk in the still fields in the moonlight and was strangely happy with her. Her simplicity and native intelligence attract me till sometimes I think I must be a little in love with her.

April 20th We dug till four yesterday but failed to get our badger out. I have learned a lot though, and went to bed tired and pleased with my day. I feel very fond of Cathy and sometimes think that I might do worse than to marry someone like her, if ever I do marry. Such a type would be the only one for a person of my egotistical ways. There are, I begin to feel, only two ways of life that are right and eternal: the religious life, and the life of man tilling the soil and in continual touch with nature. All else, cities and wealth and power, floats on the surface and is ephemeral. Those two alone live and one day nothing else will live once more.

April 23rd I lie in bed and sweat with a temperature and cold and cough. I had to crawl to Birmingham yesterday to sign some cheques, but came home and went to bed at one. I have been nursed and looked after like their own child by Cathy and Mrs Blakeman, given asparagus for my dinner and hot milk and kindness continually.

April 25th It does not affect my love for Winifrid, but this little love for Cathy is growing. It is her strange simplicity of thought and a certain secret depth of knowledge of and communion with nature that attract me. She has the simplicity of a child in the heart of an adult and it is a wonderful thing, and there is much that I can learn from it. In a quiet domestic way I love her, though I understand the limitations and blind spots her nature is bound to show to mine. It is as though a tall man lived in a village belonging to pygmies when one talks to her. In their largest hall he can just sit down, but he likes the place and so sits there with them and talks – then, to their despair and amazement gets up and, with two strides, is beyond their furthest mountain range. As this little love has grown it has been as though one were crossing a cherry orchard in full bloom to meet her, and now I hold her hand in the orchard and wander with her examining the secrets of the banks and hedges and listening to the birds singing.

April 26th Last night to see *Macbeth* with Cathy and Charles and Charles's girl of the moment, the daughter of an art master in London, and full of suburban art-commonplaces. Cathy was charming. All the way to Stratford in the car she was so excited that she could not keep still, and the play was to her reality more than life. On the way back she put her head on my shoulder and told me stories about her childhood when they lived at Wood Cottage [at the entrance to Campden House] and she spent all her days in Campden Wood exploring and wandering about.

May 6th Griggs came last night and we talked about all my new discoveries about poetry and technique, and I went home with him and we went on talking. My little love for Cathy Blakeman is quiet just now. Winifrid makes me blind to every other woman for a long time after I have seen her. The Bakers I have not seen for a long time.

May 7th Last night Charles and I slept out for the first time this year, in the orchard by the Campden House ruins, under the cherry trees, with the still moon looking down on us and sheep silver with dew gazing at us in a row mystified. The dawn was lovely and the birds sang beautifully.

I had lunch with the Bakers, the first time I have seen them since Easter. Eileen clasped me in her arms and rubbed her cheek on my beard and said I was nice. Leo depressed me by his anaemic and academic ideas about poetry, and I came home feeling that they are not now of much use to me. She is too nervy and highly strung and he had too much given up life and taken to weaving, and sees other people's ideas only in so far as they are pallid and resigned, like his own.

Last night I read (by request) to the Blakemans again. I find that Cathy knows all my *Five Poems,* and 'Idleness' and 'Night Song' by heart, and other poems not printed that I have left lying about. It is gratifying and makes one feel that one has not worked for nothing. She says them to herself, she tells me, when she is dusting the house. She says she learnt them by rote first and then began to understand them afterwards.

May 11th At about 10, just as I was going to bed, Griggs called. He had been entertaining some stonemasons who are working on Westcote House, where the Bakers are going, and was very cheerful and seemed ready to talk all night. He talked a good deal about his own work and said he must work more quickly. 'I've been taking too much trouble with my plates', he said. And people don't appreciate it and it takes too long. I mustn't be so old maidish about them.' That, from the High Priest of craftsmanship and care, amazed me.

May 29th Charles Blakeman has gone to Rome and writes that he is enjoying himself very much. He returns on Tuesday. I took Mrs Blakeman and Cathy in the car up to Dover's Hill for a pic-nic yesterday and we sat there and looked down on the Lynches and the misty plain beyond, and it was very pleasant to sit and talk to them there in the sun, and to hear Mrs Blakeman's accounts of her youth and the way she had to work then, and the kind of people who lived here, and the farmers, and those in the big houses, all seen from her individualistic point of view.

May 30th A warm rain is falling gently. The dry earth seems to breathe and so sweet smelling is the air that my heart beats hushed and fast at it. The village children are playing under the elm tree at the corner of Sheep Street, dry in its cover.

Later, a sister from the Convent has just been in to tell the Blakemans that the old Mother Superior has been ordered to move to Dudley in the Black Country. She has been fifty years in Campden and is eighty. When I heard I was shocked and tears came into my eyes and my heart was full of sorrow for her. Her nuns, the children she has taught, the grown ups she has loved and watched married and known since their birth, and who have loved her like their own mother, all those she has got to leave at the age of eighty at the caprice of this damned Catholic Church. She taught Mrs Blakemans's husband when he was a boy and she was the first visitor she had after she was married.

June 3ʳᵈ Back from Cambridge. I went on Wednesday and wandered about, saw the outside of King's in the dusk like a dream of delight, went to bed, saw my customer in the morning, and then had him self imposed on me for a tour round the town. He took me round the colleges and to the Fitzwilliam, to King's Chapel and the river, and I could not get rid of him for two hours. Some strange destiny seems to link me to Keats. This little man led me through the Fitzwilliam at an awful pace, and at last halted before a screen of pictures, and there in front of me was the miniature of him by [Joseph] Severn. Suddenly to see that face I knew so well, gazing out at me with deep eyes, like a wild creature dying in the desert, was extraordinary. I gazed for a long time silently then the little man said, 'Ah, John Keats. A funny old stick, Keats.' 'Yes', I said, and we went on.

I found that the best way back was through London, so I took the one o'clock train and got there at 2.30, and went to see Margaret Smith. We sat and talked, and went to the private view of a man called Claude Flight[85], a friend of hers. There I talked a lot of rubbish about art to Mr Flight and tried to appreciate his triangles of different colour.

I am riding in a procession at the Fete on Monday on the Ladbrooks' horse, and as I haven't ridden since I was seven I am not looking forward to it at all.

June 5ᵗʰ This morning I had my first riding lesson on Ladbrook's horse. Charlie took me out for two hours and I feel as though I had been dragged in a barrel up and down the street all morning. I chiefly distinguished myself by falling off, owing to the breaking of a stirrup leather, on Dover's Hill in front of a Girl Guides camp, and I fell on my left wrist and sprained it, and the horse kicked my leg as it went on and there is a great bruise there, and my bottom is as raw as a piece of steak. I will one day go at riding until I can ride properly. It was wonderful, riding along Dover's Hill, with nothing but the sky, the trees and the grazing sheep to see, and oneself mounted on a live creature that was as it were part of those.

---

85   W. Claude Flight, 1881-1955. One of the few British artists influenced by Futurism and Vorticism, he was a member of the Seven and Five Society, and worked mainly in linocut.

June 6th   I feel rather shaken by my fall yesterday and my wrist is badly swollen. I do not know whether to ride in the procession or not. Having only one hand to use I fear I shall not be able to control the horse. It is a matter of pride though. I will do it, to show I am not to be beaten. And as soon as I can, I shall learn to ride. Others can, so I can.

June 7th   Riding in that procession yesterday was agony. When the band started the horse started playing up, and every time it moved my whole body seemed to be torn in two. Ladbrook led the horse for me, so I was safe, but it was awful.

After it was over I slept for an hour, tired out. In the evening I drank a lot of beer with Hudson, went to a rabbit pie supper, and to a dance at Broadway, which I hated. Every time I do surface things like that now I hate it and feel wrong. As we came back, Charles, for we took him too, said the same thing, and we both decided that we shall soon cease to bother about dances and things like that.

This evening Charles and I have been for a walk, up Dyer's Lane and along the top and down Kingcombe Hill. The sheep are bleating after the rain, the hedges dripping, and the birds singing, and snails were making strange journeys from ditch to ditch as we walked along the road. We saw two feeding on another dead one. They had eaten its inside out.

June 11th   Poor Griggs. I hear he has spoiled his 'Duntisbourne Rouse' plate, one of the most charming of all his small etchings. I am going to see him to condole with him, for he will be very upset I know, because he has put more of himself into it than many others.

June 13th   I went to see Griggs and found Hudson there and the Blakers who used to live here. The plate is quite spoilt. I saw one of the few prints from it before it was and one after. It was one of the most perfect of all his etchings to me, with far more soul in it, with soul and technique living together as brothers, not, as is frequent with him, as rivals.

Cathy and my little love for her and my feeling of belonging to this simple-hearted family is very delightful. I am inclined to grow too much bound up in them all. Yesterday Charles and I and her mother took tea in Northwick Park and Charles and I bathed, then sat in the hot sun with them and talked. Charles and I slept out. It was warm and the moon misty and when we woke the bird songs were just dying down and the sun was rising over the cup of the hills to look down on Campden's roofs.

To return to the works this morning was parching agony. Only by calling on my spirit can I tolerate the agony of the senses that the place gives me. I long for simple work in Campden, so that I can be free from all that I hate in Birmingham.

June 14th Yesterday the works appalled me. Sunday has been such a warm soft day of gentle pleasure, a kind of day that I always enjoy with a kind of sleeping distrust, for I know that it cannot last and that I shall be miserable after.

In the evening I did a little more of Persephone and at ten Griggs came and stayed till after eleven and kept me up later than I had wanted to be, but I wanted to see him. He has, he thinks, saved the 'Duntisbourne Rouse' plate, for a few more impressions at least.

June 16th Griggs came last night. He is going to give me a print of 'Duntisbourne Rouse' because 'my sympathy has so helped him to save it.' I am very pleased[86].

June 29th Yesterday a wonderful day badger digging. We went first to the Quarry but did not find there, so we went off to Dark Coppice at Attlepin again and put the dogs in and found. Then we all began digging. For an hour there was hardly a sound but the whimpering of the terriers and the thudding of spades and earth. Then came long discussions; rods thrust in holes; terriers put in; more digging; cider drunk; lunch got out of bags and pockets and eaten; people coming to look on; varied advice; difficulties and doubts; and at last at a quarter to four we were within a yard of the badger. The terriers tried to draw him but could not. One by one they came whimpering out with bleeding ears and faces. We dug more, then routed the badger with a pole, drew back and waited in silence, one little bitch, wounded, still whimpering to go in again.

---

86 So much so that CW wrote a poem about it, which met with Griggs's approval.

Then slowly, cautiously, at the bottom of the trench, the grey badger came out. A spade was plunged in to cut him off, and the terriers were loosed on him to give them blood. Then, in the clamour of yelping dogs and shouting men he was lifted up by the tail, six dogs clinging to him, and bagged.

After that there was more cider drinking and talk, then it was found that there was another in the sett and we started digging again, and got him out. Still the terriers strained to get in again and again we dug and got another out. In the end we had six, tied up in bags, in the fields. We went down to the kennels at Broadway to tell the Master and to take some of the terriers back, and then came back to Campden. There, there was quite a crowd in the Square to meet us and someone had bought us a bottle of champagne, which we drunk, passing it round like a beer bottle, talking and joking all the time. Then we went into the Noel Arms and had more drinks for an hour, and at last I came home to supper tired and stiff. I am going to have one badger skinned and have the skin cured.

After supper Charles and I went to a melodrama acted by a travelling company[87] in the Town Hall: *Only a Tramp, or the Noble Brothers*, a very amusing tragedy. Next week they are doing *No Mother to Guide Her, or The Girl who Left her Home*. After that, to bed in the summer night on Doe Bank, where we awoke for the eclipse, but it was cloudy and we could see nothing at all of it.

Winifrid was absent in France on holiday at this time, and the diary is much given over to agonised yearning for her. However, CW consoled himself with a gentle dalliance with Cathy Blakeman, his landlady's daughter.

July 10th   Last night Mrs Blakeman was in bed, and Charles was out, and Cathy and I sat quietly in the kitchen, she on a stool between my knees, and talked and kissed, and it was very delightful. Then Charles came in and he and I went for a ride on bicycles in the moonlight, up through Campden Wood, up Tilbury Hollow, and along the Stow road and back at one. To-day it is hot and sunny. The summer has come at last, if only for a day or two. The Exhibition Committee meets this afternoon; Hudson, Sharpley[88] and myself and one or two others.

---

87   Of the kind immortalised by J.B. Priestley in *The Good Companions*, published in 1929.

88   Reginald Sharpley, 1879-1946. A civil engineer and soldier who took up painting, exhibiting 18 times at the Royal Academy. At the time he lived at The Martins, but died at Amberley, Glos. His painting of St James's Church, Campden, in Winter hangs in the Town Hall in Campden.

July 11th   The Exhibition meeting was in the usual Campden style, which infuriates the business part of me. At 2.30 I went along and there was no one there and no keys. At three Sharpley went and there was still nobody there. At 3.30 George Hart[89] went and there was no one there. Hudson did not go at all. Dewey the secretary said later that he had had his dinner late and as it was so hot he had had a doze after, and seemed to think that no further explanation was necessary. That is the Campden way of doing business always. They seem to think that no appointment matters, no date, no undertaking to do a thing.

Cardew came later in the afternoon and he and I and Charles went and bathed at Northwick. He and I had tea with Finberg and in the evening Charles and I went for a walk down over the flat meadows towards the railway. It was wet and hot and the birds were singing all round, more than usual for July. We found a huge horse mushroom which fed us both for breakfast this morning.

July 12th   Going home early I drove from Honeybourne to Campden through the most tremendous thunderstorm I have ever seen. In ten minutes the roads became a flood of water, crops were beaten down flat, low lying fields were flooded, and cattle were killed. Almost every second there was a blinding flash of lightning and the rain fell in one continuous stream of long drops the size of my little finger. The bottom of Aston Hill was a raging torrent. It was an extraordinary thing to drive through. The lightning gave me a headache, which has only now gone, 24 hours later. And a quarter of an hour later it was all over, fine again, but the world drenched, crops ruined, partridges and pheasants drowned, orchards stripped. At night there was steady, dismal rain and thunder still rumbled far off, like an army that has conquered and retreats because it thinks itself defeated.

July 14th   The whole conduct of the Exhibition Committee has so annoyed me that I have withdrawn my two things and resigned. I was elected on to the hanging committee and no effort was made to ask my opinion on a single point, and yesterday there was a meeting of which I was not even advised. What made it worse was that Hudson and I were talking to Sharpley the chairman at four and at six went up to the rooms and found a meeting in full progress. On my objecting Sharpley said to me that he had not let me know because he had

---

89   George Henry Hart, 1882 - 1973. One of Ashbee's original Guildsmen, he took on the running of the silver workshop in 1912, where the Hart family continues to this day.

thought I did not get back till late, though he had seen me two hours before. I took my exhibits and went off home. If he chooses to apologise I will put them in again, because they are also Finberg's, as printing, but I do not like being treated like that, and I made it plain that I did not.

July 15th Last night after visits from Griggs and Eileen Baker and explanations, I agreed to send my things back to the exhibition. All my anger had gone hours before, and I could do nothing but laugh at the Committee and myself. I was conscious of being three people: One who was really offended on principle; another who looked on from a height and laughed at it all like the devil; and another who was rather pleased to be centre of the Campden stage for a day or two.

Drinkwater and Kendon both write to say that my rhyme sheet 'Spring in the Hollow' is the best poem of mine they have seen. Wilfred Childe praises it with the extravagance of unwitting insincerity – and I myself feel that it is so little personal to me that anyone might have written it.

July 18th Yesterday I took Mrs Blakeman and Cathy out to Saintbury Hill in the car and we had tea there in the field, a strange but domestic party, watching the rabbits and enjoying the beauty of the scene. Mrs B. is like a duchess out of a German fairy story, and Cathy might have come out of one too. In the evening Cardew and I went and bathed at Northwick and later I read 'Nymphidia'[90] to the Blakemans. On Saturday I played tennis at Griggs's again, and got hot and enjoyed myself.

Entries for the next month pass in anticipation and embarking on a trip to France to stay with Winifrid and Stanley Wood and their daughters at Wissant in Northern France, where they had taken a house for the summer. On his return to Campden (and Birmingham) CW is in an emotionally drained, yet satisfied state. Here, the first inklings of the draw of the hunting field begin to emerge.

August 20th Charles and I were up at five this morning and went off to Hailes Wood. The hounds met at Wood Stanway and were drawing Thrift Wood when we got there. It poured with rain nearly all the time and we stood about and saw nothing much. Once we heard hounds in full cry in Hailes, and the sound

---

90   *Nymphidia, the Court of Faery*, by Michael Drayton, 1627.

---

was lovely. We were there till half past seven, then came back home and brought the terriers back to the kennels at Broadway.

August 22nd When I go among conscious highbrows I hate them for their self consciousness and groundless self-esteem; when I go among manufacturers and low brows and ordinary people I hate them for their gross materialism and blindness and scorn of things of the spirit. The true country dwellers, who are not one or the other of those things, are the only people I can stand, for they are themselves. They think in their own way and have souls and are real. The true countryman loves the country not for its aesthetic beauty or its colour, or nature life or hills or rivers, or views, but he loves it for all those in one, purely and un-analytically, as his home, just as, for instance, Charles Lamb loved London.

August 23rd I seem to have changed the order of my life since I came back from France. I hardly go out at all to see people. I have only seen the Bakers once and Griggs twice. When I do go out it is generally alone, for a walk, or with Charles Blakeman. He is the only permanent person in my local acquaintance, except the people I know who belong to Campden and were born in it. The others, even Griggs, melt away from my consciousness when I do not see them for a time. Cathy I see little of alone now, partly by design and partly by accident.

August 28th Yesterday Roberts and I walked round Charingworth and saw a good lot of birds. In the evening Charles and I went round to three fields where they were cutting out the last of the corn, and shot rabbits. At night he and I went to the dance in the Town Hall. I have sold about 16/- worth of poems at the Exhibition and keep on selling a few at the local shop too. I have spent £12 in printing altogether and got £7 back so far.

August 29th Yesterday I went for a walk with the Ladbrooks, the butchers opposite, in the evening, up to see their pigs and a new horse. I came home and found the house empty and got myself some supper and spent the evening rather sadly alone.

August 31st To-morrow I go shooting at Bretforton with Jack Coldicott the butcher, Edgar Hartwell from Weston [sub-Edge], the builder, and some others.

September 2ⁿᵈ Yesterday was an amazing day and I feel rather ill after it. It was terribly hot and we walked the asparagus bowers and fields of sprouts all morning, and got ten brace of birds. At lunch we drank a lot of cider and set out again, all feeling very sleepy, but only got another four brace and a hare. I shot two brace and the hare. After that we came back to the farm and the farmer brought out what he called cider, but what was really very old perry, as clear and cold as wine, and as we were all very thirsty we drank a lot of it, straight off, on our empty stomachs. Nothing happened for a time, except increased talk and laughter, and someone bet me his car that he'd race me to Evesham, and I was only stopped from taking the bet with difficulty. Then we went down to the pub in the village, and I was feeling rather drunk. There we had some more cider and then some whisky, and I felt horribly ill and went outside and was sick. I went back and found everyone else getting drunk very stolidly, went out and was sick again, then sat in the car and went to sleep. At ten I was woken by Jack Coldicott and Geoffrey Smith from Broad Campden and told it was time to go home. They got in and I drove very gingerly along, keeping my eyes on the roadside and wobbling very badly, and at last we got to Campden, where Coldicott got out after being woken up, for he had fallen asleep in the dickey. I drove Smith back up to Broad Campden, drove back and garaged my car, and went home and lay down on my settee and slept till twelve, woke, found and ate some food, and went up to bed. To-morrow I shoot at Charingworth.

September 4ᵗʰ We only got three brace of birds yesterday, but there are plenty there, though they are very wild. I only shot one brace. I have just finished E.M. Forster's *Passage to India* and do not think much of it.

I have a sort of conscience about not going to see the Bakers and Griggs, but my aversion to their arty-crafty qualities now outweighs my desire to see them. I feel that aversion just now for all except Griggs, who overtops the things which he has in common with the others. It is the petty-artist type that I can't stand, the type that can never be anything and yet thinks itself so valuable that it will not live. It substitutes an intellectual self-consciousness of an irritating kind for real self-awareness, and hides in petty intellectual snobberies from the daily reality of life.

September 5ᵗʰ Cardew came over yesterday to tea and came in again in the evening. We went to visit the Bakers in their new house and found them very consciously refined about it. I think I have exhausted any possibilities they ever had for me.

I feel quite differently now about my poetry. I used to be annoyed and sad when I got no recognition. Now I simply live and so far as it is part of my life to write poetry, I write it and that is that. By the time I have had another five years of life I shall be ready to write. The fears I have had of writing leaving me are gone. And even if that should happen it would not, in some queer way, matter now. The thing is to live fully within.

The real truth about life is that if one lives with sincerity and integrity to one's experience, denying nothing, striving to accept all, one cannot help gaining happiness of the only sort that matters, the most real and beautiful happiness because the most true. Any other sort of happiness has sorrow as its reverse, just as 'I am well' has a consciousness of illness behind it.

September 11th My cold has nearly gone. Shooting yesterday we got only five brace. I shot vilely and was nervy and shot too soon and behind my birds. In the evening I went to see Griggs and found the Bakers there, singing songs and talking folk dancing. I took a brace of partridges. The talk was of the worst sentimental arty-crafty kind. I just bore it and did not explode with despair and came away.

September 16th To dinner at Griggs's last night, and he and I talked a great deal afterwards, Nina going to bed as she always does. Love, religion, communism, art, the Bakers, Finberg, politics, and so on were our topics. At dinner Griggs joked a lot about 'poor old Jewson' and Winifrid, and I felt jealous even to joke about him and her. After dinner we were talking about love poems and he said that no great love poem could be founded on unrequited love. I told him that it might seem strange, but that I had never experienced unrequited love, and that I had never loved anyone who had not loved me. After that we got on to religion through a discussion on the origin of the creative impulse in man, and he told me how he became a Catholic, then, when he began to 'sell his Catholicism' as the Americans would say, I changed the conversation. I left at 11.30 and went in to a dance at the Town Hall for half an hour, then to bed, where I had strange dreams of my Mother and Winifrid.

September 18th   An unsuccessful day's shooting yesterday and the circus in the evening with Charles, then a dance at the Town Hall for an hour with him and Cathy, all of which I accepted as part of life, rather than enjoyed. I laughed, frowned, smiled, talked, was glad, displeased, eager, sad, thoughtful, at peace, angry, all in small degree, and afterwards went to bed.

September 19th   Toasted cheese, a pint of beer, some gin, and a session talking to Woodsend, an architect here, at the Red Lion, got me off dreaming again about my mother and Winifrid again, and about Mrs Blakeman and Cathy. Griggs has water on the knee and must rest the knee for a fortnight.

September 21st   Yesterday to Nailsworth, and I took Hudson and brought him back to Campden. At Cirencester we met Norman and Mary Jewson. Mary had on a pair of cheap brown shoes, artificial silk stockings, a brown coat, and a blue felt hat and looked like a prosperous farmer's wife whose daughters have brought home the influence of town shopkeepers' daughters from the grammar school and have tried to smarten their mother up. Jewson and I were too cordial towards each other for it to be natural.

In the evening Hudson and I spent an amusing time wandering about Campden, drinking beer, though not grossly, and laughing a great deal, and later walked over to Broad Campden with Ladbrook and met a gipsy guardsman on the way, with whom, in the fields, in the night, Ladbrook sang songs of the war; 'Mademoiselle from Armentieres', etc. We went on to the Baker's Arms at Broad Campden and drank some more beer, and came home to bed late.

The night before last I dreamt that I was shooting at Charingworth with Charles Blakeman and Keats. We were walking a field of roots and Keats shot a tomtit and I missed a partridge. It was very odd, Charles, Keats and myself, Keats in the middle in 1820 costume and a muzzle-loader, and ourselves in breeches and tweed coats.

September 22nd   I went to Griggs' last night and found him enjoying himself thoroughly, sitting in an armchair, his foot on another chair, and surrounded by Nina, the two Bakers, and two other people. He has to sit like that for three weeks and rest his knee, but he seems to be quite enjoying it. He loves sympathy and a good talk and this gives him chances for both.

The Pre-Raphaelites were like fish trained to live out of water. One feels that if they had been put back they would have died. This remark of mine seemed to amuse Griggs.

September 25th After tea a friend of Blakeman's called Nuttgens[91], a stained glass worker, and his wife and their young baby came in, and it was wonderful to see the youth and purpose in old Mrs B's eyes as she played with the baby, dandled it on her knee, held it up, talked to it. Grumpy and old as she can be, bad tempered and silent as she can be, she has a soul that has learnt to love, in the great school of sorrow. Sorrow may warp and wound and destroy, but to those whom it does make rich it gives a depth that nothing else can.

September 29th Griggs sent me a note and asked me to go and see him last night and I went and we had a long argument about the vocabulary of poetry. He quite failed to see the oddity and laughablness now of 'yon tree', 'shining orb' and such poeticisms, which explains his failure to see how bad Russell Alexander's poems are, for they consist largely of pseudo-poetic phrases strung together to give an illusion of feeling. I argued for the use of conversation, of ordinary educated society now, and we did not agree.

October 2nd Shooting all day yesterday at Charingworth with Charles and a young man called Cottrell. There are no pheasants at Charingworth but we got 5½ brace of partridges and 5 rabbits, which was not bad as it poured with rain all day and there was a howling gale too. By evening we were all tired out. But I like shooting with those two. The three of us work with a sort of instinctive knowledge of each other, just like three dogs working together. It is mere pot hunting, but when the birds are as wild as they were yesterday it calls for considerable skill, and I enjoy it far more than I do standing in a butt or behind a hedge waiting for birds to be driven over me.

Some of my shares have gone up suddenly and I am about £50 better off than I was on Thursday. Cardew is coming to tea.

October 4th Last night I went for a walk when I had done writing. It was cold and the stars were very bright and one could hear sounds far away, whistles,

---

91   Joseph Edward Nuttgens, 1892-1982. Born in Germany, he worked briefly in Chipping Campden with Paul Woodroffe, marrying his son's tutor, Kathleen Clarke, an Irish nationalist.

---

shouts, voices, that came across the fields on the still air. There was a horse champing in a field. It was so still and cold that the night seemed to be holding its breath, waiting for winter to come.

October 5th Last night Griggs came and was very troubled about Charles's manners with him. (Charles works for him in his printing room now.) He obviously daren't speak to him about it himself and wants me to and I don't feel inclined to at all. Charles has bad manners in Griggs's sense; rather he has a bad manner and no manners at all. Griggs expects a kind of deference that he will never get because he has not the way of getting it from people of independent mind like Charles, who would rather run a mile than call anyone sir. We talked for some time and then he went home to get on with correcting the proofs of the catalogue of his work that Alexander is doing.

October 7th Yesterday to Gloucester and lunch with Cardew and back early. I have read *Love's Labours Lost* and the *Comedy of Errors* and *Titus Andronicus*[92]. In them it seems to me that Shakespeare was just a brilliant young man using his gift of writing to its utmost in making stage plays as a craft. Life had not then given his genius any banks to flow between. There is little, except the Cuckoo and the Owl at the end of *Love's Labours,* and a few passages that live as poetry in those plays. I am convinced that before he wrote any of those, though, he had had some years' experience of writing for the stage, of acting, and of producing other people's plays.

October 9th Last night I went to the Red Lion and drank a little, then wandered about with vague desires and plans, vague sexual cravings, vague intentions, none of which bore fruit. I went to the Bakers', turned away; walked up one street, turned back; stood outside the Town Hall, didn't go in; wandered on; wandered back; and at last finished by standing behind a gatepost in the empty street by the Convent, listening to two lovers laughing and talking, one at a window, the other under it, till the girl's sister came to the window and called her in, and the lover went away. One cat came past; the moon was hidden, yet the sky was light; I was tired out with shooting, and it struck twelve. I came in and went to bed.

---

92   CW was undertaking a reading of Shakespeare in the order of composition, as it was understood at the time.

October 11th Last night Griggs came for half an hour and I told him I had almost finished 'Persephone' and we talked about writing plays. He does not seem to understand the drama, an essentially urban thing. Middleton Murry[93] has written to say he will read 'Persephone' for me. Our talk convinced me that Griggs has not and never will have the Shakespearean order of imagination. He is a Miltonist, of the same mould, the 'egotistical sublime'. I don't scoff at him now for this, I just accept it and think what he has missed. Charles has the Shakespearean order of imagination, so has Hudson and Mrs B., so had my grandmother, so have I, so has Jack Bridge at the Red Lion. People so widely different, they all have it, infinitely varied in degree, but of the same quality. Griggs is perpetually trying to capture life in formulae. His acceptance of Catholicism is an example. He must feel sure, have a fixed belief about things. Unless he has such, such a man is miserable all his life.

October 13th Last night Charles and I and Ladbrook went off to Stratford Mop Fair and wandered about there till twelve when it ended. The most remarkable thing was a huge bullock that weighed 30 cwt, and stood 18 hands high, and was perfectly proportioned and enormous in every limb. It was six years old and bought by its owner a few years ago as an ordinary store beast. He has taken it all round the country to fairs since.

October 17th At ten last night Cardew came in and stayed till 2.30, and Finberg joined us at 11.30 and we had a furious argument about all kinds of things, Cardew contradicting us and himself in every sentence, and Finberg being very pontifical and pompous. Our argument centred round romanticism and myself, then changed to pottery and sculpture, then to theories of significant form, which seems to signify nothing. No one knew what he was talking about, but we all talked and ideas flew about and it was stimulating. I am reading *The Rape of Lucrece*.

October 18th Lunch in Birmingham with an aunt, by which I have missed a day's shooting. To-morrow my uncle, by which I shall miss another. I am reading *Henry VI*.

---

93   John Middleton Murry, 1889-1957, writer and critic. He married Katherine Mansfield and was a supporter of D.H. Lawrence

---

In 'Persephone' I feel that I have really accomplished something. People I talk to about it too, take it seriously and want to see it. The very fact of having worked for fourteen months on one poem and of having got it done is something. I have tried my wings. I may only have flown over a molehill, but I have flown, and that is something.

October 19th I am binding my copy of 'Persephone'. Last night I got it sewn and glued into its boards, and now I fondle it and look at it like the mother of her child in newly made long-clothes. I have never bound a book before and I set myself the problem as though no one had, and thought it all out.

October 28th A delightful day shooting at Lane's at Broom Court and I am pleased with myself because I shot four hares and a brace of pheasants, one of them over the top of a row of 40 foot elms, coming with the wind, at a terrific pace, so that my hat fell off with the swing. Old Mrs Lane, stone deaf, a delightful old lady, with a squeaky voice, a beard and moustache, still talks of Stratford as though it were half a day's journey, still belongs to a 'Magazine Club' and gets the 'Spectator' and 'Chambers' Journal' a month old. She said to me: 'You live at Campden then, Mr Whitfield. It always seems to me that people at Campden are so much nearer London than we are here, so much more civilised. We are in such a backwater here.'[94] I had to write my answer on a slate that she thrust under my nose, while all the others round the plush covered tea table waited and looked on, as though I were speaking.

October 31st A good day on Saturday, marred by one horrid thing. Crossing a field to lunch, walking with Lane, he said we ought to have our guns loaded in case anything got up. I loaded mine and somehow, closing it, let off one barrel into the ground. It upset me for most of the day, though they were all very decent about it and said nothing. It was like one's trousers falling down in a full drawing room, the most unpleasant thing that has ever happened to me out shooting. Added to that I have been horribly nervy this last week and very self conscious all the time. I have written to Bomford and apologised. I suppose I am run down and need a rest. To walk up Campden street yesterday alone was an agony of self centred discomfort, as though there were a face behind every

---

94   Broom Court is near Bidford-on-Avon, about ten miles west of Campden and eight from Stratford upon Avon.

---

window watching one's least movement. I met Hudson last night and had a quiet binge and giggle with him, but did not really get tight.

November 2nd Last night I took Sam [Whitfield, a cousin] and his wife to see [Anna] Pavlova in Birmingham, a promise I made in an absent minded moment weeks ago, which they dug up. She was like a piece of the most perfect glass that seems, so fragile is it, to be on the point of breaking every moment, yet which never breaks. She is marvellous, completely in harmony with her self. When she came on stage, though all the other dancers were good, every eye turned on her, and it seemed as though the whole audience, by the very intensity of its own gaze, were creating her out of air upon the stage before it, out of air and music. She danced the Swan, which I saw years ago in London. The spirit of the swan lived and died as she danced, the spirit of a dying wild creature. As I watched I realised too that one may love the thing one kills. Love is not a gushing forth of sentiment and emotion; it is a comprehension of the unity of life; a comprehension of the fact that each thing living or dying, is part of life just as one is oneself, and that life could not exist without all things, including death. One who loves thus sees the reformer, the Shelley, the Socialist, as a grown up sees a child.

That leads me to another thing. I see Griggs like that, like a clever earnest child struggling with uncomprehending mind with forces beyond his control. His attitude to life is not a religious one, despite his Catholicism. It is an attitude which implies the right of the human will to alter life, not to suffer it; an attitude born of a nature that cannot see wholly enough to see life as a unity and accept it so. The other type is rare. It only exists in either the highest consciously enlightened being (Keats or Shakespeare) or in the simplest enlightened soul – Mrs Blakeman. In between, in the world where consciousness struts about like a clown, knocking instinct over and then putting it in its place again, there are all the types of human being upon whom one smiles, having seen their vision, as an adult smiles on a child. I have that higher consciousness. It may not be modest to say so, but it is true, I know in my heart. To have it and keep it the first need is to know oneself utterly and remorselessly. No one except the simple type can touch it without self knowledge. Such knowledge outcasts by implication all morality as such, and replaces morality with love, which is its essence.

'The crude clean comfort with which the labourer is satisfied.' Griggs said that the other night and I thought it good. The degrees of comfort are legion and each is satisfied with his own degree. The conditions of 'Greasy Moll doth keel the pot' and 'Dick the shepherd blows his nail' are to us pitiable and would afford pages of reformers' propaganda, but they are conditions in which men have been able to find themselves in perfect harmony with life. That is the thing: to be in harmony with life, with the life of each hour. Happiness is a state of mind, and is very largely independent of circumstance, or should be, if one has seen the truth on life's wholeness.

November 3ʳᵈ I don't feel eager to write and I have nothing else to do. What is the use of writing when no one reads what one writes? That is what I feel now. Poetry is the voice of a dead age, to me now. One may, given talent, ape the grandeurs of past ages, or one may get lost in the present, with no tradition to steer by; there is no alternative for us now. As civilisation grows and the language becomes more and more set, the task of giving what one writes that unexpected newness that makes poetry pleasing as well as deep grows more and more difficult – hence Futurists, Da-daists, Primitives, and the rest. In attempting an unashamedly romantic poem now I know I have set myself an almost impossible task, but to fail after attempting such a task is better than to succeed in an easier one. 'Persephone' in 1820 would have given me a name; now no one will ever read it, except my friends, and they will read it out of interest in me, or out of kindness. Yet even if I have failed in this poem I am young still, and I may yet succeed in another.

November 14ᵗʰ After dinner I went to see the Bakers about some play they are doing this year, a sort of third-rate pseudo-rural *Chauve Souris*[95], I gather. I was so uninterested in it and everything else that I told them I couldn't help them much this year.

November 15ᵗʰ Last night I revised a little, then Griggs came in and finally I went to the Armistice Dance, to which I had decided not to go. I was too late to get tight, and I went with the definite idea of being chaste. I drank a little beer and spent some time dancing with the Slattery girls, very proper and refined, and talking to the young men who were with them, then Hudson

---

95 'La Chauve Souris' (The Bat) was a popular revue originating in Paris in 1920, directed by Nikita Baliev.

arrived with a bottle of whisky and things grew livelier. The Slatterys went and their young men joined us, and Hudson and I giggled and grew rather tight. At the end, as they all went out, I caught several girls and kissed them and behaved rather wildly, and went home with Charles. This morning I have a heavy head, but otherwise feel better for it all. I enjoyed it but was conscious all the time of being not able to enjoy myself, for it was such a contrast to the life I have just got used to, a life in Campden with Winifrid only a mile away [staying with Dorothy Chatwin at Broad Campden for two weeks]. It was rather nice of Griggs to call, for he obviously did so because he thought I should be lost and desolate with Winifrid having gone.

November 16ᵗʰ Last night Charles and I went to supper with the Nuttgens. They have an objectionable coarse lavatory humour that upsets me. All their instincts to open sexual humour are diverted to jokes that are laughed at only because they are coarse and dirty. I have noticed that certain types of 'puritan' minded people have this quality. Sex is taboo, but the lavatory and the anus are permissible. There was a girl there whose father was a friend of Rupert Brooke's, but all she said was 'How thrilling' every time anyone made a remark, yet she looked quite intelligent.

November 20ᵗʰ I went to see Griggs on Friday and we talked of the old days at Wood Stanway when Winifrid was a girl. I have lately been thinking of writing C.H. Smith's life, but the obstacles of time and my brief knowledge of him make me doubtful if I could do it. It would be a fine subject though, the life of an upright, vigorous land agent in the years before the war, who was famous for never having taken a bribe, who drank a bottle of whisky a day, knew every landowner in four shires, and began work at five in the morning, even if he had been carried to bed at one the night before, and who had such daughters as Winifrid and Margaret.

Yesterday Charles and I and young Buckland[96], the son of a settled gipsy here, went to Charingworth rabbiting. It rained all day and we only got 7 rabbits and a couple of moorhens. The most amusing incident of the day was when Buckland's terrier had put a rabbit in some bushes by a pool and chased it into the roots of an old withy tree. Buckland went up and put his arm up the hole

---

96   Ernest 'Peony' Buckland, 1904 – 1978. Twenty years later he was to work as CW's gardener at Broad Campden.

---

and caught hold of what he thought was its hind leg, and pulled and pulled, and eventually fell over backwards in the water with a vixen in his arms. Knowing his ways I shouted to him to let it go, which he did – and how it went. All day he could not get over it and kept saying: 'I 'ad twelve and bloody six in me 'ands and 'ad to let it go.' The skin was worth 12/6 and I know that he has a habit of catching foxes and selling the skins.

Cardew has been and we went to the Millers to tea. A grey miserable afternoon. A discussion which gave me thoughts about Middleton Murry's theory of Shakespeare. In the Greek and Latin world, except in periods of decadence, the great individual man did not exist, and it was thus through the Middle Ages till, in England, Shakespeare came. Chaucer was part of his time, not an individual standing out from the rest. The romantic ages are those in which great individuals are the unit; the classical are those in which he is part of the whole; thus socialism is or will be a classical age, if it comes.

November 21st There is a head by Epstein of Jacob Kramer (whom I used to know in Fitzroy Square days) in the Tate. Alec Miller says that it was a study for a statue of a Jew that Epstein did, and when the statue was finished someone looking at it said 'Christ!' and Epstein said, 'Exactly. That is the title of the figure.' And so it was. It sounds too good to be true, but Miller swears that it was so.

I wish I could get Griggs to outline to me his real position towards life and religion. It would make me better able to find my own, for I know that I am the opposite. He considers the Renaissance to be the beginning of the end; to me it is the beginning of all that is significant. The age we live in is the outcome of it and Shakespeare, Newton, Goethe, Pasteur, are the types of its great men, the great individuals as opposed to great 'members of the community.'

November 23rd I am waking up again. I want to devour the whole of Greek philosophy, the whole of Kant and Bergson and Hegel and Spinoza and William James and Locke too, all at a huge gulp. My lack of education in the university sense is a great handicap. I have so little groundwork. Impatience makes me stumble on despite that.

November 27th On Friday night I went to see Griggs and we had a long talk about poetry. We discussed Russell Alexander's and I told him that I felt it was too imitative, and that he did not think enough and so on. I thought it best to bring this out into the open, and I am glad I have, for I may get less of the stuff quoted to me in future. We talked till twelve, and he admitted that it is almost impossible for a great poet to come now[97]. He said that even if he did, his energies would be diverted in some other direction. I supported for all I was worth the poet who fails in attempting the utmost against the 'good poet' who sees and accepts the limitations of his time and eventually Griggs agreed that such a man was the more admirable. Our talk livened up my mind a good deal. We also discussed Finberg's proposed new private press[98], which he is to start here, and his row with Griggs over it.

November 28th To-day I have done a little revising, and this afternoon I took old Mrs Blakeman up to see a new baby, 12 days old, at a friend's house. It was like the mummified body of an Egyptian in the British Museum. She was wonderful with it. She might have been 30, not 60. Her whole face lit up and became young, alive and eager with joy.

It is growing dark now. The sky is grey, and the Sunday afternoon strollers are drifting back down the street to their warm brightly lit homes for tea, some too to cold bare homes where the fire that cooked dinner has died out, and where an uncleaned lamp gives all the light. I am waiting for my own tea, and after it I shall read the Observer again, then a book, till supper time, then talk to the Blakemans till it is time to go to bed, facing the thought of the works in the morning.

December 1st I was busy with accountants yesterday and too tired to write here in the evening. I read [Byron's] *Don Juan* again. It is the only long poem I have been unable to put down, yet I don't know that I shall want to take it up again once I have finished it. I have decided not to write again this year, deliberately to withhold my desire to do so. I am still busy at the works and my head is full of figures and balance sheets and reserves and capital outlay and such rubbish.

I have thought a good deal about my life and poetry and what I am going to do, in the last few weeks. I have thought of giving up writing for a year; of writing only stories; of leaving the works and living at Campden as an ordinary farm

---

97 This five years after publication of *The Waste Land*!
98 The Alcuin Press.

---

worker; of leaving Campden and becoming a business man in fact, as well as by a kind of inheritance; of getting married and settling down as a husband with literary tastes and rearing a family that will hate me when it grows up; of dying; of becoming a tramp; even of joining the army and becoming a soldier; and I have decided in the end to go on as I am.

We seem to have made more money at the works than I thought we should. My income will not be much less than last year, I think. I have another fortnight of business buz-fuz before me, then a whirl before Christmas, then the peace of being once more with Winifrid.

December 3rd Hudson has left Stow and come to Campden. He is now at the Noel Arms wondering where to get rooms. I went to see him last night and found him with Mrs Haydon, his little widow, who seems very devoted to him, sitting in the smoke room, very smug. She clings to him like a leech, which he has not noticed yet. He suggested that he and I should go and see Eve Kirk after Christmas, and she at once said she would come too. She is attractive but a little common, but he does not see the latter. She and her mother live at a little cottage in Leasbourne, called Stanley Cottage.

December 6th [Philip] Chandler's tutor, Wright, an awful little bore, came in last night and talked to me just when I wanted to work. I took him out to have a drink, hoping to get rid of him that way, and did, though he did not offer to buy me one after. The sole conversation in the Noel Arms was of passing blood, gallstones, operations on the bladder, and so on, so I left. Then I found out there was a dance on, decided to go and didn't, but went home to look over 'Persephone' again.

December 7th I have often thought that we may be living in one of the most important ages of history; that we are on the brink of a life that will so change our children that they will look back on us in their old age as we now look back on the Elizabethans.

December 9th I read a little last night and then Hudson came, and we went to a dull deserted dance at Mickleton with the two men who have Court Piece Farm, Winston and White. Winston was tight and made us laugh. I have written a sentimental letter to Eve Kirk, having got her address from Hudson.

December 11th   Hudson and I seem to have come together again and have been pottering about in the evenings. He is rather improved and soberer. When I am not writing I like him to be about. Last evening I took Marjorie [Lindsay] and him and his widow to the dance and afterwards Marjorie and I came back here and sat and made love in a rather half-hearted way till twelve. This morning Mrs Blakeman was rather cross and Cathy said it was because I had had Marjorie in so late. Hudson said when I told him, 'You can take anyone in at seven and poke as much as you like, but if you do it after ten it's quite different to the old woman's way of thinking.'

Griggs has hurt his knee again. I must go and see him. I have met a young man called Gordon Bolitho[99] who has come to live here, and I hope I shall not see him again.

December 13th   What a little narrow notion most people have of prayer; a sort of outflowing of sentiment; a bargaining with a feared despot; an asking for favours from a God who must be disgusting in his flabby folly and leniency; a sort of sublimated spiritual shop-keeping. I was driven to these thoughts by a negro spiritual that Eileen Baker sang last night. I went there and found Griggs there too. I seem to be getting slightly thicker with the Bakers again now, and Marjorie and I seem to be developing a sort of relationship by accident – but I could really love her sister, a lovely intelligent, dark-eyed creature.

To-morrow meetings and nonsense. I get £150 commission this year compared with £200 last, but my salary is more, so I am no worse off. I shall be able to invest about £170 more at the end of the year, which will bring my investments up to £800. Then I still have £300 to come from my grandmother's estate, which will make it up to £1100, and give me £1 a week of my own. Three times that and some sort of job at Campden and I shall be free and safe, in a sound position to write and know myself better for at least a few years before I die.

December 14th   All the aunts and uncles at the meeting were very complimentary towards me and made a point of saying how good I had been at my job. Although I think very little of their opinion it is satisfying to know that they really do appreciate what I have done. It has snowed heavily to-day but I hope to go rabbiting at Stretton [on Fosse] to-morrow.

---

99   He later published an enthusiastic account of the Nazi regime in *The Other Germany*, 1934.

December 16th Yesterday I spent squelching around in wet fields while a wet spaniel snuffled about the hedges and put out rabbits. I also shot a pheasant. In the evening I took Marjorie Lindsay to Cardew's to buy pots for presents, and tried to work up some emotions in the car in a hard frost, as she seemed to expect it.

December 21st In the night it rained torrents and froze after, and this morning the roads and pavements were sheets of ice all over and people setting out briskly to work fell over like ninepins, and everyone was soon fumbling and slipping along the street, fingering walls of houses, which were ice too, and constantly falling down. I woke early and heard the shouting and laughter. I could not go to Birmingham as it was not only impossible to take the car out but dangerous to go to the garage.

It was so bad this morning that several people broke their collar-bones falling. Now at three there is a clear sky and the sun is shining and everyone seems rather subdued. After having braced themselves up to meet the abnormal they are suddenly submerged in the normal and rather disappointed.

CW spent Christmas with the Woods at Colwyn Bay.

December 30th I arrived home late in deep snow, great wedges of it across the road from Honeybourne wherever there was a gap in a hedge or an open fence for it to drift through. Campden was white and the streets were like ice. When I got in I found that Cathy and Charles had gone to a children's party at the Convent and Mrs Blakeman had stayed in to cook for me. As I ate my dinner Cathy came in and I was surprised at my real joy at seeing her. All the lingering sadness at leaving Winifrid was paid off by it. After dinner I went in to the party for half an hour at the request of the nuns, then we all came back and sat and talked and I went to bed at about eleven. I found presents and letters; a nice cartridge bag from my uncle; some wine from Margot; a bottle of whisky; and a facetious but good natured letter from Russell Alexander.

December 31st Last night I went in to see Griggs, found that he had set out to visit me, came back, found he had been and gone, went back, and met him by the Noel Arms. He was very frisky, and we went and had a drink there, then came to my room.

A long discussion about religion follows.

I am glad we had the talk, for religion has always been a barrier between us before. Now it will not be. He stuck to his opinions and I stuck to mine, and I think we respect each other more for it. I did not know that he was brought up a Baptist and that his sister became a Catholic first and that he tried to stop her, then followed her. At eleven we went to Dover's House and went on talking. He told me a long story about a dinner at the Cheshire Cheese[100] with Alexander and [Alfred] Munnings[101] and Jewson, and how they all went back to Munnings' house in Chelsea and Jewson was sick. I came away at half past one. It seems that Munnings may be coming to live at Burnt Norton near here, which would be nice.

This morning I have been out ferreting. It is now snowing hard. To-night I go to the Bell Ringers' Dinner, which Griggs gives every year at the Lygon Arms, and which is usually very dull, then to a party at the Bakers.

---

100   The famous old pub in Fleet Street, popular with journalists and bohemians.
101   Alfred James Munnings, later K.C.V.O. and P.R.A, 1878-1959. An immensely talented and successful painter of horses and later in life a doughty opponent of Modernism.

~ 1928 ~

January 1ˢᵗ The dinner was very dull and Griggs grew more and more nervous all the time, and that affected everyone else, and their nervousness affected him, and so on. It went on from 7.30 till 11, and I drank a lot of poor beer to try to wake myself up, but it only made me more and more depressed. When we came away I felt I could not bear the Bakers' party, which I knew would be dull in a different, more precious way. I crept up to the window and heard a recorder playing, then silence, then a burble of refined voices, and turned away and went to the Town Hall dance instead. There were a great many people there, all cheerful and natural but, though I assumed a New Year's Eve exterior I grew more and more depressed within. At 12 I went back to the Bakers and the recorder was at it again, so I came home to bed. To-day I have been and apologised and they seemed to understand.

This morning a snowball fight across the street, Charles and myself against several others, chasing up and down alleys and over gardens, then a glass of home-made wine at Ladbrook's, and this afternoon tobogganing on Poor's Piece off Aston Hill. It was lovely there, the white world, the boys snowballing, the grey sky and the rough voices echoing, and the rooks flying overhead as it grew dusk at four o'clock, and we began to set off home along the road. Now it is dark. A wind howls outside and the snow puffs down the street like dust. Everyone has gone to church and I am alone.

January 5ᵗʰ The Bakers' show last night was poor, as I thought it would be. It might have been better on a better stage after they had rehearsed it more. It was far too ambitious for the place and stage and all its chief points missed fire and its accidental ones took on.

January 7ᵗʰ An interesting thing about Griggs's work. Nearly all the inspiration for his etched plates came from one period when he was in Ireland in 1915[102]. In a garden there he made books full of sketches and notes and ever since then he has worked on those, except for some of the English churches. One great period of inspiration and the rest of one's life spent working it out. That high class sameness in his work comes from that I suppose.

---

102   Actually, 1916. See Jerrold Northrop Moore, *op.cit*, p. 112.

January 16th On Saturday I went shooting at Broom. In the dusk we stood for three quarters of an hour with our feet in quaggy grass in the flooded fields waiting for the duck to flight. They came, high over my head and I did not get a shot. They settled on the flood-water further down and Roger Roberts who is a boy at Shrewsbury achieved the ambition of his life and shot one. He was so pleased that we all felt we had had a successful evening. How he will talk next term.

January 18th A wonderful day's coursing at Slaughter, up on the hills, the distance misty, the sky clearest blue, and the earth moist and soft where the sun had looked over the walls and thawed the hoar frost. A low growl of Cotswold voices, broken every now and then by old Jefferies shouting or some steward's shout of instructions as he went by, and punctuated all the time by the solitary bookie's 'I'll take 4 to 1. I'll take 4 to 1', which never ceased. He was a little red faced man with bad teeth and an untidy moustache stained with nicotine, a towny blue overcoat, a rather dirty bowler hat, and black boots made of leather that was suitable only for a pavement. He trudged along, an odd object among the healthy farmers and youths, the smart young women and their men, the queer people who seem to own greyhounds, over stubble, plough and grass, up hill and down, muttering all the time, 'I'll take 4 to 1', and followed by another little man who looked somehow subservient even to his dingy authority, and who entered the bets in a dog-eared account book.

Shakespeare wrote poetry but wrote as Chekov did, because he loved and desired to recreate the world. He would have written in prose if he had lived now. So far I have written largely because I have loved myself and have thought to magnify myself in the eyes of others by telling them of my own feelings. That is not the way to write anything any good. I am changing and I am sure now that the change will take place without destroying my writing. I find that a new desire to write is coming to me now because I am learning to love this world with a love that finds its best joy in recreating it by writing. I knew it yesterday as I watched the crowd, the faces, the horses, the dogs, and the terrified hare and the rolling hills.

January 29th Yesterday afternoon I sat and talked to Hudson and in the evening we went to the Red Lion. I got permission from Winston to 'shoot every bloody thing' on Court Piece Farm, which he is leaving, and all day to-day I have been mooching about it with a dog and a ferret in a drizzle. There is nothing much there, except a few wild duck, which I am going after in the morning with Charles, and we only got four rabbits, but I have enjoyed myself immensely. Hudson was in one of his hedge peering moods and was very delightful and amusing. He has a marvellous way of looking just like the animal he is thinking of, and he made us laugh a lot by being a pheasant under a tree, a rabbit, then a ferret.

February 2nd I think I shall start a descriptive piece to be called 'The Village', and describe Campden and its life and country. The only difficulty would be to get some sort of form into such a poem, and prevent it being a mere catalogue.

February 3rd Last night there was a Cricket Club dance in the Town Hall, to which Charles and I had decided not to go, but a Mrs Buchanan, a widow who arrived here in June with a mother and twins, called and asked if I would like to go. No one quite knows whether she is a widow or not. Her children were born in Belgium, and her husband is said to have died since they was born, by some; others say that he is in prison for false pretences. However she is an attractive young woman, and I said I would go. I danced with her and she began to tell me how she loved towns and particularly Manchester, and to complain of Campden and its quiet and the muddy paths, and my hopes of liking her fell flat. But I took her home after the dance and she had soft lips and a soft front and that was pleasant enough. But she also had little green beady eyes that looked naked in the moonlight, so I closed my eyes and trusted to my sense of touch and smell and came home at three to bed. I don't think it will go very far. There's something sly and suspicious about her – and those little green beady eyes in the moonlight still haunt me.

February 9th Griggs came to see me last night. He thinks that years are the same as age; he garbles the platitudes of his Church dogma and refuses to think for himself; and the result is that he blankets himself in a maze of dogmatic half-truths which 'great theologians' have invented to shield the suffering heart from life. He would rather have comfort than truth. I should like to see him cast adrift, alone and weeping, because he still might find a more dangerous and better path through life. If he were a woman I would trouble him till I had torn him out of his cotton-wool covering of cant and lies and self-deception, and left him naked. Then there might be some hope for him. Then he might produce one or two plates in his old age as great as Samuel Palmer's last ones, great in soul, not only fine in craftsmanship.

February 13th I went to see Griggs on Friday night and sat with him till one. He was very depressed and told me Campden was a dark, narrow place, with no one but gossips and evil speakers in it, and that I was the only person he could talk to and feel that he was being understood by. Tears came into his eyes as he spoke. 'You are the only one I could show my weaknesses to and not feel ashamed. You understand and you are sincere,' he said. I was quite touched by it all.

February 15th I went to see the Bakers last night and found them gloating over a new wireless set. Griggs is disgusted with them for having got one.

February 17th It is a beautiful clear day and yet I am depressed and miserable, with moments of strange exaltation, which seem never quite to mature. I went out to another factory this afternoon, about a mile away. What a terrible world that is; dust, dirt, noise, dirty children, mangy dogs, bloated and pale men and women, starved ones too; and the pitiful sun that makes the country a paradise, shining on all this filth and horror at the same time and only making it seem worse than it is. Before I can say that I accept life I have got to accept the idea of living in such a place myself and loving it and losing no part of my consciousness of beauty's existence in all things.

February 20th Yesterday I went out ratting at Court Piece and we caught 32 rats in an hour in a heap of manure. In the afternoon I went to look at the shoot at Heythrop, and after tea Cardew came and stayed to supper. I did no writing except a little planning. I begin to think of printing a volume of descriptive poems, about 50 pages. I have enough to fill one now[103]. I have just heard that the £200 which ought to have come to me on the death of a Chatwin uncle now goes to the Official Receiver at Cardiff because of my father's bankruptcy and my mother having made no will.

February 24th My life is a day to day progress like other lives, and I feel I have nothing to say here, and I see nothing great before me to live for. My only ambition now is to live on after I die as a writer of quiet nature poems, one

103   This was to emerge as *The Village*, the first book put out by the Alcuin Press, issued in 100 copies later in the year.

who was not much known, but who loved England, and was loved by those who knew him and his work.

March 5ᵗʰ I have been going the pace rather the last week or two and I finished up on Saturday night, after being up till four or five on other nights, by getting rather drunk and being ill and coming home at nine and sleeping on my settee till twelve, and waking in the morning in bed, hardly knowing how I had got there, and rather weary of gadding and a bit ashamed of myself. I got up well before breakfast and went for a long walk and that made me feel better and gave me more self-respect. But what a fool a man feels in the presence of nature, in the bright sun on a spring morning, after having been drunk the night before. The very rabbits seem to cry him shame and the larks seem to look at him like innocent maidens who are shocked to find for the first time that life is not as pure as they have been brought up to believe.

March 15ᵗʰ On Monday night I went to the Parish Council meeting, to elect Parish Councillors. As soon as I got there someone proposed that I should take the chair, and I went and sat on a rickety stool behind a desk in the cold schoolroom and stood up and made a little speech and, with the aid of the Clerk, conducted the meeting so that, as one woman said afterwards, 'It weren't no bloody good at 'orl. You moight 'ave bin in bloody church, it was that quiet.' But others seemed to think I did it quite well and were pleased. The time before there was an awful row in which the chairman joined, I believe.

March 19ᵗʰ I saw Griggs and Jewson and Alexander and walked about talking to them in the garden of Griggs's new house [New Dover's House] – which at the moment looks rather like a barn that has fallen down and not yet been rebuilt.

April 2ⁿᵈ Yesterday evening Cardew came in and we had a quarrel. He was arty and Baker-sodden and superior with that cold-blooded watery superiority that self-conscious aesthetic people get. I told him to go home and that he would find me in a better temper next time. Half of it was acting on my part. I have written to him to-day and apologised.

In the evening Hudson and Winston and White and I went up to Stow and spent an hour or two very merrily at the Talbot. I knew it would be rather a swift party, so I tried old C.H. Smith's old trick and drank a tablespoon of olive oil before I went. It worked wonders and all the others wobbled and stuttered and I stood up quite quietly and talked and they couldn't understand it.

April 3rd   I feel as though I once had a brother who was John Keats, but that I now have one called John Clare[104].

April 8th   Another amusing chase round the country for a shoot, to Guiting and Swell and Stow.   Beer in a lovely old house at Barton [House, Barton-on-the-Heath] where a Mr Swallow lives, a haulage contractor and poultry keeper. There is a marvellous and unrestored room with the oak panelling painted green, and an Adam fireplace green and black, sitting on cheap Edwardian chairs at a table covered with a bilious plush cloth, with a fern in a pot on it, we sat and drank and talked.

April 9th   This afternoon I have wandered about the hedges and watching creatures in a pond and looking up to find a different and more beautiful view of Campden each time, the hills behind bathed in sunshine. I counted over 30 arable fields from a place above the Leasowes, more than last year.

April 10th   I have decided to learn to ride this summer. I have seen Strafford at Westington Mill and he is going to give me lessons in the evenings in May and June, and will charge 5/- a lesson, and later on he will let me take his dealing horses out to exercise in the early mornings.

April 27th   Last night I wandered about the fields at the back of Campden. It was a warm night as in June; one of those nights when one hears birds singing in the dusk all round, and the cuckoo far away in some orchard; when it is so warm that one can for the first time in the year sit on some bank by a brook and brood for hours.

April 30th   All day yesterday I went and walked round the shoot at Roel Farm with Hudson and White and a 6-inch to the mile map of it. It was warm and beautiful and as I went through the covers and over the big open fields I felt particularly happy. In the evening we went to the Farmer's Arms at Guiting

---

104   John Clare, 1793-1864. Labouring class poet of the countryside in Eastern England.

and later back home. We called to see old Arkell at Donnington Brewery[105] and went down his bit of river with him, watching the great trout rush down the current and suddenly turn, facing it, under some log or clump of reeds. Then he took us out on the lake in his old boat and talked with a quiet seriousness of how the Lord had made the world. It sounded like the voice of a soldier of Cromwell's. He has a real soul, Arkell, hardened though it may be by bitterness and solitude, for he loves his farm and place and his only son is an idiot. The hardness has been tempered by a communion with a loved world of nature for fifty years or more and is a fine thing in him, part of the man.

May 7th *(In Rotterdam)* Yesterday I spent with Dorothy and Margot and in the evening I went to see Griggs at the Arts Club and found him and got him to go to see Charlie Chaplin with me in 'The Circus' and he sizzled and fizzled and seemed to enjoy himself a lot, and so did I.

This morning I flew over from Croydon, my first flight, far better than going by sea. One is an individual all the time and is treated as such at the Airport and Customs, and as a means of transport it is comfortable and to me not sick-making. It was very queer to see the world all laid out beneath one, yet to feel oneself still of its own air, as it were. The little Dutch and Belgian towns, seen from the air, were charming, and one could see the people in their gardens and walking in the streets clearly.

CW writes of the charms of Rotterdam and The Hague; of his host and hostess, the firm's agents; and concludes:

This is a charming country in its neat way, all green and fresh and tidy, with water and tidy houses, tidy roads, tidy canals, clean streets, fine houses in the old parts. But it all has a dullness that one cannot escape, dull countryside, dull faces. Holland is like a perfectly kept allotment garden of vast area.

May 16th *(Back in Campden)* I have been for a walk with Charles. It is a marvellous evening. All the sky black and threatening, except for one slit over Dover's Hill, but the light from that covers all the fresh trees and the hillside down towards Westington with an unearthly yellowish glare, and Campden, its chimney tops touched by that light, sleeps below. We talked of the year before

---

105   The Arkell family have been brewing at Donnington since 1865. This was probably Herbert John.

last and the wonderful mornings we had then after we had been sleeping out. It seems years ago. Charles is so young beside me now, still full of hope, still only just beginning to live.

There is little of life in Campden during the next few weeks: a bout of 'flu, nagging jealousy of Jewson, to whom CW was convinced Winifrid was becoming close, and the politics of the appointment of a new chairman of S.B. Whitfield & Co occupy the diary. In the last, the appointment of CW's friend and mentor Reginald Roberts of Dorsington was the result, a satisfactory one for CW, who felt he had out-manoeuvred his cousin Sam and his uncle Harry.

June 12th On looking back at my old poems I see now how terribly bad they all are by any reasonable standards, worse than I ever dreamed, technically. I am quite sure that the only ones worth keeping are the ones I have chosen for printing, and I am pretty sure that my only chance for the future is to keep to such quiet things. I have come to earth with a vengeance. I think I shall probably do better for it. I shall walk with the wild creatures among the woods and in the fields and, loving them, speak every now and then to make a mirror for their beauty.

It is strange how one's friends always annoy one when one is in the egotistical stage of one's life by picking out the lesser things that one does and trying to turn one to it. Griggs and Hudson and Winifrid repeatedly have told me to leave such poems as 'Persephone' and 'Adonis' and to write only nature poems. I have scorned such advice and been enraged by it many times, thinking them all wretched Philistines. But they were right.

June 25th   Griggs was very talkative and cheerful as we drove home *(from a week-end visit to Hilcot, where Winifrid was staying.)* He talked of Stanway and the old days there, and made me feel almost as though I had been there and known Winifrid in her youth. He seems to have taken a great fancy to Dorothy (Chatwin). He told me an amusing story about a drunkard:

> — Why did you begin to drink my man?
> — To drown my sorrows sir.
> — I should have thought you'd have drowned them all by now.
> — Yes sir, but the buggers 'ave learnt to swim.

June 26th   All day meetings and lunches; solemn faces; protests and growls; obsequious givings way; false flatteries; silence on my part; tea and the departure of the last uncle, the chairman affair settled and Roberts elected; a sigh of relief from myself as I found myself alone in my office and free to take up Surtees' *Handley Cross,* which I am finding very absorbing.

June 28th   Finberg in a great state of fluster and importance came and promised half of the proofs of my book [*The Village*] this morning and asked me to let him have them to-morrow to print. Nothing has come. He is a little ass. Relying on someone else's promise[106] he has got my paper ready and even wetted it, and now it will be spoilt. Sheer bad, stupid, too self-confident management. I wish I could like him better, but he is such a conceited ass.

June 30th   Last night the proofs came and I tried to correct them, with visits from Finberg, Jewson, Dorothy, Margot and Marjorie Lindsay to help me.

July 2nd   I played six sets of tennis at Griggs' this afternoon and was not as bad as I expected to be. Finberg has printed one side of the first sheet of my book and I am very pleased with it. The one or two things I have written lately seem to me much better, though humbler than my old work.

Last night I spent an hour walking up and down the tennis lawn with Griggs talking, as the evening grew dusk, and the moon rose, then went and sat with him for a bit. Cadbury[107] has been very good and has agreed to buy the houses in the street, by Barnes the blacksmith's, and do them up and make a small trust of them for the preservation of Campden houses and so on[108].

July 4th   A walk with Charles to Broad Campden last night. We went in to the Baker's Arms and sat there for half an hour and had a pint each. It is strange how totally different the men in the bar there are from those in Campden. In Campden you get a mixture of tradesmen and labourers and small masters and horse-dealers and farmers; at Broad Campden there is nothing but labourers, pure and simple, stinking of corduroy and sweat and tobacco. The bar there is

---

106   Finberg's own printing press had yet to arrive; the work had been sub-contracted to a Bristol printer.
107   William Cadbury, 1867-1957. Quaker head of the Bournville chocolate company and philanthropist.
108   See J.N. Moore, *op. cit.* pp. 205-6.

---

dingy and old, lighted by the fire and one candle. There are no taps or counters, but the beer is brought in fresh from the barrels outside. There is a low growl of talk which ceases as anyone enters, and then works up again, many addressing their settle-neighbours without the least sign of listening on their part. I sat next to old Gibbs, the only employer there, a half-retired old farmer and he told me there was a litter of cubs near his house, and described them vividly and with feeling. Then he added, 'And I finished watching them, and shouted out to them "Now you little buggers, get in your 'ole. The 'unting season's coming."' Then he added with a surprised air, 'Ah, and they did too guvnor.' They stole a fowl of his wife's and she grumbled. He said, 'Well if you was shut up in a 'ood and 'ad nowt to feed on bit rabbits you'd want a change wouldn't you?'

July 11th   Last night Finberg then Hudson and Russell Alexander. I have agreed to go with Hudson to play cricket for the visitors at Sapperton on Saturday. Finberg and Hudson stayed very late and we had a long and tedious argument about England's degeneracy. I held that England is still only on the eve of her real greatness and that in a thousand years English will be the chief language in every country in Europe, in India and practically all over the world, while Englishmen will still be the strange practical dreamers who suddenly do what the world is saying needs doing, while the world is still talking – and then let the Chinese or the Indians take the credit for it. I may have talked a good deal of rubbish, but I went out to buy some cigarettes at 10.30 and found Strafford and Winston and Jack Coldicott at the Red Lion and had several whiskies bought me in a very few minutes, which excited me.

July 13th   We bathed again at Northwick and slept out. As we went towards Doe Bank a little white terrier bitch that belongs to Bridges, who rents Doe Bank too, came out of the dusk in the street and jumped around us, licking our hands, and then followed us up to the field. When we got there she pushed through the gate and ran on ahead of us to our tent and went straight in through the small opening and lay down on my sleeping bag. It was just as though she had been shut out and had thought it all over and had come deliberately to meet us. We pulled our bags out into the open and she stayed in the tent, then, just as I got into my bag, she rushed out and curled up under my left arm. I pulled the cover over myself and her as best I could and so we slept all night. She woke when I did and came home with us and went straight on to the Red Lion not attempting to come in with us.

July 16th Saturday [14th] was queer. At first I felt physically sick just after Winifrid arrived, something to do with my memories of Sapperton and my jealousy of Jewson, then I pulled myself together and tried to use my will and act as though she was not there. That way I was all right. Then she came and sat by me and with the mere touch of her arm made the world a different place to be in and all the rest of the afternoon passed off well. Griggs was tight and jumped about like a wild schoolboy, and yet still looked like a staid and respectable etcher.

After the cricket we went back to the pub with Russell Alexander and had some beer till he was in the right mood, but as soon as I saw his game I was furious and walked off and Hudson followed. I didn't want to stay because Winifrid would have thought us both tight, because I would have hated it all, and because Hudson would have lost his temper over pen and paper games, and because I was sick of Sapperton and arts and crafts people trying to be jolly so falsely. We got off at 8 and went to Fairford Wake and home by 12.

All yesterday [15th] was nice; the morning bathe at Northwick; the park with its pedigree sheep that looked as though they had been combed and brushed; the quiet Guernsey cows; the great trees; the stone lodges; the people diving and swimming, and a woman with a baby under a tree watching.

With regard to Cathy I am still torn between a doubtful duty and a very real affection. Deliberate self-deception is one of the weaknesses of the undeveloped mind and she has it badly. She said, 'You don't know how much I love you. You never will.' I take this and yet I can give her nothing and as a result I often feel as though I were devouring her, but I like her love so much that I cannot stop myself.

July 18th Last night at the Baker's Arms at Broad Campden, old Bricknell the landlord was talking of C.H. Smith, Winifrid's father, something about a terrible number of whiskies that he once drank for a wager. Then he went on about C.H.'s father, Russell Smith, 'Ah, 'e was one of the shin-kickers up on [Dover's] 'ill. 'E began to teach old Jim Taylor once and took 'im by the 'and and nearly kicked 'im to death.' Such is our little immortality.

July 22nd Yesterday was a terribly busy day in the way a day can be busy when one does nothing. I worked for two hours after breakfast and more or less finished my 'Haymaking' poem, then began a sort of life which Eileen Baker aptly describes as living like a puppy. I went out to the post, met Winston and went to Gretton with him, came back for lunch, lounged about on the seat at the corner by Sheep Street with Hudson, went to [Fred] Symes the local tailor's, changed into tennis things, played tennis at Griggs', went to the Bakers for tea, then to the Red Lion, then to gather a bunch of white jessamine for Mrs Blakeman, then to bathe at Northwick, then home to dinner, then to sleep alone on Doe Bank. I woke at 6.30 and came down home and talked to Cathy.

July 29th Yesterday I took an advance copy of my book to the Exhibition. I have sold 30, which will give me £15 towards the £30. I played tennis at Griggs', went rabbiting at Roel, bathed, went to Griggs at night. He likes the book.

CW spent a week in early August with Winifrid at Hilcot and much of the holiday month bird-watching with a newly-acquired pair of binoculars, and reading Jane Austen. Winifrid comes on to the stage and withdraws, causing CW relief and anguish in turn as she does so, and maintaining her 'right' to continue seeing Jewson as being balanced by CW's relationship with Cathy.

September 3rd A long letter from Frank Kendon and some very useful criticisms and much pleasing praise of my book. Russell Alexander was at Griggs' and talked a lot of nonsense. He is the most real bore I know. Kendon says, 'your observation is marvellously accurate, but your economy of observation, your sense of exactly the right thing to say, is at present your genius.' All that and more that he says is very pleasing and as others have said the same things sometimes I am inclined to believe it.

September 9th Yesterday shooting at Roel again and we got 30 rabbits, 3 hares and 1½ brace of partridges and 2 pigeons, and finished up tired and terribly thirsty. We all had tea at Guiting and sat and smoked and talked, each basking in a sort of inner pleasure in having spent the day well; Lane, Charles, Roberts and his two boys. I brought 20 of the rabbits home and Charles and I paunched them. I have sold a few and shall take the rest to the works on Monday. I feel remarkably fit after two days walking and shooting, though not subtle minded.

On Friday [13th] night I went along to make sure the Griggses are coming to dinner and found A.J. Munnings the painter there. He is a most delightful man, has the delicacy of soul to love Jane Austen; the English spirit to love Surtees; the depth of humour really to know and understand Rabelais and Don Quixote; and the most active imagination. He got a little drunk and began describing Handley Cross and Mr Sponge to Griggs, and I have never heard such wonderful description. What rather flattered me was that he seemed a bit bored with Griggs' solemn romanticism and woke up when I got there and talked about these things and badgers and shooting and hunting with a wonderful creative enthusiasm. I wish he would come and live here, as he talks of doing. He is the sort of man I would like to be, if by being it I could avoid losing a certain gentleness of affection for the world that he lacks. I met him again in the morning and took him to the Red Lion and he held forth at great length to the people in the bar about privies, and all the kinds he had seen, to everyone's amusement. Talking of a house he said he wanted 'the kind of place I can shit in my own park.' What a world of meaning concentrated into a few words of rather coarse humour; the Shakespearean imagination, the biggest example of it I have met yet. And how alive he is compared with the self-conscious Miltonic. He writes wonderful hunting songs and ballads but never prints them. Griggs has heard him sing them in London and says they are marvellous.

September 10th I was thinking this morning of the various things that I have had reported to me as having been said about me: 'A nice steady young fellow. A bit of a character and a good sportsman. A wild young bugger. 'E's got more money than you'd think. 'E's 'ot on the women. 'E's a good business man. 'E's got his head screwed on tight. That bloody poet, I can't stand him. That bugger with a nanny beard. Well 'e stands it alright and don't mind 'aving a good laugh at 'imself'

This amused analysis is among the last entries for 1928, after which CW writes that he has decided not to keep the diary for a while. His life seems happier, and with the reading of Surtees that he undertakes during the autumn, his growing interest in hunting begins to occupy the foreground of the diary.

An entry on September 13th reveals his deep response to the hunting field; the response of a poet.

September 13th They killed 5 cubs this morning, making 15½ brace to date. It was a wonderful morning, chilly at first, and as we drove along the flat road to Meon [Hill, Mickleton] among the market gardens we could only just see the top of the hill peering through the mist. As we went up the hill we rose above the mist and from half way up could see the whole of the Evesham Vale as though it were covered in downy snow, the tops of the elms and the roofs of the houses and here and there a church spire standing out isolated above it all, looking very weird and lovely. Above was a clear sky and the sun was shining on us warmly on the hill. When one of the cubs ran to ground in an unstopped earth the Master dismounted and went to the place in the middle of thick brambles and stood over the earth and blew his horn and the hounds surged round him, and as he blew the third time the terriers were brought up and as he tailed off in a strange sad way the notes of his horn were like a dirge. The effect on me was extraordinary. I imagined the quivering cub down in the rabbit hole, smelling and listening to the people above, waiting, terrified, and not knowing what would happen. I saw the people, the hounds, the spades, the terriers, and I knew that in a few minutes the cub would be dug out and thrown to the hounds. I was not sorry for it, nor did I feel anything against killing it, but the knowledge that it must die, the sense of the lovely clear autumn morning, and the strange simple descending notes of the horn all seemed to combine to make a pure thing, sad but perfect. In a few minutes hounds had been called off and had found again, and in a few minutes after that, while the cub was being dug out, they killed almost at my feet.

~ 1929 and 1930 ~

In January CW began to take riding lessons every Sunday from Strafford at Westington Mill — 'a horse dealer with bow legs and a hook nose who was at Charterhouse and who has been in every imaginable parasite trade from selling watches and giving away half-crowns at country fairs to selling cars and acting in music-hall turns.'

In the summer, the Woods rented Mary's Acre at Broad Campden, and Winifrid and CW were thus able to spend a lot of time together, mostly on riding expeditions, a contented period with only 'Jewson the vinegar in its sweetness'. Here, an almost farcical event occurred, which nonetheless was a watershed in their relationship. One Sunday evening, having agreed to take Winifrid to Birmingham the following morning, CW drove over to Broad Campden and found Jewson's car in the drive. He climbed on to a water-butt and, through a small window, spied on Winifrid and his rival inside. From the clues that he picked up, he adduced that the relationship was not happy, and when Jewson's car had gone later, went in and spoke to Winifrid, not revealing that he had been snooping, but only that he had seen Jewson's car there — deceiving her for the only time in his life, as he put it. Winifrid refused to give up Jewson and CW replied that he would, and could, wait for as long as needs be, feeling as he went home that he had 'won'. The next morning, when he came back to collect her, it seemed to them that indeed he had, and they referred to that moment as 'The Miracle' afterwards.

That summer, Stanley Wood sold Dinglewood School at Colwyn Bay, and by chance the Woods discovered that the house at Wood Stanway had become available to rent from the Wemyss estate. While it was being made ready the Woods spent the autumn at Cagnes-sur-Mer near Nice. CW spent Christmas at Wood Stanway, and the Wood family went to live there in March 1930.

Riding lessons continued and in the summer of 1930 there was a riding tour, with Winifrid chaperoned by a complicit aunt Dorothy, over towards Sherborne and Chipping Norton. By the autumn CW felt that he was ready to launch himself on the hunting field, having bought a cob called Joey from Strafford, to be put at livery at the Red Lion for £2 a week, kitted himself out and negotiated a reduced subscription of £10 to the North Cotswold Hunt, on the grounds that he would be an occasional participant: he attended 15 meets in the season of 1930.[109]

---

109   At Bibsworth, Honeybourne, Campden Wood, Mickleton Hills, Springhill, Nineveh Farm, Wormington and Rook's Pool (twice each), Paxford, Stump's Pool, Campden Market Square, Didbrook and Ford.

~ 1931 ~

The first four months of the diary for 1931 are largely given over to hunting. While the account, and those that take up a large proportion of the diary for the next few years, may well be of interest to historians of hunting, I have decided to omit virtually all of this, since although it was central to CW's life at the time, and for the next few years, it is of less interest from the Campden perspective that I am trying to keep in view for readers of today.

New names appear in the text, notably Bob Jeune, nephew of Lord St Helier, Charles Napier, the Wardens, and Miss Norah Sylvester, a redoubtable farmer from Broad Campden.

At the end of the season in April, CW characteristically does his sums: £50 for riding lessons; £65 for Joey's keep; £20 for clothes; £10 subscription. In all 22 days hunting and 8 days cub hunting.

A new volume of poems, entitled 'The Wood Gatherer' was nearing completion, attracting helpful criticism from Edmund Blunden and Frank Kendon. When the hunting season is over, many diary entries are devoted to close observation of nature. As he puts it: 'peace, with outside lives that are separate from our own; to see ourselves in terms of another life that is not burdened with consciousness; that is the way for me now.' CW's changed outlook on life is summarised in the following elegiac entry:

June 19th What a picture one conjures up in one's imagination after reading George Eliot and Surtees and the early Dickens, of the country England a hundred years ago. The country was still an agricultural land living on its own produce and governed by the landowners, who were directly part of the earth by which the population lived. Sport, uncontaminated by the needs of pandering to a town population; fox hunting in its growing prime; wealth picturesquely used by a few and on the whole, in the country at least, charity and kindness enough to make life tolerable to the poor; local influences like rings of ripples spreading a few miles and meeting others; everything individual and full of character; and the countryside remote from the towns, and full of untouched beauty, while in the country towns there was society and what one can only call now the fascinating boredom of such places. The villages were groups of almost self-supporting communities with their landowners and small gentry and doctor and parson and yeomen and peasants. And though classes were clearly defined there was room for ability to raise the strong individual from one to another. What a world it seems to us as we look back on it from these strange days, what a world to have lived in.

August 8th   The wettest and most depressing summer I can remember. In July Dorothy and Winifrid and I went on another short riding tour to Fairford and Charlbury and it was very marvellous. I have spent the holiday week at Wood Stanway and it was like going home. Life is very good, containing as it does so much that I have longed for for years. I am leaving the Blakemans at the end of September, and going to live at the Live and Let Live Hotel[110] in the High Street, where I am going to have two unfurnished rooms and my own things. Mrs Blakeman asked me to go as she is getting too old for Cathy to be able to look after her and me as well. I am sorry in a way because it will be like leaving home, but the hotel will be more comfortable and will fit in with my present life better now.

September 7th   To be called [for cub hunting] I tied a string round my leg in bed and let it dangle out of the window for Ladbrook to pull in the morning. Two girls must have found out, for I was woken by a pulling that nearly had my leg off and loud giggles in the street outside. I don't know who the culprits were.

September 29th   I am moving to-day to my rooms at the Live and Let Live Hotel, which look very nice. The sitting room has a view out towards Broad Campden and the bedroom is in front and though small, it will do. The bathroom is next door to it. There are four or five other guests' rooms and I like the Griffins, the people who have the place. They have come home from Southern Rhodesia, where he has been mining. He drinks a bit as most colonials do, but is nice and Mrs and the daughter are charming. There is a son who writes and has occasional epileptic fits.

October 21st   'The happy man is the man who lives objectively, who has free affections and wide interests'. Bertrand Russell. Slowly, through long struggles and days of analysis of my own mind I am reaching that goal. I am in

---

110   At present, Stuart House, High Street.

a far happier state now than I was a couple of years ago. It is my experience of love that has been the touchstone of any wisdom I have attained.

Hunting again occupies the rest of the autumn. There is no mention of the works; little indeed of Winifrid, although CW did again spend Christmas at Wood Stanway.

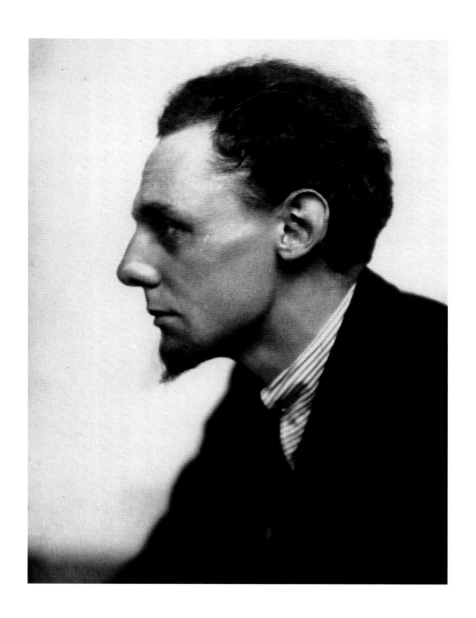

The Aspiring Poet.
Christopher Whitfield, 1926.

Winifrid Wood, 1925.

'One of the most loveable men I know.' Oliver Baker.

'A woman full of earthly peace.'
Mrs Blakeman.

F.L. Griggs.

Sitting comfortably, 1903.

Hunting Man. Tatler, 1939.

'The loveliest site in Campden.'
Tithe House site seen from
St James' Churchyard, 1939.

The Tithe House, July 1940.

The Tithe House, garden side.

The Tithe House interior.

L.D.V. Parade, Summer 1940. CW in foreground.

S. B. WHITFIELD,
MANUFACTURER OF
Metallic Bedsteads, Cots, Chairs, &c.,
GLADSTONE WORKS,
WATERY LANE, BIRMINGHAM.

S.B. Whitfield Works, 1876.

S.B. Whitfield Works,
November 1940.

Wedding Day 17th January 1942

Bohemian businessman,
France 1938.

Businessman historian,
Droitwich 1961.

~ 1932 ~

January 2nd   I did not go out [hunting] on the Tuesday after Christmas because of the snow. They did hunt however and had quite a good run from Buckland. After that hunting was stopped by snow till to-day. There was a large field out at Childswickham after the Wire Dance at the Lygon to which I did not go. At present I can only just afford to hunt at all. My income this year will not be more than £500, out of which I shall have to pay £150 tax on the previous year. The works is doing very badly and is feeling the slump very much and is unlikely to make any profit this year, so I shall have only my salary.

January 16th   The meet to-day was at Trooper's Lodge, but an old woman there was killed last night trying to save a child's life when it was nearly run over by a car, so we met further on, at the Spring Hill turning. It was a fearfully windy day with cloudy mist racing across the sky and a fine drizzle at first which became a steady rain later. We were all gloomy about the day's sport, but found at once in Brown's Gorse and ran to Sezincote Warren and across Bourton Downs. There were only ten of us at the start, because everyone had been misled by their making for the Stow road at first. We ran across the Downs to Smallthorns Farm, then to Snowshill Hill, on between Sheppy Grove and Oldhill, over Buckle Street, through Welshman's Hedge and to ground in a rabbit warren near Stanway Ash. A 3½ mile point and about 4 as hounds ran, in 35 minutes. It was very exciting for me as I was with hounds the whole time. I rode with them in sight, just a field down wind from me. It was one of the best hunts I have yet seen. Hounds simply raced and I had about 20 walls and Joey jumped splendidly.

I have decided to rough Joey off at the end of February as I am hard up, then turn him out as soon as I can and get him up at the end of September again.

January 21st   I dined at Clement Parsons' at Broadway, the brother of Alfred Parsons[111] the artist, last night. He told me among other things that he had a friend whose father saw the burning of the Bastille [in 1789] at the age of 6. The friend is now 75 and must have been born when his father was over 60.

---

111   Alfred Parsons, 1847-1920. Landscape painter and garden designer; part of the Anglo-American group of artists at Broadway from 1885.

February 3rd   I see quite a lot of Griggs and often take him and Nina down to dinner at Wood Stanway, but I have lately come up rather more against his proselytising Catholicism. His whole being is riddled with the poison of Christian dualism. Everything he conceives must have an opposite. He is a mass of antagonisms which fight a vicious warfare within him, living on the territory of his soul. He is dead. He is like an orchard of good trees ravaged by blight, in which a few fine fruits still grow among the leafless branches. Apart from his Catholicism I am very fond of him, but that does sometimes spoil him for me. I suppose I have an absurd Calvinistic hatred of Catholicism in me, inherited from my Unitarian ancestors. I have had a number of Catholic friends, but when I see their Catholicism naked I turn against them till they hide it decently again.

February 28th   Now that hunting is over I can look at myself and, as my 30th birthday approaches, take stock of where I am. It is not an exhilarating thing to do now. I am in the middle of my life, or nearly so and I am dissatisfied and depressed about it. It seems to me that I have achieved practically nothing. I am neither poet nor business man nor country gentleman, not cultured man, nor well read man, nor happily drunken man, not promiscuous lover, nor anything, but a bit of all. I belong to no group, no stratum in society, no category. I am too much of a writer to be a good man of business, too much a man of business to be a good writer, too much of a sybarite to be anything.

What have I achieved? I have something like £170 a year of my own now and not long ago I had nothing. I have written and printed two volumes of poems and burnt many more, and these two volumes have brought me kind praises but no repute. I have not got one of my poems into any periodical and no publisher will take them at his own risk. I have learnt to ride a horse across country and go fairly well with hounds. I have read thousands of books and enjoyed them, but I have a memory only for the thoughts and feelings they have given me and not for their contents, and I cannot use my knowledge of them to talk to and equal those who read much.

It is a sad picture when I compare it with what I hoped for and believed myself capable of ten years ago. I am better off, more comfortable, more secure, but I am a failure in everything I have attempted really. And what is worse is that now I have no aim left, am working for nothing, concentrating my energies on nothing. I drift from day to day, from January to February with no aim, no earnest desire, no purpose. I am empty of illusion about myself and I see nothing I now want to achieve except an increased independent income which will finally set me free from the works, which I still hate as I always have done. But even that freedom which I used to want so that I could write and become a fine writer or even a great one, I now only want so that I may escape from a job and a place that I hate, in order to live a more pleasant life in a place that I love. There is only one thing that makes up for the loneliness and emptiness of all this, and that is Winifrid.

April 28th I have a constant longing to enter the calm of achievement in all things and to rest there. I long to attain some sort of finality, to escape from life into a closed and finished state of being, no more becoming but become, and beyond the threat of change. It takes the form in my daily life, of longing to get my clothes finished at the tailors; to get certain things done to my car; to write and round off a poem; to type and bind up my poems for last year; to feel that my own investments are safe, and a round sum; to get my £200-300 a year and a cottage of my own into which I may escape from the turmoil of my days; and yet as each of these things is attained, so far as I have attained them, not one of them has brought me the content I have dreamed of, and at once a dozen others spring up and call me on to further effort.

March 1st I am reading [Sir William] Rothenstein's *Men and Memories* and have just joined the Times Book Club, which, through Elliston and Cavell of Oxford[112], delivers here weekly now.

Only one thing about Winifrid's being at Wood Stanway is a constraint to me: I tend to lose touch with the people and life of Campden itself. I spend so much of my time at Wood Stanway now, practically every week-end, that is largely my home, and yet I am not there enough to root myself there wholly, as it were. I am in Birmingham all day during the week, and so I only touch Campden at night. In the winter I am hunting and shooting as well, and often in the evenings I do not want to go out to the pubs, but to stay in and read or write. So I have got out of touch with the local life here that I love, and in which I have found so much solace. I must see more of it now, for it is a life that is deeply satisfying to me, the life of these Cotswold

---

112   The leading department store in the city, closed in 1973.

---

labourers and farmers, horse dealers, poachers, bookmakers and their attendant women. They and the actual physical world they live in are quite different seen through my Stanway-Winifrid eyes from what they are seen through my Campden-Hudson-Blakeman eyes. The Stanway-Winifrid mind sees the world more as a lovely spectacle of tree and field and wild creature, fair and intimately known, part of a realistic but romantic nature poem; the other mind sees the world more as a melting pot for the nature of men and women, a more real and Zola-esque place and a little sordid, but fine despite that, with its beer and facts and corn and horses and money, cattle, boots, stones and trees. Both these worlds are necessary to me for my full being.

I have just invested another £175. Now that we are doing so badly at the works I do not hope for any commission, while my salary only just covers my needs. I am having all my income from my investments paid into a separate account at the bank and reinvesting it regularly. I now have £3597 invested and an income of about £160 a year from it. I do not think the works will pay any dividend for a few years now, owing to the slump, and may not even survive it. It will last at least another three years though, and in that three years I must save enough to give me £200 a year net, and I can do that easily, and that will make me quite free fundamentally.

May 3ʳᵈ   One of my most cherished pursuits is to capture for myself the seeing eye of different periods, to try to penetrate into the mind and soul of different sorts of people at different past times, and so gradually to accumulate a sort of composite impression of what it was like to live in each past age; a synthesis, made up of guesses and implications and penetrating into the daily life of the past.

May 7ᵗʰ   The night before last I went with Ladbrook rat shooting at the rubbish dump up on Westington Hill, then came down to the Baker's Arms at Broad Campden, where he and I represented Campden in an amusing shove-halfpenny match which we lost by three points. It is sad how the peculiar and subtle atmosphere of the villages is becoming merged into a sameness now. Once the Baker's Arms and all its people used to be quite different, the pub of a small village, while the Campden pubs had the quality of pubs of a small country town. But in the last few years the Baker's Arms and many like it have become modern and much the same as country pubs anywhere else, in

Campden or Chipping Norton or Stow. The subtle differences are all going now, and terribly fast. It is an age of sameness, in which to be individual is almost to be at a disadvantage.

Last night to see Griggs. He is just back from London where he has been at the R.A hanging committee. Hudson has not got anything in this year he says.

This year has been the warmest winter, the wettest summer, the latest spring, the driest February, and the coldest early May that I can remember.

May 9th I am taking Winifrid to London on Thursday, and so we shall miss the Stow Fair, which I have always been to, usually with Hudson, but it will only mean missing getting rather drunk, and I am glad about that. It used to be the custom here to buy a pair of boots at Stow Fair, goose-grease them, and hang them up in the kitchen till next year, to soften and waterproof them.

May 21st Last night rabbit shooting at the quarry and I shot a young one, then a drink with Hudson and then to the village dance, where we sat and watched and I danced two dances. In the middle Rachel [Wood] and St Aldwyn[113] came in and I brought them home for a drink. This morning pouring rain has set in for the day. My day so far: 9. Woke and lay in bed thinking about the people whose voices I heard in the street and wondered what to do all day. 9.30. A bath and I dressed and shaved. Breakfast. Read a bit. 10.30. Did my accounts. Saw Dorothy who had a message from Winifrid. 10.30 to 11.30. Walked about the street in a mackintosh. Paid Elsley the ironmonger 4/-. Took four empty beer bottles back to the Red Lion. Paid a cheque into the bank. Paid Haydon 1/4d. Bought some cigarettes. Weighed myself (10st 12 lbs). Bought a small very good pair of field glasses for watching birds. 11.30 to 12. Read The Field. Took my shoes to be mended. Kept meeting people in the street and chatting with them and making silly jokes about the weather. 12. to 1. Went to the Red Lion and drank a pint of beer and saw Strafford, Ladbrook, etc.

May 22nd To-day after more torrential rain floods in Sheep Street and a dismal Scuttlebrook Wake last night at which I stayed until 11.30 wandering about in the rain talking to people. This morning the old chestnut tree opposite

---

113   Michael Hicks Beach, 2nd Earl, 1912-1992. Succeeded his grandfather in 1916, aged three.

Guthrie's the [black]smith[114] fell on a caravan, but no one inside was hurt. The tree slowly heeled over at about ten and one large branch penetrated the roof of the caravan and knocked the breakfast off the table. The damage to the caravan and a lorry near, which had brought some of the booths for the wake and had not gone, is said to be about £200. The County Surveyor came and the men worked most efficiently so that by one the lorry and caravan were set free. There was a huge crowd, nearly everyone in the place, watching it all, and everyone was sad and disturbed at the fall of so familiar a tree. A curious gloom was everywhere and at first people talked in hushed voices, as though the fall of the tree were an omen of something ill to happen. Then the busy clamour of work changed that and everyone watched and gossiped and gave advice that was not taken, and blamed causes for the tree's fall that had nothing to do with it. The real cause was the lopping about 20 years ago of several boughs on one side of the trunk, which had caused the whole of that side to rot and die to the roots. Old Bob Guthrie the blacksmith with whom I sat under the tree years ago one midnight and drank cheap port, listening to all his tales of old days, was very sad and seemed to connect the tree's fall with his own coming death[115]. For some time he has been saying how he is tottering and is worn out and ready to die, and now he seems to think the time has come. The tree was planted in November 1812, or so Jose Griffiths[116] says. People who do not usually talk to each other were talking eagerly and there seemed to be in everybody's mind a feeling that it was a sort of duty to stand about and gaze until the clearing up was done, and the fine tree cut up and carried off.

This afternoon the biggest circus I've seen in Campden came and is in Badger's Field now: three elephants; 70 horses and ponies and three charming pony foals, very small and sleepy and with such spindly legs. Further excitement and everyone gathered in the field watching the tents being put up. Campden has been in a great state of excitement all day, with these two events, and the pubs will buzz with talk and argument about them to-night.

May 25th   To-night I have been watching two common whitethroats in a hedge near Strafford's [Westington Mill], searching every twig and working up and down, hardly still for a moment, and singing in their constantly repeated

---

114   At the junction of Church Street and Leysbourne, near the iron pump.
115   An unduly pessimistic forecast: he died in October 1935, aged 82
116   Josephine Griffiths, 1864-1949, of Bedfont House. Author of *Chipping Campden To-day and Yesterday,* printed at the Alcuin Press for T.R. Elsley, Campden, 1931.

---

little notes all the time. The cock seemed to be chasing the hen as well, and combining his evening meal with the preliminaries of his courtship, and working himself into a small warm ecstasy of love and excitement.

On Monday the circus which was very good considering the wet and dripping tents and the sea of mud the poor horses and men had to work in. The elephants grotesque and queer in wet English fields, grazing by twisting off the clumps of grass with their trunk-tips and putting them in their mouths.

May 26th To the Red Lion and after a mumbling talk with Will Haines there and as I walked up the street with him, I got his permission to put a bridge over the brook above the bathing lake, for the Wire Committee. Tall, thin, stupid and shrewd, he hardly said anything all the time, but agreed in the end. Now I have to write to Prentice's landlord and see Major Noel and I ought to get the work done by August.

June 16th To Ledbury this morning and this afternoon to a badger dig in Weston Park. Old Jefferies there, and Wally Stanley, and Will Haines and Plumber Haines and Fred Hart[117] and George Hiatt and his son John, and Ladbrook and Lucas from Evesham and Grinnell and Blakeman and Tom Hopkins and a dozen others. They got three young badgers out, one of which has gone to a decent home at Hiatt's, but I pity the other two. I am glad they could not get at the old ones or the other young one. A bathe after tea, with Blakeman at Northwick, reviving our memories of the many times there before.

June 29th Yesterday I flew over Campden in a plane that came to the football field by the station and gave flights for 10/-. It was bright sunlight in the evening and it was delightful to look down on the place and to see it all laid out beneath, with its gardens and orchards and houses and trees. I went twice, once with the daughter of the people who keep this hotel [The Live and Let Live] and once alone. Jack Dudfield from Dorn near Moreton [while telling a story] used two words I've not heard: *glurry*, meaning slithery like a Cotswold road after rain; and *wuthering*, meaning fussing or bothering or being unnecessarily cautious and nervous. And, speaking of some land he said, 'Ah, one sheep's fart be worth a cow's turd on that land.'

---

117   Frederick P. Hart, 1879 - 1971. Lt. Commander R.N. (ret'd) and a prodigious collector. Lived at Trinder House, High Street.

CW was not feeling well for the next six weeks. A combination of a major reorganisation at the works and uncertainty about whether Winifrid and Stanley Wood would remain at Wood Stanway after the expiry of their lease lowered him, as the next entry shows.

July 28th I am beginning to show signs of wearing out I feel, even at this comparatively early age of 30, and though I should not care to die I should hardly care if I were told that I must. What I would give for peace and health and quiet in my mind for a time.

July 30th Now I seem to have recovered again, except for the temporary after effects of a dance at Weston-sub-Edge on Thursday, at the end of which, rather tight, I walked into a brook in the grounds of the village hall. I saw M there and it is several years since I have seen her to speak to. I must have been rather in love with her then for I was quite excited at seeing her, just glad to see her and talk to her and hear her rough soft voice again. She has been married to a farm labourer for six years and has had three children but still looks young and quite good looking and fresh and her figure hardly changed.

August 5th This hotel [The Live and Let Live] is full of old maids who sit about painting all day in the town. They have no more art in their souls than sex in their bodies or powder on their faces.

August 20th Dinner at Clement Parsons' at Broadway on Friday night. Very pleasant and polished and luxurious and full of the sense of easy and cultured existence that attracts me more and more. Tennis at Reynolds' at Alveston[118] yesterday which, though without culture as he is a self-made tube maker[119], was also pleasant. Three courts on the lawn that stretches out to the flat tree planted park, cut off only by a white iron fence. Great elms all round; sheep and cattle close all the time; pigeons cooing; jays shrieking; wine from their own grapes; parlour-men; polish; good food and luxury. But I'd rather have a life of my own alone than the life these people lead, constantly jostling each other in each others' houses, year in, year out. No space for the soul to grow in, no spiritual privacy. No souls to grow at all perhaps.

---

118   Presumably Alveston Grange, now an hotel on the outskirts of Stratford upon Avon.

119   The Reynolds Tube Co. had been acquired in 1928 by Tube Investments Ltd. It specialised in butted tubes, which are thicker at the ends than in the middle.

Business and, subsequently, hunting dominate the diary entries during the autumn. There is an interesting sidelight on Campden pub talk in December.

December 2nd   It is astonishing how the men in the pubs here still talk of the [1914-1918] war as an almost present event, and the one event of their lives — yet with all seriousness too. Many of them were in the Yeomanry and went out to Palestine and the Near East. To-night a long talk in the Red Lion with Margetts[120] and Ladbrook about their experiences, full of humour that was serious yet light, profound in its understanding of the sadness of life, and brilliant in its denial of all pedantic gloom about man and his fate.

---

120   Arthur Margetts, market gardener in Station Road. He sold his produce at R.S. Margett & Sons, later Potter's and now Jaffé & Neale, bookshop.

CW had spent Christmas with the Wood family at Wood Stanway. He was invited, with the family, to see in the New Year at Stanway House, where CW noted the evident sadness of Lady Wemyss, who had lost two sons in the War. He and the younger members of the party went on to the Cobweb Club in Cheltenham and danced until the small hours.

January 5th This hotel [The Live and Let Live] has gone bust and the Griffins have left, and I am living alone in my rooms in it and feeding out, waiting to see if I can buy part of it and turn it into a house, in which case Dorothy [Chatwin] will come and live here too and act as housekeeper for me, which will be nice, because she and Winifrid are such old friends and she knows all about us, and so we shall be free here when Winifrid comes.

January 17th I have bought part of this hotel that I want, and soon hope to get settled in with Dorothy. I shall at last soon have a house of my own and my £200 a year, and so I shall have achieved some of my aims in life.

Again, there is little but hunting until the Spring.

March 13th We are now installed in this house in the main street, Dorothy and I, and it is quite comfortable and I like it, though the fact that it has no garden is a draw back in some way.

Hunting came to an early stop on April 15th on account of the hard ground. CW records that hounds had been out 119 days and killed 62½ brace of foxes including cubs. CW himself had hunted (at a cost of £88) on 31 days. By the spring CW's social life opened up again.

April 25th Fred and Nina Griggs came to dinner and they stayed until 11.30. Very charming. I enjoyed this evening more than any evening I have yet spent in this house, except with Winifrid. We had a good dinner and I got some good burgundy and sherry and port, and Dorothy made excellent coffee. They say they are thinking of moving house to London if they can find a house there, for financial reasons. I am very sorry, for they are the closest friends I have here now, and I am really fond of them both.

May 3rd I have been to a doctor in Birmingham about myself because I have been feeling so ill and off colour and what I can only describe as 'poisoned' lately, for some time in fact. He says that I have a diabetic condition and has ordered me to diet and take no sugar and has given me some medicine too. He told me to see my dentist as he thought the cause was in the roots of some teeth in which the nerves were killed some time ago, and I have had all my teeth X-rayed and am to have several out.

May 12th I feel much better already for the diet and the medicine, but I have to have four teeth out, probably more. I dreamt last night that Michael St Aldwyn had refused to pay me back the £200 I lent him, and hope it is not prophetic.

May 14th To-day Dorothy and I have been entertaining people to meals. The Sharpleys to lunch – he has two pictures in the R.A. – Mrs Bennett Clark to tea with a Mrs Williams, and Griggs after tea for a drink and St Aldwyn for dinner. St Aldwyn offers me his horse Hercules, me to have him till the end of March next and if he is sound then pay £30 for him. I think I shall accept. Joey goes to George Hiatt at Aston Subedge to be hunted occasionally and to be worked on the land, and to be sent to the Kennels for the hounds to eat if he is too unsound.

June 14th I went to see Griggs last night and saw his new [zinc] plate of 'The Trent', a really lovely work, the most gentle and poetic he has done since 'Duntisbourne Rouse' I think, one I could sincerely say I loved with my heart.

I would give a lot to be able to sell say £100 worth of shares and walk off and cross to France and wander there from place to place for six months, cut off from my bondages and the temptations of business and money. But besides my own underlying caution I am responsible for Dorothy too and she cannot now afford to live by herself, and I am tied to Campden more than I know till I think of leaving it. I must accept that and be happy. If one accepts one's circumstances one can be happy at the bottom of a well.

June 17th I have reached one or two apparently disconnected conclusions and plans: to sell this house and get a better one with a garden in a year or so when I shall be able to afford it; to turn to writing again seriously and to let the elements of my life be part of my writing; possibly to write a semi-autobiographical novel; to go on with my work in Birmingham till I am 37 and wholly to accept it as part of my life while I do; and to turn back, as well as to my writing, to my own inner life, which I have neglected so much lately.

June 18th The Cricket Match at Stanway[121] was very good. Brilliant fooling by men such as those is more enjoyable to me than to watch serious play. I got away afterwards and so escaped from the falsely jolly evening that I knew would happen, and had supper alone and read my Wordsworth book [Hugh l'Anson Fausset's *Wordsworth, The Lost Leader*] and went out to see the Chandlers at Hidcote. I go to dinner there on Wednesday.

July 3rd I go out to-morrow to Swindon with Jack Coldicott and Bridge [landlord of the Red Lion] to look at horses. Coldicott goes down there every year and buys young hunters, and I am hoping to find something that may do for next season, but I am afraid the price may be too much for me, as I have not yet made up my mind to spend more than about £50.

July 4th Reading Rushen's *History of Campden*[122] I find that a list of men who were capable of bearing arms in 1608 made by John Smith an antiquary of those days, contains the names of Edward Whitfield aged about 40, a 'caliver man[123]'; and Thomas Whitfield, unclassified. In August 1629 Thomas Whitfield appears again signing a memorandum in the Church Register conveying the South Chapel to Sir Baptist Hicks for use as a place of burial. They do not appear again in the book. Campden being one of the channels through which the Welsh wool trade flowed, they may well have come of the same family which sent my ancestor, another Edward Whitfield, to Birmingham to seek his fortune in 1753. Both the Campden Edward Whitfield and my ancestor who went to Birmingham were blacksmiths.

July 5th I have had the first of five teeth out, a molar with great carrot roots, dead and decayed at the roots. Two more to-morrow. My jaw aches.

---

121 Between a team of New Zealand Test players whom Lord Wemyss had brought over, against a Gloucestershire side.
122 Percy C. Rushen, *History and Antiquities of Chipping Campden*, 1899 and 1911, the standard history of the town until CW's own, published in 1958.
123 A caliver was a light form of arquebus, fired without the stand that the heavier weapon required.

Reading Keyserling[124] it seems to me that Christian man will never 'convert the heathen' till he himself has attained something greater than Christianity.

July 13th I begin to wonder whether any really valuable action on my part about my life must not include my giving up living in Campden, which is in itself an escape, giving up my money seeking, my hunting, and all my hopes of personal comfort and retirement and, after having performed that act of renunciation, taking part in the creation of socialism in England. Under certain conditions I could do that and find greater happiness and completeness than I shall ever find in any secluded retirement. It is perhaps the only vital path for me to take, but whether I shall take it or not I do not know.

The next two weeks are occupied by a holiday trip to Scotland with Winifrid and Dorothy, travelling as far North as Inverness. CW's reaction — it was his first visit — was enthusiastic and he remarked that the Scots 'poor as they are.... have the hospitality of Christians and gentlemen...[with] far better manners and more intelligence than even better class English people, and more interest in the outer world too.'

Back in the Cotswolds, CW was in pursuit of a horse, and encountered a Captain Clarke of Hawling Lodge near Cheltenham.

August 1st Clarke a charming man living all alone out there, with dogs and horse and a tame badger, which sleeps on his bed and goes walks with him like a dog, and which he takes into Cheltenham in the car with him. He says it lies curled up on the back of the hood quite happily when he goes off shopping.

For much of August CW was unusually busy at the works in Birmingham and following this had the remaining dental extractions performed. This left him weakened and depressed. By October he was better, and looking forward to hunting on a new horse that he had acquired, but it was to prove difficult. Winifrid, who had also been ill, was also being more than usually capricious; she had been dabbling with Indian mysticism. Added to CW's worries, the works was losing money and there is little in the diary apart from hunting concerning his life in Campden. A poignant vignette on the hunting field on Armistice Day reminds us of the solemnity attached to this moment, only fifteen years after the Great War's end.

---

124   Count Hermann Keyserling, 1880-1946. Pan-cultural philosopher, very popular in the 1920s.

November 11th The Armistice Silence very impressive out on the hills, the horn blown sharply twice, and then silence and the bare heads, and only the sound of a bit in a horse's mouth or a hoof touching a stone, or a saddle creaking.

The grey horse was sold in Cheltenham without warranty, for £15. CW finally bought a reliable if elderly horse called Peter from Cresswell for £50 and was delighted with him.

December 28th Peter sound [after a touch of lameness] I set off to Milcote Station[125] today in sleet and a bitter wind and caught up with the hunt horses. It cleared up a bit at Long Marston and I left my mac at a house there – and got wet later. We had a marvellous day. We found by Milcote House, a huge field out and a lot of Warwickshire people, and the fox crossed the Avon and hounds followed him but scent seemed poor so very few followed. Later they came back over Welford Bridge and drew Welford Brake blank. Later we found in Welshmans and got away. We then had a hunt of nearly two hours, slow at first but fast later on, round Dorsington, on towards Pebworth, across the Hoden, back for Honeybourne, on to Badsey Station, and on into market gardens where hounds had to be stopped to prevent damage. I don't know how many fences I jumped but I should think at least 30. Peter is a marvel and never turned his head. Alas, towards the end of the hunt he began to go lame on his near fore again and walked the first two miles home lame. Then he winced and the next moment he was trotting sound. Hunting on him is a totally different thing from hunting on any horse I have ridden, even Joey. One can take one's own line and jump the fences just as they come. On him I feel I am really only just beginning to hunt in the full sense, really ride to hounds, and not merely keep near to them by every ingenuity one can think of. On him one just gallops on and goes anywhere where there is no wire, and knows one will get there easily and safely.

---

125   On the former Honeybourne to Stratford railway line, now the 'Greenway' track.

CW had taken to writing satirical rhymes about local characters.

January 13th

Griggs:

So anxious to be jolly all the while
He always laughs when he need only smile,
And in between denies his jovial nature
By gloom and mournfulness in every feature.

The Vicar[126]:

He sold his soul in youth, quite undismayed,
And still waits on, still hoping to be paid.

The Bakers:

Cockney weavers earnest in the life
Of intellectual and domestic strife.
They know the bird songs, if it's but by name,
And think the wren and robin are the same.

Wakeman:

Here's Wakeman, landlord of the Noel Arms,
Whose daily costume looks as though he farms.
Aiming at Pickwick he alas has grown
Winkle the bounder to the very bone.

February 17th   A story recently heard out hunting told me by Charles Napier: A farmer and a girl he was courting were out for a walk, and looked over a hedge and saw a boar on a sow, mating. 'Oi'd like to be doing the same as that old boar,' he said. 'Well, why don't you?' said the girl. 'It's your own sow.'

CW had mentioned seeing Audrey Chandler out hunting ten days earlier, but he would presumably already have been acquainted through his friendship with Ben Chandler. His report of their next meeting is somewhat equivocal, considering that she was the young woman he would marry eight years later.

---

126   Canon George Hitchcock, at Campden 1916-1934.

February 18ᵗʰ A perfect afternoon. I did not go to Wood Stanway but walked out to the Chandlers at Hidcote[127] for tea. Audrey was looking very smart in a new brown dress. I rather like her. Winifrid says I ought to marry her, but apart from the fact that I don't want to marry at all, and that it would be unfair to marry while I belong as I do to Winifrid, I don't know that it would be a success. [Ben] Chandler brought me back.

Hunting again fills most diary entries until near the end of the season. CW had written to the Evesham Journal objecting to the proposals that had been put forward to convert Haydon's Barn (the Tithe Barn opposite the Church) into a public hall. As will be seen, CW eventually bought the site from Ben Chandler, who had bought it in order to protect it from development, and built the Tithe House there in 1939/40.

March 26ᵗʰ My letter to the Evesham Journal [February 27ᵗʰ], and the others that followed it have stopped the proposal to convert the fine old [tithe] barn into a public hall.

April 10ᵗʰ To walk across this street, down an alley, past a walnut tree, and out into the fields that come so close that they are a sort of garden to the houses, and to hear the thrushes singing in the evening, after being all day at the works is still very wonderful. I went this evening, with all the joy that filled me ten years ago, and walked up to look at Peter [the current horse], now blistered[128] and in the field on Doe Bank. I think he is improving. Fred and Nina Griggs to dinner to-morrow night.

April 16ᵗʰ My committee in Birmingham and all its work now finished and a new era of prosperity for the works beginning I hope, but a lot of work to do yet before I can slack off. All day in a stuffy hotel room with 20 men all smoking cigars and the windows shut. This evening Campden seemed a paradise, so cool and clean and fresh. After dinner to Griggs, who showed me the sketch for his 'Clavering' etching[129], and we had long discussions about art and books.

---

127   The Chandlers had lived at Hidcote House, Hidcote Boyce (3 miles from Campden), since the mid-1920s. It was restored for them by Norman Jewson
128   A method of reducing swelling by applying a blistering agent to create an inflammatory reaction. Not in use nowadays.
129   'Memory of Clavering' see Moore, *op. cit.*, pp 245-6.

April 24th Work is getting less worrying and more of a routine nature again, that others can do, and I am freer. I stopped to look at Peter this evening on my way home, and I have hopes still of his being sound. Dorothy has gone to Bearley. We have hopes of getting a cottage in Leasbourne, a quieter part of the street, soon, joining on to the Griggses, and I look forward to being there greatly.

April 30th A lovely evening and a clear sky and still air and fresh green everywhere and birds singing. I have been to dinner with the Hugginses[130] at Berkswell through lush green Warwickshire countryside.

May 1st Home early and a walk round Pool Meadow before dinner. A perfect evening and a soft warm haze over the vivid green of everything. Campden very beautiful, like a woman one loves and has loved for many years and loves more as the years go by, because one has loved her so long that her very being is her beauty.

May 3rd I am happy – because I am English and because I can come home and listen to the thrushes and blackbirds and hear the cuckoo and look at and talk to the horses at grass, and then sit in my room [at the Live and Let Live] at dusk and read, with the town outside one window and the fields outside the other, brilliant in the late evening light and echoing with bird songs.

The continuing entry seems prescient, although CW had not, at this stage, mentioned European politics in his diary. Hitler had been appointed Chancellor in Germany less than eighteen months earlier.

That which England means to the average man was threatened with destruction in 1914. It was the same sort of thing as that which a woman he loves means to a man. Seeing it threatened he fought and would have fought until he was exterminated to keep it – and he won. If it is threatened he will fight again and if he loses be exterminated rather than be absorbed by an alien spirit.

May 5th Last night I stood by my door, Campden still and dark, only the lights in the windows here and there, and the outlines of the roofs against the

---

130   Lt Col William (Bill) Huggins, D.S.O., M.C., D.L. 1890-1965. Married Elizabeth Cadbury and lived at Berkswell Grange near Coventry. He, like CW, came from a Birmingham manufacturing family. One of his four sons was Jeremy Brett, the actor.

sky. I felt deeply part of its quiet and gentleness and beauty and at the same time aware of Birmingham and its factories and suburbs and my own life there in the daytime, thirty miles away across the fields and woods, and to my joy and surprise the two did not fight each other in separate halves of my mind but lived together in me at peace, part of the whole that I have found life to be. The synthesis is at last becoming accomplished and I am becoming whole without destroying either part of myself. I am glad. I am becoming in this way worthy of freedom from Birmingham.

May 8th There are vague stirrings in Campden that may lead to our move to the house in Leasbourne, Stanley Cottage. On Friday I lunch at Farmcote [above Winchcombe] and shoot rooks with old Burgess who lives there.

That evening, CW went to the theatre at Stratford for a performance of Romeo and Juliet *[directed by W. Bridges-Adams] with the Hugginses, Stanley and Winifrid Wood and Dorothy. This resulted in the following entry and rhyme:*

The theatre was awful, Shakespeare murdered, mauled, mouthed, insulted and ruined. The actors could not speak; every suggestion and subtle meaning was hidden in a slur of syllables; the whole thing was painful and bad.

> This theatre with Yankee money built,
> To expiate their English-speaking guilt,
> Where Adam's puppets strut the barren board,
> And men and women watch, genteelly bored,
> Shakespeare's a corpse. If Shakespeare's ghost could come
> And see how we insult him in his home
> What thundering satire he would write of us.

May 11th I shot 21 rooks with 50 shots with my .22 rifle and I am rather pleased with that. A very good lunch, served by spotty youths in livery, everything grown on the farm; lamb, vegetables, asparagus, butter, apples and ale. Lovely Jersey cow butter. Cresswell as mad as ever. Old Burgess a nice old man with a whimsical sense of humour. This evening I heard the cuckoo at 10.15 at Broad Campden and have never heard him so late before.

May 14ᵗʰ The Sharpleys to dinner to-night. To-morrow to *Henry V* with the Hugginses to which I am not looking forward after *Romeo and Juliet* being so bad. We eat rook pie to-night.

May 15ᵗʰ Surprisingly *Henry V* was good as *Romeo* was bad. A very fine production[131]. The straightforward simplicity of the play appealed to Bill Huggins and he said that he would lean it by heart if there was another war so that he could repeat the parts to his men. I said that I thought the effect would be spoilt by his having to speak through a gas mask.

May 29ᵗʰ One step further towards a move; I have written to Miss Stanley the owner to ask if I can have the cottage after the 30ᵗʰ September 1935, till when I shall take over the present lease.

Scuttlebrook Wake on Saturday night was moved from its immemorial site in Leasbourne out into the Recreation Ground by the police in conjunction with certain old maids and I am very cross about it and shall do all I can to get it brought back. It makes me angry when people interfere with time-honoured rights like that.

June 10ᵗʰ To-day to the Griggs' and took Nina to Stanton this morning and there at Sir Philip Stott's[132] went and ate fresh strawberries warm off the bed, and as I came home a cuckoo came over the street as though it was a wood drive, calling out, a refreshing experience again of those joys that were such a daily pleasure of one's childhood.

That cuckoo through the air, this air in Campden of living in a town and yet in a garden where the houses and the street are just incidents in the surrounding country; fields behind each house and the birds and the silence and the sun and the basking dogs lying in the street, and the swallows in their nest just above my bedroom window, who talk to each other in the night just as sleeping lovers do when they are half awake. It is all so fair and so wonderful, this place, that it enchants me just as it did ten years ago when I first came to live in it.

---

131   Directed by Robert Atkins.

132   Sir Philip Stott, 1ˢᵗ Baronet, 1858-1937. Engineer and architect from a Lancashire cotton-spinning family, he moved to Stanton near Broadway in 1913 and was instrumental in preserving that village.

June 13th We seem to be rather nearer getting the cottage in Leysbourne by the end of July now. I went to look at it again to-day and it is very nice and could be made charming with a little money spent on it. It is just the place I have always had in mind to retire to and I hope I shall go there.

June 14th Have been rather successful with my Campden poem at last. It is for Griggs, for his Campden book[133]. I hate using place names in poems or the titles but in this one it is fairly natural.

My present plan about the cottage is to take it for three years until I am 35, by which time I ought to have my £5000, after that I want what I have earned — leisure.

June 16th I have heard from Miss Stanley who says I can have the cottage, so I have only to settle with Mrs Haydon its present tenant to let me get in by the end of July. It will be a great relief and a proper step which fits in with all my plans.

June 17th This is the history of my day yesterday: Breakfast; put the electric kettle right; read the paper; went to the bank to enquire about a little building site; came home and wrote to the man whose name I had been given; went to see Mrs Haydon and agreed that she should move out of the cottage in a month and that I should give her £10; measured my future bed room and found I could get my furniture in, though I am not sure about myself; came back and told Dorothy; wrote to Miss Stanley and agreed to her terms and asked her to send me an agreement from Sept 25th to sign (£30 p.a.); made a list of all my furniture and planned how to get it in; talked to Dorothy about it all, very excited and relieved to be leaving this noisy house soon; went and had a drink at the Red Lion; had lunch; slept for ten minutes; went to Mickleton Club Sports with Hudson and Ladbrook and won 2/- on the jumping and had tea; went for a walk and had a look at Peter and came back through Westington; climbed over the Red Lion garden wall on my way back and had a talk to Jack Bridges and advised him about enlarging his loose boxes; had a drink and played with the dogs there; came home; slept for a quarter of an hour; changed and had dinner; went off to Mickleton Wake again with Hudson, and

---

133   See note to the entry for April 4th 1924. For the text of the unpublished poem, sent out by CW as a Christmas card in 1934, see p. 259.

also Bill Becket and his wife, and drank in the yard of Barlow Stanley's pub in the crowd of seething people; had a walk round the Wake, a Hogarth scene; saved Hudson from falling off a merry-go-round; went to the dance and found it was over at 11; came home and went with Hudson to Bill Beckett's and drank bad dandelion wine; went to bed and read a book called *Poetry Direct and Oblique*[134] and could not take it in properly; went to sleep.

June 22nd   Yesterday to London and to the Horse Show at Olympia with the Straffords, and to the Academy and back to Birmingham on Friday morning. The Horse Show was good, but all the plush and flowered gilt glories of the [Earl of] Lonsdale['s] period are gone now and it has become as much a business venture as a circus. Another of the great solemn splendours of the Edwardian era gone.

During the last week of June CW took a holiday with Winifrid and Dorothy Chatwin in Eastern England, reporting Lincolnshire as 'very spoilt by new buildings and pylons and masses of mean houses and bungalows outside every town' in contrast to the Dutch 'who have achieved a standard of taste in a flat country that puts us to shame'. Lincoln and the Yorkshire abbeys were very much appreciated, however.

July 1st   Stanley Cottage is now settled as from the 25th Sept, and we only wait for Mrs Haydon to move out so that we can move in. I have drawn plans of all the rooms and have fitted all our furniture in. I shall let this property [The Live and Let Live] and the shops that go with it for three years when we have moved in at a total of £120 a year with luck. After three years I shall either buy the cottage or build one. I should by then have in all my £5000 saved, including the property, and by then too Dorothy will have found a cottage for herself.

July 8th   I have been to see the Oliver Bakers at Bearley with Dorothy. He begins to look very old and weak and transparent. In the evening to see the Campagnacs, who have lately come to live here from Liverpool, where he was a University professor[135]. A nice, ironical, detached man.

July 21st   To-day I have moved by myself, in suitcases and boxes in the car 950 books, the bookcases, have put up the shelves, put the books on them, and have also moved all our prints and pictures, about 50, and have sweated

---

134   By E.M.W. Tillyard, 1889-1962, literary scholar.
135   Ernest Trafford Campagnac, 1873-1952, Professor of Education at Liverpool.

all day and drunk beer like water. Now at 7.30 I have changed, had a cold bath, and am clean and fresh in my dinner jacket, and feel I have earned my rest.

July 28th We moved on Thursday and got all the furniture in by one. By midnight with an interlude of dinner at Dr Birch's[136] we had got straight in a marvellous way, except for Dorothy's spinet which would not go into its alcove in the dining room downstairs. That has been seen to since, and we are straight now, all the prints and pictures hung, and even the alterations beginning in the garden. It is perfectly charming and I love it. Not a thing jars. It is quiet; the furniture looks well everywhere; the garden is just large enough; it is cheap; and the relief to be away from the other place, which I hated for its noise and discomfort, is great. I have a tiny back bedroom, into which I can just get my things and myself, and an upstairs sitting room in front; Dorothy has the top bedroom and the dining room as her sitting room. That is all there is except for the kitchen and the bathroom and W.C. combined.

This afternoon I cut down an old plum tree near the kitchen window, then began and painted the water butt green. That led to painting all the spouting at the back, and two doors, and my face and my shirt, and it has taken me till 10. Charles Blakeman has just called, having come back from Edinburgh, where he works now in a stained glass studio[137]. I am very happy and have never before felt life to be so full of promise and so satisfactory in all its aspects as I do now.

July 31st I have been in the garden every evening. It is good to become more intimate with the earth again and to sit out there when it is too dark to work, but light enough to see the form of things, and the moths and bats that flicker against the summer sky. I was up at four thirty and went cub hunting and am sleepy. I took Blakeman and Ladbrook and Bridge. Hounds killed one cub and several got away. They hunted well, except for the usual early season young entry who wandered about disconsolately outside the covert wondering what it was all about. A lovely morning and the vale grey and silver, with splashes of sunlight slanting across it.

---

136   Dr Birch practised at The Gables, High Street.
137   That of Herbert Hendrie, 1887-1947.

August 16th This evening finishing off the small garden near the cottage until it got dark, then to Griggs', where the two Guiney sisters[138] were, from Oxford. I do like them. They are two really true women in whose lives laughter and sorrow are one. The younger sister is pale and consumptive and the elder, a mountain of a woman, gives her whole life to looking after her, but there is no sentiment, and yet feeling and love are there all the time.

August 25th To the theatre at Stratford with Betty Huggins and two girls and Leslie Huggins, Bill's brother, the music master at some public school,[139] and a Victor Bonham Carter.[140]

August 28th Tom Benfield, Griggs' gardener, is working for me here just now, and he is a delightful old man. He calls all plants blokes: a strong bloke; a weak bloke; an awkward bloke; a measly bloke; a poor sort of bloke; a nice bloke; a pretty bloke; an untidy bloke; and so on.

September 1st When I was gardening this morning Bill Jefferies the running huntsman came in and said: 'You've done too much of that guvnor. You'd better come after they partridges.' So we went out and shot 1½ brace on the allotments and his ground in the Brach. This afternoon I went with Roberts to Stuart Slatter's at Meon and shot another 1½ brace. A lovely day and typical of its time; frosty morning and evening and hot day, and clear, and glorious hazy views from Meon; small tortoiseshell butterflies enjoying the sun; rooks flying lower and more overhead than in summer; pigeons clattering from the trees; starlings on the chimney pots chattering and curdling. Autumn is almost here and the cobwebs are wet with dew in the mornings.

CW had traded his unsatisfactory horse Peter for a new mount from Strafford at Westington Mill.

October 16th I have decided to call my new horse Taffy because, when I was showing it to Ladbrook in the stable, I said it looked to me as though it had a bit of Welsh pony blood in its veins, and at that moment it lifted its tail to rear, and Ladbrook said: 'Yes, it's sure to be a Welsh horse for it's got a leak in its arse.'

---

138   Grace and Ruth, from an Oxford Catholic literary family.
139   Stowe School, Buckingham, established in 1923.
140   Victor Bonham Carter, 1913-2003, writer on country subjects, farmer and campaigner for authors' rights.

He is settling down now in his stable, leads well at exercise and looks well. On Thursday at Meon I shall find out more about him.

A broadcast of Campden last night, a scene in a pub, a vile travesty of the place and people. A highly sophisticated young man comes into a pub, motoring through, and asks a series of questions in breathless haste, which are answered by the old men of the town. What would really have happened would have been that all the men in the bar would have stared at the young man, would have answered one question in a way that would have made him nervous about asking another, and then would have kept quiet until he went. When he had gone they would have said: 'Who was that bugger? Cocky young bugger, weren't 'e?'

October 19th I set off on Taffy at 9 this morning for Hinchwick and arrived when hounds were running by Beechy Bank. On the way I saw a fox in the gorse by Brown's with a mole in his mouth, sitting and listening. Then he went off quietly but decidedly towards Bourton Wood, carrying the mole. I joined the rest of the field by Sezincote Warren: Major [Weld-] Forester, his wife Lady Victoria, Mitchell, Parson Murry, Pickering, Wetherley, Peggy Alexander, Stella Warden, Hotton, [?Dr Colin Houghton], Colonel Edwardes and a crowd of 50 or so.

And so hunting begins to occupy its usual dominant place in the diary during the autumn and winter. CW was delighted to be invited by the Master to wear the hunt button, writing that 'it gives me as much deep satisfaction as a letter from a publisher saying that he had seen my poems and wanted to publish them'. Concerns with the works, which was still losing money, and meeting again an old girlfriend, Audrey Robinson, combine to exclude much mention of Campden at this time. CW again spent Christmas at Wood Stanway.

~ 1935 ~

As was his habit, CW recorded his investments and expenditure at the start of the year. Investments stood (at cost) at £4002, and his expenditure during 1934 totalled £505, including taxes. CW's determined aim was to have investments of £5000 (about £300,000 by today's values) so that he could live independently, and he planned to have achieved this by the end of 1936.

January 2nd Apart from my car [£65], which is essential if one is to live a life of any freedom at all, and hunting and shooting, I do not think I could possibly have spent less. I have only done it because of my determination to save enough to live on without the works, but that determination has been one of the most consistent factors in my life, ever since my Father left and I saw the possibility of doing it.

January 31st The charm of this cottage for me is that I can live so many lives in it from John Clare gone up in the world to a country gentleman gone down. Campden itself lends itself to that too. I am anything from poet to foxhunter here; jolly good fellow to studious recluse; lecher to Puritan; deist to agnostic; dandy to sloven. I am balanced in the middle of all these personalities and only need the weight of a sentence or a word or a picture to sway me one way or the other.

February 15th I have been working hard at the works. I have, in my own mind, taken on the task of saving the business and giving all I can of myself in reason to it for the next two years. By then it will either be stable enough for me to stay away more or I shall leave it altogether and admit my failure. I think I shall succeed, but I must keep my balance carefully and not let it get hold of me.

February 22nd Alastair Miller the son of a sculptor here [Alec Miller] to dinner. I like him and think he ought to do some good work one day if he can only break himself and survive. His second book of poems disappointing but he talks well and seems really sincere.

During this more settled phase in his life, and with the end of hunting, CW's thoughts turned again towards his writing, revising some old prose workings and thinking about new projects.

March 13th I have gone more and more into my own private world lately and that is the way I shall go, living only really important life inside myself and with myself. Most of my poems are creations of that world. I shall call my next book or a book of prose essays *A World of One's Own* I think.

So it was to be: a collection of evocative pieces based on CW's memories of his childhood at Bearley, Warwickshire, of life in Campden and the countryside, published by Country Life in 1938, with woodcut engravings by Geoffrey Miller.

Two weeks later, another project emerged that was also to see the light of day.

March 22nd I think of starting a prose Persephone *(a constant poetic theme of CW's)* who would be a woman who had married a man who did not attract her before she had developed enough to know her own mind. He would be her Pluto. She would have a lover in the country to whom she would go each spring.

Mr Chambers and Persephone *was published in October 1937 by the Golden Cockerel Press, with wood-engravings by Dorothea Braby. In a review, H.E. Bates described it as 'a small masterpiece' and compared it to David Garnett's* Lady into Fox.

April passes with Winifrid much preoccupied with a daughter's illness, and becoming ill herself; CW as a consequence found himself depressed but found solace in working at the garden of Stanley Cottage.

May 5th A very grand Jubilee [of King George V] procession, a lovely day and crowds of people out, an ox roasted in the Recreation Ground and dinner to all over 60. I had old Polly Waine[141] our oldest inhabitant in the sitting room to watch from the window, and gave her a whisky and some cake and drove her up to the dinner in the car afterwards.

May 7th Yesterday Winifrid came here for dinner and we went out and joined the torchlight procession up to the bonfire and saw the fire lit and watched it blaze. Then on to Broadway Tower where there was another one, and sat there, warm at fifty yards from the blaze.

---

141 Mary 'Polly' Waine, 1843-1937. CW maintained her story that her soldier father had fought at Waterloo; this was a popular Campden legend, although it seems not to be true. See *Campden Characters*, CADHAS 2011, pp 53-54 for an account of this feisty lady.

The following entry gives an interesting insight into the perils of business flying at that early date. CW went to Glasgow for a hospital trade exhibition.

May 17th Back from Scotland, a very interesting flight there via Belfast, and coming back quite mildly exciting. After setting off in lovely clear weather, though with a fine sprinkling of snow on the hills outside Glasgow, we crossed to Belfast in bright sun and from there to the Isle of Man. But after that we ran into sleet and snowstorms and had to fly 20 feet above the sea and nearly hit a trawler, only missing its mast by a few yards, and could not land at Liverpool, but flew on to Manchester in thick fog and were sent on from there by train.

May 27th I came home at about 10 and left the car in Miss Coldicutt's garage, where I keep it, and went to bed. About a quarter of an hour later I was called up and told that the car was on fire. I went out after putting on some clothes hurriedly and it was blazing. The firemen had got it out of the garage with great difficulty because the brake was on, but they had it out on the grass in front of the garage soon after I got there. They could not put it out and in an hour it was completely gutted. It is of course insured, and I ought to get £100 to replace it with, but I must get it settled quickly as I need the car every day and the insurance does not cover hire.

May 29th I have got £90 for the car and £14 for the things in it and I shall get a 1934 model of the same car, a Morris 10, and can replace the things I lost easily for rather less than I have been paid, so I shall really do quite well.

June 1st I have got a 1934 Morris for £116 for which the works will pay the difference of £31 and I am very pleased with it. I got it up to 70 miles an hour when I brought it out here yesterday.

June 15th Scuttlebrook Wake in full swing to-day outside our windows, a maze of stands, a babel of shouting and hammering, and to-night flares and crowds and loud speakers and music. We keep open house with drinks in the sitting room for friends to come in.

June 16th The Wake last night very good, and interesting to watch all the packing up and to get to know the gipsies, some of them quite well. We had in for drinks: Fred and Nina Griggs, Audrey Chandler, Tom Robbins, Strafford,

---

Mrs Strafford, Jack Foster from the Seagrave [pub in Weston sub Edge] and his wife and daughters, Charlie Ladbrook, Tom Barnes, the Police Sergeant, and Basil Fairclough.

July 26th Have been to see the Carrol Perkins[142] next door and have met T.S. Eliot[143], a very quiet, wise and gentle man. He said little the whole evening but all sense and with no shade of consciousness of himself as a famous author, but as a man, being himself, naturally.

CW took a fortnight's holiday in the Lake District with Dorothy and Winifrid.

August 11th Fred Griggs called and I am going there to tea and afterwards am taking him down to Netherton [near Elmley Castle, Worcestershire] to do a study for an etching of the chapel ruins, now in the garden of a house there.

During the next few weeks CW was mostly hard at work with the essays for A World of One's Own. *He was also diverted by an affair with his early love, Audrey Robinson, by then a married woman living in London. Cub hunting has begun.*

September 21st I started at 6.30 this morning after coming home at one from Wood Stanway with Fred Griggs last night and rode over to Sedgecombe [at Broad Campden]. We had a run round by the railway and killed. Later I came home and about one when I was gardening I heard them in Congrove and ran out and saw them kill in the orchard. Another fox was bolted from the drain and hunted into some sprouts at Catbrook and lost. The whole of Campden turned out for this, John Skee the fat landlord of the Lygon Arms leaving his bar unattended, and some of the shops were left empty too. How they ran and puffed and panted and enjoyed the hound music.

CW had a bad fall while out cub hunting towards the end of October and this resulted in a lingering cold, some pain in the back, and a general feeling of malaise, which continued well into November. He was depressed at his lack of progress in writing, even in his diary.

---

142 John Carrol Perkins had been minister of King's Chapel, Boston, Mass. His wife's niece Emily Hale was Eliot's muse during 40 years.

143 Thomas Stearns Eliot, O.M., (Missouri) 1888 - (London) 1965. A great poet of the mid-20th century. Eliot took the title and some suggestions of place for one of his *Four Quartets* from Burnt Norton, three miles north of Campden.

November 20th I find it increasingly hard to write in this diary as one should – freely; somehow as I settle down to it it all slips round the corner of my mind, as it were, and I have a sense of having nothing to say that I have not said before.

As to life, I look into the abyss and it is not pleasant, and yet is inevitable; the abyss that death is the cessation of personal existence. And I wonder sometimes and fear too lest I may become the subject of melancholy as I grow older. I have no straws left to cling to except those that may be blown my way: writing – and it threatens to leave me at any hour; Winifrid – and she is subject to the same cessation of existence as I am, but not necessarily at the same time; money – and one loses it, or continually wants more; nature, books, my own being – they all melt away and fail one if one fails them.

I am, as most men are, dogged by a fear of life that I never really look in the face, and it is when the cloaks against it, chiefly Winifrid and writing in my case, show signs of impermanence that I shudder and feel I may go melancholy-queer one day. I rely too much on too vulnerable things to be safe, and having no faith in anything beyond, having no fixed idea to cling to, of God or of life after death, I have in the last resort nothing. No man who faces the truth can have, but one has not truly faced the truth till one has faced the fear of life without these things and by conquering it, achieved sanity.

CW's aunt Dorothy Chatwin, his companion at both the Live and Let Live and Stanley Cottage, had bought a cottage for herself at Stow on the Wold, and was to move in mid-December.

December 2nd Carpentering in Dorothy's bedroom, which is to be mine when she goes. I am busy arranging things for the change and have not written anything. There is the house to be got right, and there will be dinners and dances at Christmas, and I shall not be in the trough of the wave until half January is done, and I can only begin to work in the trough.

December 3rd Hacked up to Naunton with Stella Warden starting at nine and got there in 1¾ hours. Saw Hudson there, rather beery and unshaved. He is living there and painting, but drinking a lot.

December 13th Dorothy moved yesterday and I spent all day getting straight afterwards. I am very pleased with the change. I feel a different person with the house to myself. My furniture all fits in well and looks far better spread out.

I have discovered about myself and the house I live in that the house is my body and its windows, especially its upstairs ones, are my eyes. It is a body that does not move, and its front bed-room windows are its real eyes. Its garden is its behind, and my garden feels like a Victorian bustle sometimes.

My narcissistic nature takes great pleasure in arranging the furniture here and getting everything just so for myself. I suppose the typical old maid is really narcissistic, just as I should become, and probably shall if I go on living by myself.

December 16th I went to see Dorothy at Stow yesterday and she is settling in well and likes her cottage. I should not be surprised if Hudson is living with her soon. They are fond of each other and it would do them both good, except that she has such a Victorian conscience and would be ashamed if it were known. If he did not drink so and were not such a wash-out of a creature it would be a good thing if they were to marry.

December 18th [Cousin] Sam [Whitfield]'s small son Jeremy aged six, an interesting child, precocious but natural, said the other day, 'I don't think I believe in God Daddy, he seems so unlikely.'

December 19th My total money invested is now £4327, an increase of £320 this year. I aim at investing £350 in 1936 and then reaching the £5000 early in 1937. My first investment was £150 in 1925, so I shall have averaged nearly £500 a year for 10 years, which is a pretty good effort out of my income as it has been. If I go on working after 35 I shall aim at another £2500 which will make my income £350 a year and that I think will be enough.

The weather over Christmas was 'an unbelievable series of fogs, frosts, snowstorms' but CW managed to hunt on Boxing Day – the meet was at the Fish Inn above Broadway in those days – and once more before the New Year.

~ 1936 ~

January 8th   The total eclipse of the moon seen from Bordesley Station in Birmingham of all places and so most uncharming.

January 19th   The frost is worse and old men look very wise and say it has begun just as it did in 1895. I messed about in Campden and had tea at the Strafford's and went later to the Campagnac's, then to see Griggs. To-day the Kennards to lunch but Mrs Cook [housekeeper] put on a rather crude meal of cold beef on cold plates, with tepid vegetables. After they had gone I went down to see Brian Parker at Aston sub Edge and we went out and tobogganed on Poor's Piece till it grew dark, and had some very good fun, though there was hardly enough snow.

January 21st   The King [George V] died last night at 12 o'clock. No theatres, dances, racing etc. I wonder if they will stop hunting for the week. I am very impressed by the reverence and real respect of the men at the works and in the pubs here. He was truly a father-substitute in the best sense in their minds. What wonderful lives of public service, those of his Grandmother [Queen Victoria], his Father [Edward VII], and himself – and the Prince [Edward of Wales] too has begun, and will be a good and popular king I think.

January 30th   The first day's hunting to-day after three weeks all but two days. We met at Foxcote House [near Ilmington, Warwickshire] which has been closed up for years and now has tenants, who gave us good port. The old owners were a Catholic family called Canning, and they had a chapel there and a priest living there alone for years. The present owners are not Catholics and the chapel has been 'unconsecrated' quite ceremoniously by priests, etc[144].

February 4th   As I see them my essays (*A World of One's Own*) and the characters and my three books of poems are a sort of document of English country life now that may be fascinating or valuable in 100 years, if not now. Certainly the characters are pretty complete as a set of people living now, and they have some wit and life in them.

---

144   The chapel was built in 1814. Philip Canning Howard died in 1934. The altar from the chapel is now at the Church of the Assumption and St Gregory, Warwick Street, Soho, London. The present owner of Foxcote is an American owner of a lingerie brand.

As I enjoy my life alone, so I loathe my works life more and more and want to be free from it – but not free merely to be idle. And writing is not enough now, and it is late to take up another country money-making occupation. So I want enough money on which to be able to hunt and get about and travel a bit. Yet to get that I shall have to drudge on longer in Birmingham. I am in a cleft stick. I ought to have cleared out in the Fitzroy Square days and risked it. I have just read Lord Lytton's *Anthony*. How I feel, in my social scale, the state of energy and indecision of power and aimlessness that he felt. He was just a year younger than I am.

March 3rd Last night a dance at the Town Hall, got up so that Catholic children may go to Weston super Mare and make themselves sick with sweets in June.

March 19th I have finished off work in the top garden, have tidied it up, dug the beds, cut the lawn, and put 2ft wattle hurdles along the lower part of the wall, making a screen, so that I cannot be overlooked at all, and it looks quite well, besides being effective. I have also weeded the paths and rolled them. I worked from 8 till 5, with half an hour for lunch, and am tired, but feel well again and happy.

April 18th This morning I finished the alterations in the garden which I began when I came here and laid the last stone. The satisfaction of finishing is great. To have done a respectable job with one's own hands is good. Now I can potter and enjoy the spring here. All I have done could have been done by a man at the cost of £20 or so in a month I suppose. I have taken 18 months and it has cost me £3 and it has been done with my own arms and hands and legs and will.

April 21st It is snowing hard outside to-night and the world is white. A cold and horrid spring so far. Have read a rather good book called *England have my Bones* by T.H. White[145] and have sent him my own *Woodgatherer*. He seems to understand the country properly.

April 27th T.H. White writes and thanks me for *The Woodgatherer* and seems to want to meet me.

---

145   Terence Hanbury White, 1906-1964. At the time he was a master at Stowe School. He is best known for his Arthurian trilogy *The Once and Future King*.

April 29ᵗʰ There has been a Red Throated Diver shot here, an immature bird, with his throat still white. He was taken for a wild goose by Dudley Haydon, who shot him — a pity, for they are fairly rare.

May 24ᵗʰ Cold; fires in the evening; wind; clouds; sun; little rain. Yesterday and to-day I planted out marigolds, snapdragons, asters, zinnias and pansies in the garden.

May 27ᵗʰ Very cold still. The amount of noise that a small boy can make is amazing. There are several playing at being dogs out on the grass opposite this cottage and when I looked out to see what all the noise was about I discovered that it was all being made by one small fair haired child of five.

May 31ˢᵗ At Griggs' last night and the Shanks[146] and her daughter there, the daughter rather like Audrey [Robinson] and very attractive but only 18. I like Shanks. He twits Griggs about his Catholicism and asked him last night: 'Does your Wesleyan upbringing permit you to say that, Freddie?' about some remark Griggs had made very pompously.

June 3ʳᵈ Yesterday the hills were white with hail and there was a sharp frost at night, and it thundered for an hour and all the electric light went off, and an oak was struck by lightning on Draycott Hill — such is June this year and such has been the Whitsun holiday week I have had at home.

June 6ᵗʰ Scuttlebrook once more, and an extraordinary and very eventful day.

CW had been rabbit shooting on Dover's Hill in the morning and on the way had stopped to talk to Elizabeth Fairclough, whom he took shooting with him. Elizabeth and Basil Fairclough had arrived in Campden a few years earlier with their young child and were living at Dover's House in the High Street. They had met at Oxford where Elizabeth, a strictly brought-up vicar's daughter from the Lake District, was teaching music and Basil was an undergraduate. She became pregnant and they married but since the birth of her (unexpected) child relations between them had been chaste. Basil was independently well off and had worked at the Alcuin Press and at Gordon Russell's in Broadway.

---

146   Edward Shanks, 1892-1953. War poet, novelist and a prominent figure in London literary circles.

I came home and Basil came in and looked round the garden and went. I went down to the Red Lion and had a drink and came back for dinner, the wake blaring outside and the crowd increasing. I then went in to Miss Sunderland-Taylor's (the retired headmistress of a girl's school who has adenoids and is my next door neighbour)[147] for coffee and Dorothy was there, and the Campagnacs. I had my dining room turned into a bar and beer and whisky all ready on the table, and saw that all was well when I came back from next door, and then went off into the crowd. Then began the busy meeting of friends and the bringing in of people for drinks, talking and chattering and listening to and passing on local bits of gossip and jokes. The Griggses, the Chandlers, Biddy Slattery, young Griffiths[148], Tom Robbins, the Pembertons[149], and Elizabeth and Basil [Fairclough] all came in and many others. I was distracted and busy, first talking and entertaining, then going off into the wake for a time. Elizabeth is shy of people and I noticed that she looked *distraite*. She hung about a lot, but I was too busy to take much notice of her. She asked if she might go up into my sitting room 'to choose a book' and I, thinking she really wanted to go to the W.C., did not go up with her, but stayed downstairs talking and forgot about her.

Later on, when there was no one else in the house for a bit I went up and found her still there, sitting in the window watching the wake below. I sat and talked to her, conscious of an emotional tension, but detached and separate, still under the illusion that ours was just a sentimental friendship in the first stage of its development. Then we sat on the settee to look at a book, myself still preoccupied with the task of finding her one she would like. She leant back and I suddenly found myself kissing her.

Thus began an intense affair, which lasted through the summer. Elizabeth admitted that she had conceived a passion for CW more than a year beforehand and more or less threw herself at him. CW, for his part, although bemused at first, soon found himself in love with Elizabeth. Winifrid's reaction was initially one of resignation and letting go; CW, for his part, was torn between a new love that promised some sort of future (Elizabeth's fragile marriage notwithstanding) and the fourteen-year old relationship with Winifrid, which he realised — as she must also have done — held no long-term prospects, despite its deep roots.

---

147   Alice Maud Sunderland-Taylor, 1872-1942, at Stamford High School 1909-26.
148   Guy 'Dinkie' Griffiths, 1916-2003. Son of Scudamore and 'Rubie' Griffiths of Bedfont House in the High Street.
149   Guy Pemberton, architect at Broadway who worked with Sir Guy Dawber.

This summer also saw the beginnings of other changes in CW's life.   The affair with Elizabeth energised him to write, in the space of only a few weeks, his novella Mr Chambers & Persephone *marking his move towards expression in prose, reserving poetry in future for the private sphere.*

The diary this summer mentions the first intimations of war.   Recording his thoughts after breakfast in a York hotel during a business visit in late June, CW writes:

As I read [the paper] my mind was full of E. and W. and life, and I read something that made me realise that the last war was only the rumbling of the thunder compared with the next, which I felt is bound to come, and as I knew that I felt I could face it whatever its terrors, could still love men, even those who brought it about.

Of CW's life outside the personal sphere there is little of significance recorded this summer: an evening in early July at Stanway when Lady Cynthia Wemyss gave a lecture on 'Ghosts in Literature' at which Lord David Cecil, H.G. Wells and Max Beerbohm were present; a June night witnessing the birth of a calf at the small farm at the Brach belonging to Bill Jefferies the running huntsman, which became a chapter in A World of One's Own; *a visit to the cinema in Cheltenham with Bill Jefferies and Charlie Ladbrook to see a Chaplin film, probably 'Modern Times', released that year.*

In late September CW bought yet another horse, this one from a Mrs Ellison of Broadway, for £25.

September 20th   Am very pleased with my new horse [Muggins]. He is a big brown gelding, well bred, said to be by Hurry On[150], and to have belonged to the Duke of Gloucester[151] who sold him for £250 before he [the horse] made a noise. He is at least 12 years old but has the best legs of any old hunter that I have seen. I rode him to-day and like him very much to ride, though he is a bit rough. But he is a really good looking horse with a lovely neck and an intelligent head. Mrs Ellison is a well-off, yellow-faced, bad tempered old hag who lives in Broadway and deals for a hobby, and looks as much like a man as she can. I have heard of some good horses being bought from her and Alfred, her groom, is an honest sort of creature, and would not have let me buy a wrong 'un.

---

150   A famous, undefeated thoroughbred, 1913-36.
151   Prince Henry, Duke of Gloucester, 1900-1974. Third son of King George V.

The excitement of a fresh season is in my mind and I am looking forward to it with an eagerness I would not have thought possible in the summer. I am going to ride as boldly as I can make myself, and I feel really established in the hunt now, for this will be my 7th year. Why one loves hunting it is difficult do say, but once one does it is part of one for life; the joy of it made up of so many things that analysis is impossible, but it is England and English in every part, even in its contradictions.

On October 29th, CW noted that there were 25 hunters in stables in Campden for the season.

November 10th   About war in Europe now. I feel that wars are highly probable, and that they will be wars, because of man's power over matter, of a terrible and devastating nature. I do not think that man can yet prevent war, or that he will be able to do so for thousands of years. Before he does so humanity will be destroyed and reborn many times; men will suffer, be born, create small tranquillities, die, and go on again; what we know as society will be unrecognisably changed; there will be long dark periods of semi-barbarism; and in the end man may acquire control enough to balance his creative and destructive urges and so prevent wars. A gloomy picture, it may seem. But it only concerns me and other individuals as the state of the water it lives in concerns a tadpole in a pond. The tadpole's function is to survive, or rather to cause the race of tadpoles to survive – even in that he is a will-less creature. Such in my view is man too, but he knows it, though only dimly.

November 18th   I found Bill and Betty Huggins in the full excitement of a house party [at Berkswell Grange], and switched myself into the proper vein of silly hilarity, dressed for dinner in my pink coat, and dined. The dance was pleasant enough but mostly bright young or middle-aged things were there and no one very beautiful or very interesting, except an intelligent looking German who was a friend of Bill's and was staying there, a Count von Moene[152], about my own age. At about one I went and found him sitting by the day nursery fire alone, and we sat and talked European politics for an hour; Russia, Hitler, Freud, Spengler and so on. He spoke the most perfect English, though with

---

152   I have been unable to trace this gentleman, even allowing for alternative spellings such as Moehne or Möhne (CW did not know German.) He was apparently in the German secret service, (see entry for 17th September 1937) so perhaps it was a cover name? The Möhne is a river in West Germany feeding the reservoir that was breached in Operation Chastise (The Dambusters) in May 1943.

an accent. A little man with a good head, an expression of being sufficient to himself, and keen brown eyes. He seemed to think that unless there is some sort of United States of Europe formed against Russia in the next ten years there will be war for certain, which will result in the destruction of the Europe we know and the complete dominance of Russia over the whole continent. He was sure that Russia could not be destroyed or beaten. It is too huge. I agreed, for I have thought so for years. Russia has the strength of isolation that we had, from our 20-odd miles of water up to say 1918. She has it because of the thousands of miles of her territory and her widely scattered towns and her extraordinary wealth of resources of every kind needed for war.

November 20th By profit taking and reinvesting I have £5104 invested now, and an income from it of £251 a year, so my object is achieved which I set out for in 1925, in which year my income from my investments was £2.7s.6d. My new object now is to invest another £2000 to give me a total of £350 on which I really could live as I want to – if I don't alter my standards before I have it. It will take me about four years.

November 23rd To the Red Lion this evening and we started arguing about the weight of Bill Jefferies' boots, Charlie Ladbrook, Bridge, Tom Keyte and myself, so we sent for the kitchen scales and each put down 6d and a note of the weight and he took them off and we weighed them there and then, the winner to buy drinks all round. They weighed 7lbs and I lost my 6d but had a Bass that cost 7½d, which caused some amusement.

December 7th I am so sorry for the poor King [Edward VIII]. It is such an inexorable conflict. The year is coming to an end quietly for me. I feel I have accomplished more in it than in its predecessors and that next year I shall again. I feel I am really getting measurably near to achieving some at least of the things I have aimed at all my life. Frost has come and the ground is as hard as a brick and the air a few yards away from my fire as cold as that of a cavern.

December 10th I had to spend the night in Birmingham last night because of the fog, the first night I have spent there for years.

I have burnt all E's letters to me and mine to her, which she gave back to me. I want to get rid of the thought of her. She was a wrong turning in my life from which I managed to turn back in time. She wanted to come and see me the other day when Basil was in London, but I put her off.

December 28th A nice Christmas: Wednesday night a long discussion with Griggs about art and living and all the different natures that one carries within one, and how, when one is like I am and responds to one after another and often two at once, one is a dilletante and gets nowhere, though life may be very full. Griggs told me how he had been able to choose and so to canalise his energy, and we argued and talked till late; Thursday hunting and in the evening going from pub to pub and house to house and drinking all sorts of things till about 3, with Bill Jefferies, Lawrence Ladbrook, Arthur Margetts and various other people, all of us quite silly and half drunk and Christmassey in the pagan sense; Christmas Day at Wood Stanway till, in the evening, three young men staying there and I came up and went to the Red Lion for a couple of hours, and they left me there till 12; Boxing Day hunting again and dinner at Wood Stanway; Sunday at my Aunt Lucy's in Birmingham, the dullest and most alien day of all, and to the Oliver Bakers for supper; to-day from 11 till 4 beagling at Catbrook. Now Griggs is coming in and I am going to a dance later. To-morrow work for a short day and dinner at Wood Stanway, where I take the Griggses; Wednesday work; Thursday hunting and to dinner at Griggses. That is a bare account, but somehow I can't take the trouble to write it all, for there is so much. I will put it into an essay one day.

~ 1937 ~

As was his habit, CW began the year with a financial summary and he celebrated the New Year in robust and festive style.

January 1ˢᵗ My investments are now at £6265, including the £1150 shares in the works that I now have, at 20/- each. If one assumes a 7½% income from those the income is about £350, and I am determined that the works shall average that now. I have spent in 1936: Housekeeping £132. Car £46. Clothes £63. Pocket money £70. Various £90. Hunting £114. Books £10.

January 2ⁿᵈ Audrey [Robinson] came down from London by train and we had tea here, then I took her down to the Lygon at Broadway to get her room and change. I called for her at 8 and we came up here for dinner, and afterwards talked and sat in my room and were very happy together. There was no need to get to the dance until 10.30. Suddenly, though she was in evening dress and I was in pink coat and boiled shirt, we decided to go up to my bedroom and make love – which we did very successfully and with great joy. Then we dressed and set off for the dance and joined the Roberts' party. We danced nearly every dance until 4.30, had a very good supper and bacon and eggs twice and lots to drink – champagne, brandy and so on, and I left her there and got home at five. I got up at 9 and went down to fetch her later and took her to the train at Moreton at one. When I got home I lay down with the intention of resting for a bit – and slept from two until seven. Now I don't know whether it is day or night or which end of the year it is or what day of the week.

January 6ᵗʰ I went to see Eliot's *Murder in the Cathedral*[153]. The play is not a play. Every character in it is T.S. Eliot preaching his philosophy and his theology. It goes slowly and one has no interest in the action. No one is alive. All are plasterboard – and American-Mediaeval plasterboard too. But the play is saved by the technically very interesting blank verse, a new blank verse, compounded of Milton and [G.M.] Hopkins it seems, full of back pressure and short, recoiling syllables, and very well spoken all through by everyone. The verse interests me enough to make me decide to get the play and study it further.

---

153   At the Duchess Theatre, London, produced by E. Martin Browne; it was partly televised.

January 11th To-morrow I go to Lincoln and on to London and back on Thursday night. Life is very full of activity and business, but I feel strong and well. I think my health grows better every year now. I accept this work as it comes and have set out to make £5000 [profit] this year, for the tide has turned at last and I mean to make the best of it while it flows.

January 15th Lincoln Cathedral was lovely on its height above the sordid mess of houses and factories that obscure all views of the old town. To see an old print of Lincoln, say in 1800, and to see the town now fills me with sadness. Yet the thought struck me there that we are possibly the backward looking romantics whose love of beauty demands that a town should be 'unspoilt', while the people who lived in the town when it was unspoilt were looking ahead and desiring a world very like the one we have. Goldsmith certainly did this and there were many Goldsmiths in his day. And in the 17th century who but a few Sir Thomas Brownes[154] desired the past back or thought of the present as anything but progress? Which of them would not love and praise the beauty of the Cinema Palace or the comfort of the villa — and forget the ugliness?

January 18th In bed since Friday night with 'flu and a temperature which won't come down and an aching head and eyes. But I have been cheered this morning by a letter from Owen Rutter of the Golden Cockerel Press saying to my astonishment that he likes *Mr Chambers* and would like to publish it by itself. He read it 'with very great pleasure and delight' and likes it so much he would 'pass it over with regret'.

January 25th My first day's work [since the onset of 'flu] and I feel very tired and stuffed up after it and almost in despair at having to go back and take it all up again, having to talk to people as alien to me as I can imagine, to deal with them, to struggle in the maze of competitive business, and to live to standards I despise. It is all hard and grows harder, but if I have any sense (in one sense) I shall stick to it while the tide runs and then — if war or some cataclysm does not come — I shall be able to enjoy my freedom. How I shall enjoy it I only realise when I have had a week away, even ill.

February 5th A letter from Heaths [literary agency] saying that Country Life are still considering my essays and like them and may serialise them in

---

154   Author of *Hydropathia, or Urn Buriall*, 1658.

Country Life with illustrations and then do them in book form. The mere possibility of having two books published this year is almost too much for me. I glow with anticipation – then the thought of neither of them being published at all, for nothing is sure yet, damps my spirit. If only it happens it will make me happier than anything else could, and it will make me write too. I know that, for even the hope makes me ready to write and full of ideas. I go to the Roberts' dance to-night and hunt to-morrow. Am well again now.

February 14th Have finished off my two stories and sent them off. I have typed and typed till 12 at night, Thursday 3000 words, Friday 2000, Saturday 2500 and to-day 3000. I don't know what the Cockerel will think of them, but I think, as far as I can see at present, that they are fairly good and I have a strong hope of seeing them published with *Mr Chambers*. In ten days I have written over 10,000 words and typed them, not bad for work in one's spare time, mostly in the train and at night. God, how I hope these two books will get published. It will alter my whole life, I feel, and fulfil my ambitions, repressed for years.

I have been over to the Straffords [at Westington Mill] for tea and I met old Mr Tattersall[155] there, the last of the Tattersall family in the famous horse auction rooms in London[156], a charming old man, like a duke, in loose old man's clothes and a carnation in his buttonhole.

February 20th *Mr Chambers and Persephone accepted by the Golden Cockerel Press*. I don't know any more yet, date of publication or terms or anything, but I am very jubilant and told several people out hunting and felt anybody's equal. Went and told Griggs and he was very glad. Winifrid sent me a telegram. He must have phoned her. Now I only have to get my essays published for the turning point in my whole life to be made. The Cockerel don't think the other two stories will go with *Mr Chambers* well enough. I am rather glad. They will form a nucleus for another volume.

---

155   Edmund Somerville Tattersall, 1863-1942. A friend of Sir Edward Elgar.
156   Founded at Hyde Park Corner in 1766 (the same year as Christie's) by Richard Tattersall, a former groom to the Duke of Kingston, and still in business today, at Newmarket.

February 22nd [Charles] Nauman at Campden House[157] a very nice man with a little wiry frame and bright blue eyes and grey hair and the air of a Conrad character and a soul behind his wealth and his eight horses and three cars. I saw books like [Charles Morgan's] *The Fountain* and [Francis Yeats-Brown's] *Bengal Lancer* on his shelves.

February 27th Sleepy and tired after the Warwickshire Hunt Ball and a drenching out hunting to-day. At dinner last night Bill Huggins proposed my health and Betty put a crown of laurels on my head and it was all very laughable and flattering and embarrassing. I got home at 4.

March 2nd Have finished off my 3 essays and sent them off to be typed. Nothing from Country Life yet. I went to Wood Stanway last night with Griggs who <u>will</u> forget that the evenings are my chief time for working and who comes in when he is bored and stays till 12 or 1.

March 5th A letter from Heaths stating that C. Life want to see my last three essays and will then make a decision. It looks more hopeful, but I wait in anxiety. Anyway, hunting to-morrow and my Uncle Tom and Dorothy and Winifrid to dinner, then off to Ireland for a week, away from everything but myself. I have got nervy and want a holiday, which it will be, though I am going on business. I hope to get some hunting and shall take my things. I shall have to take a holiday this year, I think. I have not the resilience I used to have.

March 10th [In Belfast]. On the way up from Dublin here I fell in love with the country and have a new story in my head as a result. One day I shall come to live in the south of Ireland. It is what one seeks everywhere; a land out of the insane track of European nerves and fidgety efficiency; a country that lives on its farms and its land; a country with a soul. It worships no typewriter, nor any Austin 7, nor chromium plate, nor steel, nor money, but the spirit of man alone with nature. I felt all the emotions of falling in love as I watched it from the carriage window. The North though is more like England or Scotland; the germ of greed has entered its blood, though it is a paradise of simplicity compared with much of England now. To love England, the countryside of it, one has to re-create it in one's heart, eliminating and

---

157   At Coombe. 1¾ m SW of the town, built for Sir Baptist Hicks in 1628. Comprehensively and successfully remodelled by Norman Jewson, 1934.

rebuilding; but Ireland is herself and recreates one's own heart as one loves her as she is.

March 11th Down to Dublin last night. This morning snow and sleet and slush all day and my hopes of a hunt gone. Have been all day with our new Dublin agent, a charming man called Lanigan-O'Keefe who looks like a cavalry subaltern and hunts and fishes as much as he works, but he works as well, and is fairly cultured too, and extraordinarily hospitable. His uncle is High Commissioner for Southern Rhodesia and his mother was one if the initiators of the Irish Sweepstakes. He took me round several hospitals, all wonderfully equipped, with sweepstake money, but now very much hedged in by red tape. All the doctors were charming and all seemed to have unlimited time to sit and smoke, and the conversation is about anything but business – hunting, fishing, politics, books. Later O'Keefe took me to see the mixing of the Sweep tickets at the Mansion House, in a great hall, full of elaborate machines into which the tickets are fed by pretty girls in gay uniforms. There are 5000 girls employed in all, in the offices and for work generally. The tinsel and ceremony were rather spoilt by the drenching weather. These Irish are the most hospitable people I have ever met and they work to live and do not fret themselves into a fever for the sake of money. I like them.

March 14th All night travelling, breakfast in Birmingham, and home through a snowstorm, to find Campden in 6in of snow. I am very tired.

A letter from the Cockerel giving terms for *Mr Chambers*. They propose to do a limited edition at 24/- and pay me 5% on it, and an ordinary edition at 8/6 and pay me 10% on that on the first 1000 and 15% on more. I shall accept. There are to be several wood engravings by Dorothea Braby[158]. Nothing from C. Life yet.

March 16th I have just realised that if the Cockerel sell 1000 copies of Mr Chambers I shall get £50. It seems incredible and far more so than backing the winner in say the Grand National. I can't believe it at all. I have never thought of money coming from what I write, and it seems absurd and laughable and improbable. I have only thought of getting published.

---

158   1909-1987. CW later regretted the choice.

April 1ˢᵗ A contract at the works for £11,000 worth of beds with which and normal luck we should make £7000 this year, so that I shall have about £900 to invest. Early next year I should have £300 a year of my own. But I think I should be foolish not to go on for another two years and make it £400. With that I should be free altogether and should use my income from any directorship I might keep on for the purchase of real luxuries. I see release in measurable distance and I think I can wait till it is complete now.

April 5ᵗʰ Very busy at the works and confident that this wave of prosperity will lift me finally out now, always provided that war or catastrophe does not come and forbid it in the end.

April 27ᵗʰ

Visitor:	(to Charlie Ladbrook) 'Can you tell me where the urinal is my man?'
Ladbrook:	(a new urinal is now being built [in Sheep Street] 'Yessir. Just around the corner sir. But you'll have to wait a bit.'
Visitor:	'How's that?'
Ladbrook:	'T'aint quite finished yet sir. They be putting the roof on this week.'

May 12ᵗʰ The local Coronation Procession has just wound drearily past, all dressed up for fine sunny weather, and the sky is grey and the day cold. I think I must be the only person in Campden who did not listen in to the service this morning.

May 15ᵗʰ In Cheltenham this morning I met a Miss Severn. Introduced to her, I could think of nothing to say but, 'The only Severn I know is the Severn who went out to Rome with Keats.' 'That was my great-grandfather,' she said. It fascinates me to think that in shaking hands with her I was only three handshakes from Keats himself.

May 24ᵗʰ [During Scuttlebrook Wake] on Saturday night Agnes and Biddy Slattery, Higford Griffiths, Audrey Chandler, the Griggses, Bill and Garnett Keyte, Charlie Ladbrook and Bogie Haydon, Wally Stanley and Bill Jefferies, Jack Bridges, the Policeman and a lot of others came in for drinks. I went to bed rather drunk at one and could not sleep for the noise of the packing up outside.

In the morning, not feeling at all well or clear headed, I set off to lunch with Owen Rutter[159] [at Wargrave, Berkshire]. A nice man with a nice house and rather negative wife and a loved daughter. He has spent a lot of his life in Borneo as a district magistrate and now lives retired and writes and has his partnership in the Cockerel. Had long and interesting talks with him and looked through the whole of his collection of Cockerel books, saw some of the woodcuts for *Mr Chambers* but do not like them very much.

May 26th   Yesterday to London and first to Heaths [literary agency] in Piccadilly and arranged for them to go through my letters to the Cockerel Press and draw up an agreement if they think it necessary. Then I went to see Carrington[160] of Country Life, taking the drawings Henry Payne[161] had sent me (very poor) and he told me that he liked my essays and was definitely going to publish them, but that he did not want the book to fail through having the wrong artist. He has approached Clare Leighton and Agnes Miller-Parker but they are both booked up. The young artist Geoffrey Miller whom he has found has done a good specimen and if he can do the figure drawing he will probably get the job. Later I went and met Christopher Sandford[162] of the Golden Cockerel Press at Romano's, for lunch. He is a nice Irish person about my own age, wide browed, with rather a receding head. He seems to like my work. He wants another long-short later if *Mr Chambers* goes well.

He is also in the Chiswick Press, which bought the Alcuin Press from young Finberg in Campden, and told me that for the first seven months Finberg lost £700 for them and that they then discharged him and put in a working manager who wiped off the loss and made £500 in addition in the next five months. He says, which is true, that though Finberg is a lazy and useless creature, he is one of the few printers who have really good taste.

June 5th   Aunts to lunch. Rather a blank week-end. Last night out with Griggs to the Lygon at Broadway and then to the pictures at Evesham, then back to Dover's House to drink and talk till one.

---

159   1889-1944. He had recently become a partner in the Golden Cockerel Press.
160   Probably Noel Carrington, 1895-1989, book designer.
161   Henry Arthur Payne, R.W.S., 1868-1940.
162   1902-1983. A partner in the Golden Cockerel since 1933, he later founded the Folio Society. Lived at Eye Manor, Herefordshire, a Carolean house near Leominster noted for its fine plaster-work. He became my sister's godfather.

CW spent much of June writing and correcting a collection of short stories which would eventually appear under the title Miss Piper's Trouble, *published by John Lane The Bodley Head in 1940. Meanwhile, arrangements for the publication of* A World of One's Own *had at last been finalised, and Geoffrey Miller appointed to illustrate the essays.*

July 29th   Miller came on Tuesday night and I spent all yesterday with him with enjoyment. He is a sort of cockney Charlie Blakeman, 32, a serious craftsman, without very much feeling but pleasant ideas about the sort of subjects I like, bearded, with rather narrow, widely spaced brown eyes and a good head, rather like D.H. Lawrence as a young man. We have settled and discussed the illustrations for the essays and he has now to see Carrington and to settle with him how many to do and the terms. I took Miller to Great Alne station and the Aqueduct at Bearley and the station there to make studies, also to several other scenes, and afterwards to Shakespeare's birthplace and tea at Stratford, and I think he enjoyed himself. His mother has a sweet shop in Reigate and he married a fellow student with small means of her own.

On July 30th CW went on holiday to France, flying from Croydon in an 8-seater aeroplane to Paris. Here, he stayed at the Hotel d'Alsace where Oscar Wilde had died, visited the Exposition Internationale, Versailles *and* Chartres, *as well as several night clubs. He witnessed a miracle play,* Le Vray Mystère de la Passion *performed on the parvis of Notre Dame by 500 actors to an audience of 10,000, according to CW's enthusiastic diary entry. He was back in Campden on August 3rd.*

August 4th   Now I am back in Campden. It took me only six hours yesterday to come from Paris here and the transition was a shock. This morning, no sooner had I got up than Roberts came to see me to talk over business, and when he had gone Griggs and Russell Alexander came in for a drink, so I have hardly had time to collect myself yet.

Relations with Winifrid were at a low point during much of August. She had taken up with what would now be described as a 'walker', a man called Vereker, described by CW as 'a sickening little white-faced nancy-boy'. Furthermore, after fourteen years of apparent tolerance, Stanley Wood had turned against the relationship. In the immediate aftermath writing, cub-hunting and a severe cold occupy CW's time, but this seems to have been a distinct turning-point in his emotional life.

September 17th When I was at the works to-day Bill Huggins rang me up and asked me to lunch. He had Count Moene with him whom I have met before, and Betty. Later they called for me and brought me home and had tea and looked round Campden and had a look at Muggins. Moene gave me an invitation to go to Germany to stay with him. He is a very charming man and speaks perfect English, is said to be a crack air pilot and show jumper and is in the secret service, so Betty says. He has a brain. [Huggins] says Germany is awful now, on war rations. You can't get an egg for breakfast and the place is lousy with soldiers. He has just been there to stay and was all over the country and as far East as the Polish Corridor, motoring and shooting and playing tennis and everyone was marvellously hospitable to him. Yesterday out cub hunting Elizabeth Devas told me of Leningrad, where she has been; pavements full of weeds; great ornate houses falling to ruin; people dressed like tramps; food short and everyone looking very pinched and miserable. So one learns about this odd world.

September 19th Went for an hour's walk this afternoon and met the Cardews and had tea with them at the Blakemans. They are typical of the petty craftsman-artist. They can see no idea but with their own odd bias and have no power to lift themselves above their own little environment. Their small inferiority complexes make them insist on their little theories and be deliberately odd, and they achieve nothing but the second-rate.

October 20th I came down [from London] with Charles Nauman [of Campden House]. He is an interesting man. He has been ill lately and for years he has been seasick out hunting, and has had pains round his heart. They have never been able to find the cause and now they think there is no physical cause, but are psycho-analysing him, Dr Crichton-Miller[163], and already the pains have begun to go.

November 11th Went hunting. The Armistice Silence was impressive as it can be in a small village [Long Marston] at a meet. One could not help feeling that it was the type of man hunting stands for who made the sinews of England's resistance during the war, as one watched the group of 100 or so there on their horses. The only break in the silence was Muggins staling. Slowly, as the first minute passed he stretched forward and then let forth a cascade on the road – to everyone's amusement after.

---

163   Hugh Crichton-Miller, 1877-1959, founder of the Tavistock Clinic in London.

December 1st Aunt Lilian [Langbourne][164] keeps her copy of *Mr Chambers* in a drawer because the woodcut on the cover shocks her and she is afraid it may shock her friends or visitors.

December 3rd I danced last night at Ragley[165] with the Huggins party and got home at four. The house is a gem of 18th century architecture and the rooms are still furnished with things that must have been bought when it was built. The ballroom is a dream of form and grace, and the whole place a warning to this pettifogging age and yet its parent. Anthony Eden was there and his wife, and my respect for him has gone up considerably: he went up to his room about twelve to go to bed as he was very tired, and he found a couple on his bed, who leapt off, embarrassed. He said: 'I am so sorry to upset you, but I am very tired and must go to bed — but my wife's room is next door, through there, and she won't be up till the ball is over.'

In the autumn of 1937, CW fell in love with Winifrid's daughter Griselda (Grizel), 24 years old and working for the Oxford University Press. Both were serious about the relationship and it was not long before marriage was being discussed, despite Grizel's understandable hesitation when she learned that CW had been her mother's lover for many years; it seems remarkable that she had not realised that this was the case. In a display of what CW saw as her 'greatness' but perhaps in a certain sense relief, Winifrid had given her blessing to the relationship.

As Christmas approaches, CW records:

December 22nd I look back on my great love for Winifrid and see all those years as a country in which, like some knight of old, I have been under an enchantment, the enchantment of my illusions and complexes. Beautiful as that enchantment was and indescribable as was the beauty we created out of it, it is as the years of immaturity compared to the years I now foresee. I feel years younger, and all my impulses find strength for their carrying out. I am alive, which I have been only at rare intervals before, rare and beautiful intervals. I am childishly happy in giving all I can to her, and in taking her ingenuous sweetness and her mature sophistication in return. I hunt to-morrow and meet her at Oxford and bring her home.

---

164   Widow of a P&O Captain, who lived at Malvern.
165   Seat of the Marquess of Hertford, near Alcester, Warwickshire.

December 29th   Christmas at Wood Stanway, with Winifrid and Stanley in the background and Grizel in the forefront of my mind. So life moves, strange and deep and unpredictable. When I think of marriage I am sometimes aghast, or incredulous. Money is in the background of my uneasiness, but it is a faint uneasiness only. On Sunday I took Grizel to lunch at Malvern with three of my Whitfield aunts and they all liked her. If we do marry we both want the greatest privacy and simplicity. My contemplated leisure and retirement I see now would have been dead things, and that is one of the most important discoveries I have made this year. One must not make stagnation, poise, or peace a goal, but must find them by chance, and use them as stepping stones to further activity, not as shelters from life. One must, to be alive, either face the pressure of it and survive it, or face it and go under. Anything else is death. I realise that if we do marry I shall be tying myself to the works for years, but I do it with my eyes open and no more fear in my heart than the first fence of a hunting day.

So 1937 comes to an end, one of my fullest years. The works has recovered; I have had nearly £2000 gross income in all for the first time; my first book has been published; I have another coming out next year; I have two others written; I have a lot of new clothes; a total of £6200 saved; and the promise of more books to come and another good year at the works. My love for Winifrid, after being wounded till it could not live on, has given place to my love for Grizel; and the alarming and horrifying burdens of marriage have been faced and accepted in prospect. Now I wait the decision that I feel sure will come from Grizel very soon, and wait it with the greatest peace and confidence. I feel on top of life, though it is hard and full of demands. So I will remain.

Woodcut illustration by Dorothea Braby
for 'Mr Chambers and Persephone', 1937

~ 1938 ~

January 1ˢᵗ   My investments are now £7312 including my shares in the works at 20/-. Assuming 7½% from the works, the income is £385. I have spent during 1937: House £140, Car £53, Clothes £25, Self £83, Various £86, Hunting £100. I look forward to saving about £1000 this year with luck. This year contains, maybe, a new life, a multitude of adjustments, and an impalpable future. I am happy about it beneath my doubts, but I have doubts, mostly born of winter fatigue and the opposition of an established present life to an imagined future one.

January 4ᵗʰ   A cheque for £10 from the Cockerel, my first royalty, and a nice letter from Rutter, and also the pleasure in seeing my name in the acknowledgements in Oliver Baker's new book on Shakespeare's Warwickshire[166]. I am well into my story about Joe Martin's Revenge and shall do Mabel's Christmas to-morrow, which will finish the reconstructing of *Miss Piper's Trouble*[167], as I now call the book.

The love affair with Grizel started to fade during the winter months as the prospect of marriage began to focus her thoughts on the lack of independence it would entail, just when CW had gradually reconciled himself to giving up his. By mid-February CW was writing:

Grizel seems to have gone back into her own self contained life quite finally. And the odd and merciful thing is that I have too in a way. Is ours a case of two introverts saying to themselves: 'Now I have offered and tried to marry, and now I am free to live by myself?' I find a great sense of peace in the prospect of being able to think only of my own life again. It is a fine sunny day and I have taken a day off to be at home, simply that, and I am savouring the delight of it; the feel of the sun on a silver jug; the sense that I need not worry about money; the feeling that I am to all intents and purposes free from the works; the feeling that I have in finding my own self contained in myself, there for myself alone.

April 11ᵗʰ   Fred Griggs came in for an hour and seems ill. It was terribly sad to see him. He seems to have gone to pieces suddenly, partly through drink,

---

166   *In Shakespeare's Warwickshire and the Unknown Years*, Simpkin Marshall, 1937.
167   The title story was based on Miss Chinn, the Griggs' governess, who was a member of the Plymouth Brethren, a conservative evangelical Christian group, emerging in the early 19ᵗʰ century.

---

partly through financial worry, the result of his extravagance. Now he fears he is losing his sight. It is awful.

CW was about to leave for Paris again when he wrote:

May 20th Poor Fred Griggs has been very ill in London, a stroke or something, though I find Nina very reticent about what it is. He is very ill and may not live, I gather, and hardly knows anyone.

On May 21st, CW was in Paris for a second time and after a day there took a train to Auxerre in the Yonne, where he bought a bicycle and set off to Avallon, Saulieu, Moulins and Vichy. He took a train to Le Puy, and spent a further week in the South, visiting Avignon, Arles, Nimes, Aigues Mortes and Montpelier. On returning to Nimes to watch a bull-fight, he sold the bicycle for half the price he had paid for it. While he was in France, CW records his intimations of war:

May 26th It is amazing how, every time one looks at a paper, it is full of references to England; the firmness of England over Czechoslovakia; Germany and the attitude of England; what England will do; what England ought to do. It seems that we have for the time being averted the threat of war, but I don't like the thought of the future at all. I can't see how war can be avoided indefinitely. At the cinema the news film: Hitler in Rome; the King and Queen; the Italian and French armies; the British Fleet; all war.

He was back in Paris on 7th June and received news from Dorothy Chatwin that Fred Griggs was not expected to live long; the next day CW saw the obituary notice in The Times.

June 8th Now I go back to a Campden without Fred.

June 11th I came back yesterday, flying over by Imperial Airways and having lunch on the plane, then down through a green and lovely England in the car to Campden. Eight hours from Paris home. Here I am in my little house, not yet aware of myself, not yet really here, and I feel almost as though I were in someone else's house that I know well, it is so familiar and yet so strange.

Nothing seems to have happened here during the weeks I have been away, except Fred's death. But that, that he will no longer come in to see me, no longer be there to go and talk to at any hour of the day or night, drunk or sober, is appalling and I can hardly believe it yet. I shall have to go and see Nina soon.

June 12th Scuttlebrook Wake last night was a dismal affair for me, haunted by the memory of Fred. It is extraordinary how he is brought to mind by everything I do or think. Though I have often avoided discussing certain things with him, and though we have often disagreed about things important to us both, he has been for years a sort of standard to set my thoughts to, justifying them, not by whether he would agree with them, but by how they looked to me when set beside my conception of him and his standards. And he has been the only man, except Hudson perhaps, with whom I have ever reached any real degree of intimacy.

Evening. Have been down to Wood Stanway and have seen Nina. She is wonderfully calm and poised so far, but she has not yet fully realised her loss. There is no will and only an absolutely insolvent estate. I may have to help. It seems to have been a long drawn out series of hopes and despairs during the last few weeks. Apparently the collapse Fred had in London about six weeks ago was a stroke. Then some doctor said he must have his teeth out, and they took them out in a nursing home. Then he was allowed to go out and there was an awful dinner at the Café Royal when his mind seems to have gone completely, from what one gathers. Then he was brought home and put to bed and he had a cerebral haemorrhage and another stroke and died, apparently of a clot of blood on the brain. That is all I can find out.

June 19th As I sit in my little back room writing this, the garden hot with summer outside the window, the swifts and swallows circling above, the bees buzzing, and the scent of some pinks I have put in a jar filling the room, and as I look around the little room that I have made, I am pleased and happy and feel once more that I <u>must</u> get away from the works soon.

June 21st I can't accept the works any more and feel tempted to leave now, but I know I shan't. I shall wait till next year and I know I shall have to make an effort to do it then. I intend to give in my notice about December 1939, then I could leave in June and go abroad for a few months at once. Much depends on my success or otherwise in writing.

June 23rd A pleasant day at home pottering about, putting up valances to my dining room curtains, altering rugs, making a garden table and reading in my little writing room. The freedom of living alone is such a delight that I should now find it hard to live with anyone. To do what you want when you want, to have a sandwich at two o'clock and to read until four, then for no reason but that one feels sleepy, to go to sleep till six. It is all a delight, and doing it, one's affection for so many small things, and scents and sounds is like a delicious silent chamber music.

June 26th Yesterday I went rabbiting on Dover's Hill and I couldn't shoot at all. I had 15 shots at rabbits, easy shots, with my .22 rifle, and only got three, but I had a pleasant walk. Later the [Geoffrey] Millers arrived [for the weekend]. She is charming, a lady, tall, with a soft mouth, brown dyes, dark hair, and a curiously gentle eastern manner – she came from the Far East and one can't help thinking there is Oriental blood somewhere. He is irritating and pinkish red in politics as so many weaklings are, and bone lazy. He's taken about five times as long to do my woodcuts [for *A World of One's Own*] as I took to write the essays.

Two manuscripts had been turned down; one a book of 'Characters', the other a short novel called 'Sherbury'.

July 2nd It is very depressing for I have reached a stage when, if I don't get another book accepted, I shall find it hard to go on. A terrible amount hangs on that. If I fail I shall be nothing in my own eyes, for to be recognised as a writer means everything to me. I have no love now and I am alone. I have sacrificed a social life to a previous love, and there is only writing left to me as a serious occupation. If that fails I shall drift into marriage. I am having my last Thursday at home till September, for staff holidays begin now. We seem to be doing well at the works and I should be able to save at least £700 this year, but only that, the money, gives me any satisfaction in that. To be successful in business, apart from the fact that it gives me money, is nothing, is almost a wrong thing to my mind, for myself at least.

July 3rd Dinner at the Carrol-Perkins, the American couple who take the house next door in the summer, with the Cresswells and a mad American widow of a dramatic critic, who made me coin the phrase, 'Yes, but you see

Shakespeare is <u>not</u> quaint.' That should be shouted in every Shakespeare lover's ear from youth to age. I have the page proofs of *A World of One's Own* and it looks rather a nice book. I think it ought to sell, especially for Christmas. Am going to tennis at the Lorraine-Smiths this afternoon, girls who always attract me when I see them, but when I go there I find myself saying to myself, 'Que fais-tu dans cet galère?' for we have nothing but local gossip in common, and hunting and horses. However they are nice, amusing people and they have a pleasantly vague sense of life and little idea of time, and there is a stagey atmosphere about the whole house that attracts me.

July 4th Roberts went to a wedding on Saturday and saw among the presents a copy of *Mr Chambers and Persephone*, given by people he did not know.

July 6th I find myself depressed and aimless and have been so ever since I came back from France. For one thing I am only going on at the works as a sort of formal kind of continuation of something that is over and done with. Before, between hate of it and need for money, and out of the general conflict of my feelings about it I gave myself the illusion of being keenly concerned in its efficiency. But now that is at last achieved, now I have pulled the place out of its slump, now it has made good profits again under my control, it is as dead as a finished book for me, and any writer will know how dead that is. But I've got to go on for another year or two because I still need more capital than I have so far saved.

As for writing, till I know whether 'Sherbury' will be published, again I can't start anything else. I may of course be making the discovery, which I made about poetry ten years ago, that I have worked myself out in the little I have done. I should not be surprised. If I can't write what will get published I shall, in the end, stop writing even prose. I don't like the thought but it may be true. I begin to wonder whether I have any really deep urge to write, one that will last. I think that if I write another novel and one or two books of stories I should be finished. In the meantime I can't rouse any enthusiasm in myself for the work yet. I feel lost and make no effort to find myself. It is like having walked out into the middle of a great marshy lake.

July 11th Last night on the way back from the station at Moreton I called in at Temple's at Upton Wold [near Blockley] and spent the evening with him very pleasantly. He is only 23, farms 350 acres, lives alone in that big house with two awful Harrods imitation oak carved armchairs, a huge wireless, two wolfhounds, two hound puppies, a Sealyham, three sheepdog puppies and their mother, and a housekeeper.

Roberts told me that after he had seen the copy of *Mr Chambers* at the wedding *(see July 4ᵗʰ)* he overheard this: Bride. 'Oh, how nice of you to give me Christopher Whitfield's book. I happen to know him a little.' Guest. 'Oh, how interesting. He's an ironmonger isn't he?'

July 17ᵗʰ [After a dance given by the Huggins' at Berkswell Grange.] The dance was for some German friends of Bill's, Count and Countess Praschma[168] and her sister, who reminded me of Charles Morgan's heroine in *The Fountain*. The two sisters are great-grand-daughters of Prince Metternich and know Keyserling.

July 22ⁿᵈ On Wednesday Betty [Huggins] and the Germans came down for tea. Sophy Praschma's sister, a charming young creature who made me think of Cleopatra, is Princess Ratibor[169]. She is the unmarried one. We had a very pleasant tea party and I packed up some things and went back with them for dinner and a farewell dance. We spent a riotous evening after a lovely dinner which ended with peaches and champagne, the peaches, pricked all over, revolving slowly as the bubbles got stuck on the roughness of the skin underneath, then eaten on a plate with sugar and *Kirchwasser*. We danced and fooled until two.

The most amazing thing to me was Katie Ratibor's attitude to Hitler. She is a girl of brilliant intellectual ability. She learnt Russian so that she could read the great Russian writers in the original, and speaks five other languages. Her English is perfect. We talked of all sorts of subjects and Hitler came in by way of Vienna. At the mere mention of his name her eyes changed and face became that of a woman who has lost her critical power through love. 'What Hitler tells us to do we know is right' she said. 'Hitler is the mother and father of the German race.' The Catholic Church? 'I am a Catholic, but the Church, though magnificent, is old-fashioned and out of date, but <u>Hitler</u> will reorganise it so

168   Princess Sophie of Ratibor and Corvey, 1912-1981, had married Count Friedrich Leopold Praschma (1900-2000) in 1937.
169   Princess Marie Agathe of Ratibor and Corvey, known as Katie, 1911-1971.

that it will be alive again.' She went on, while, spellbound by the credulity of so intelligent a woman, I listened and made no remarks. She was like a woman in love. One could say nothing.

July 29ᵗʰ On Sunday at Wood Stanway the idea for a new book came to me; the crystallisation of a solution of ideas that has been in my head for some time: 'The Island' (*a long-running project*) and Percy Lubbock's[170] *Earlham*, and an 18ᵗʰ century house and a lake and C.H. Smith in it, and decay of beauty, and love... I don't yet know what sort of a book, but there is one coming.

This idea, known during its writing as 'Cora Rhys', was eventually published as Lady From Yesterday *by the Golden Cockerel Press, with wood engravings by Lettice Sandford, Christopher Sandford's wife.*

August 4ᵗʰ Nina [Griggs] and Russell Alexander are coming to dinner. He is staying with her. I went in last night and we played croquet and the [George] Harts were there too, but the sadness of the place without Fred was awful. I could not forget it, could not get the idea out of my head that he would come round the corner of the house at any moment and say Hello. The place is haunted by him and by one's memories of him. I can't think how Nina can stay there.

August 14ᵗʰ I went to see the Oliver Bakers this afternoon at Bearley. I have never seen anyone so frail and old and transparent and yet still living as he is now. He is a man who meant much to me when I was young, with his quiet antiquarianism and his Quixotic gentle ways. I went into the garden of our old cottage at Bearley too, for the place was empty, and walked about a bit. It was strange to be there after 14 years. It is all overgrown and neglected, and has been spoilt for me because the orchard has been taken into the garden. In the loft over the garage is still the painted background of trees and fields that I did on the wall for a setting to my model railway.

September 6ᵗʰ This week seems to be a momentous one for us in Europe. If no war comes, and I do not think it will now, there may be peace for a long time. The powers of aggression have brought into being by their activity forces

---

170   Percy Lubbock, 1879-1965, man of letters and step-father of Iris Origo. His book *Earlham* was based on memories of childhood holidays at Earlham Hall in Norfolk; it won the James Tait Black Memorial Prize in 1922

which will stop them. The change of opinion in America is one of the strongest factors. So it is always; a strong positive force creates the force for its own opposition.

September 8th Have finished 'Cora' to-night, 64 pages. I think it is all right. I shall read it through to-morrow. A walk round the allotments after partridges but there were very few and they were very wild. I only shot one and it fell in some sprouts and I could not pick it up.

September 12th Hitler is making his speech at Nuremberg but I have decided not to bother to go out and listen to it on someone's wireless but to read it in the paper in the morning. Have been working on 'Cora', touching it up. My old 'poisoned' feeling has come back rather badly. If it goes on I shall have to see a doctor about it – if there is no war. If there is, then nothing like that matters, nothing that concerns individual life. Then the only thing will be to give oneself up to the preservation of freedom and culture and to the destruction of tyranny. One must give up one's life in principle, that is unquestionable, give up all claim to it oneself, then the rest will not be hard.

September 14th   War seems to be nearer. It is awful and impossible to believe. At Winchcombe Show a rumour went round that France had declared war on Germany and that Germany had invaded Czechoslovakia. I went to Wood Stanway to listen to the news. No mention of that, though the news is grave enough. Then at 9.45 the news came that Neville Chamberlain is flying to see Hitler tomorrow. There is some chance of saving the situation yet. If it comes I have, in theory at least, given up my personal life and can quite freely undertake whatever my duty may be.

September 15th This visit of Neville Chamberlain's to Hitler[171] seems to have cast a temporary quiet over everything, and once again one can think of tomorrow, though not yet of next week or the week after.

September 18th The shadow of war hangs over all one's thoughts. If it comes and they want me I shall join the R.A.S.C. [Royal Army Service Corps] rather than a fighting regiment. Somehow, though I can face being destroyed

---

171   The Prime Minister's first face-to-face meeting with Hitler, not that from which he returned waving the 'Piece of paper', on 29th September.

I can't stomach being directly concerned in the killing of others. But I think they will make a compromise this time and avoid war, though it may only mean a greater [war] later on. Germany <u>may</u> grow to be the dominant power in Europe without war, and that may be best, if we can take second place and remain a free core of culture.

September 23rd The news sounds very bad indeed. I fear there will be war and can hardly face the thought. I don't see how we can evade war now. It is terrible.

September 24th All the time the shadow of war over us all; war visiting England, which has been untouched for a thousand years; destruction, barbarism – in order to shut up a horde of maniacs once more. Why can't people live at peace at last?

September 25th Yesterday after cub hunting I went shooting, all with a feeling that it might well be for the last time. But today the news seems a little better. A week to wait for the Czechs to accept what seem to be reasonable proposals, things having got to this pass.

September 26th Still the shadow over every thought. I find myself quietly preparing, as if for death. I am making a will, going through my MSS, paying my bills, etc. I find I can face war quite quietly, realising to the full through my imagination that it would be the end of life as I have known it.

September 27th War seems inevitable. I have made my will and shall take it to the bank on Saturday. I shall join up if wanted and not wanted more than in Birmingham. Have finished off my copy of 'Cora' and shall finish my book of letters received [from writers, critics, etc.] by Saturday. I went to the Red Lion and for half an hour we forgot there was a blank at the end of this week. That is it: a blank, a void, the unknown, this life already renounced. It is a strange experience to go through. I can read only the newspapers and Shakespeare. *Antony and Cleopatra* again to-day, as full of marvels as a new play to one's eyes. I am quite happy, though afraid of the unknown.

October 1st Cub hunting at Springhill. An unreal feeling about the sun and hounds and the whole scene after the nightmare of the last few weeks.

October 2nd [In London] Now it is over one can breathe. I feel as though I have been hit on the head and have not yet recovered. A stunned feeling. Nothing seems quite real that is ordinary, for one had faced something so appalling. The woodcuts [in *A World of One's Own*] are worse than I had feared. I could cry about them, for they quite spoil a book that I have worked so hard to make it decent. They are slipshod and they are bad and make me long to hit the wretched Miller. They will inevitably be associated with the book in people's minds.

Last night, dinner with Roberts at Boulestin's was very good. While we were there Harold Nicolson[172] came in to dine and word went round that all was well. Later at a night-club a man came in with the early edition of a morning paper, and there we read that it was so. There was an almost audible sigh of relief, then people went on dancing. One can breathe again and think of leisure and all the things of leisure and dream of the peace that may reach into the future if only sanity and good fortune come back to men.

To-day I have been to a cocktail party at the Whitworths[173] here, in Church Street, a very nice couple. She hunts and is charming, and he is in the BBC.

October 3rd A nice letter from Sandford about 'Cora'. I hope to get it published by the Cockerel next year. Nina came in to-night. She seems very lonely and lost and I don't know what she can do. She ought to marry again to be happy, but who would marry her, with no money and six children, poor dear?

October 6th Cub hunting at Coombes [Campden House] after a late night. A perfect October morning, a sort of living symbol of the peace that has returned to us since those awful days. A gentle wind, a clear sky, and views out over the Warwickshire Vale that were just sufficiently hazy to quicken one's imagination. Life is open and free again and one can look out on it as an open scene into which one will ride, living in the movement of one's horse as it clears the fences and strides over the ridge and furrow, the plough and the big grass fields, which give one time to think how to get out of them best. It is good. If only I could get away from the works and live more of it. But the prospect of new taxes seems to make that more remote.

172   Sir Harold George Nicolson, K.C.V.O., C.M.G., diplomat, politician and writer.
173   Robin Aymer Whitworth, 1911-1996, married Cecily Blunt in 1934. A distinguished BBC producer, later my godfather.

I hear that there was not a bid for Griggs' house [New Dover's House] at the auction on Tuesday. Poor Nina. I suppose she will stop there for the winter now. She came in the other night and was very sad and like a child that has lost its father. I kissed her and consoled her and tried to make her feel that I understood. 'You are very good. You understand so much. You are quite necessary to me, Chris dear,' she said. And she went back and wrote me the sweetest letter. It is good to feel one is of some use.

If with France ten years ago we had once again suppressed Teutonic growth we should not have had this crisis. But as it is I feel that Neville Chamberlain (who is some sort of cousin by marriage) has shown English realism and opportunism and idealism to the full. We have saved our skins without losing our souls.

October 23rd Bob Parker-Jervis and his wife from Paxford asked me to dinner. They had some people staying with them, and were short of a man. We had a most riotous evening. We were to go on after dinner to a dance at the Beechams [at Compton Scorpion Manor] near Shipston, the married son [Adrian] of Sir Thomas [the conductor], but the women would not go, so we three men went, not at all sober after a cocktail party and our dinner, and found a rather small dull party going on. Old [Utica] Lady Beecham and the unmarried brother [Tommy] were there, and a few other people. Charades were in progress and we, full of our dinner and wine, woke the party up and the charades became alive. There was supper and champagne and a lot of talk and laughter and nonsense and in among it some sense. Mrs Beecham sang very charmingly. They asked me to dinner on Thursday. [Adrian] Beecham paints well. I've wanted to know them for some time. Everyone mocks at them and laughs at them, but they are nice, for they have brains and are creative. They ride in the most amazing fashion, all wrong, and dress all wrong too, and yet go quite well.

October 27th The party at Nina's [before a sale of Griggs's furniture and her being reduced to living in a few rooms only] was Margaret Smith, Winifrid and Stanley Wood, Norman Jewson, my old rival, and myself, and there was such a sadness about that one had to drink quite a lot to forget that Fred was not there. We all sang round the piano; 'The Farmer's Boy', etc, as we used to do in his lifetime, and it was both cheerful and depressing. Poor Nina, she has such courage and such a hard life before her.

The Golden Cockerel Press had agreed to publish 'Cora' and CW was spending the week-end with Christopher and Lettice Sandford at Eye Manor, near Leominster, Herefordshire.

November 1ˢᵗ Eye is a lovely house, a Charles II building with a Georgian porch, it stands with the little sandstone church in its garden, and the front lawn slopes down to a ho-ho wall and the fields. The garden is big and could be very fine but Christopher can't afford to do much to it. The loveliest feature of the whole house, apart from its fine broad staircase and its panelled walls, is the magnificent [plaster] relief work. In every room, both on the ground floor and on the first floor there are plaster ceilings wrought into the most amazing wreaths of flowers, fruit, Cupids chasing their quarry with a pack of hounds, and so forth, and there is hardly a blemish in one of them. The atmosphere of the house too is friendly, like the Sandfords themselves, and the children are charming. I have never seen a nearer equivalent to an eighteenth century 'happy family' in modern costume. I have seldom enjoyed a week-end more.

Hunting had begun again on November 1ˢᵗ, in a week of exceptional heat, and begins to occupy its usual dominant space in the diary.

November 12ᵗʰ I find myself thinking of marriage quite often, hardly seriously, but thinking. Meanwhile I go on writing, chiefly out of habit, and give much of my thought to hunting and little to anything that my conscience can call real. Yet isn't it perhaps the best way, to create a deliberate illusion, known to be such, because, or if, one has not the heart to do anything else? The crisis of September has not left me the same person. One <u>can't</u> think too much or too far or one would lose oneself in despair.

November 14ᵗʰ We are getting busy again at the works and should have a good year – if war does not come. But I feel appalled about the state of things in Europe. It cannot go on. One feels with everything one does that one may be doing it for the last time. Is this the last season's hunting before convulsion comes? That is the kind of thought that runs in my head and poisons the meaning of everything now.

November 22ⁿᵈ Our board meeting at the works and the accounts. It looks as though I shall be able to save over £1000 this year, and the present year, which began on October 1ˢᵗ, is going well so far. If it happens again I shall be free with over £400 a year. The question then is whether to go on till I have £500 at which I should be able to live as I do now without being dependent on any other source of income, or to leave then. I could get the £500 with ease by the time I am 40 now [in 1942]. I wonder what I shall do, or if war will come and disrupt all my plans.

November 29th The meet was here in the Square and we spent all day messing about in Weston Park. An appalling day. A few fences to jump in the vale when hounds looked as if they'd gone away, but nothing else. I came home fed up and found the Warwickshire [Hunt] all over Campden, having made a five mile point from over by Shipston and killed in the open in Haydon's orchard by the church [among the ruins of Old Campden House.]

December 10th I think that of all the moments when I am most conscious of all that England and her freedom, her very existence, stands for, the hour when I am hacking home from hunting is the most poignant. Then, as I look at the woods and farms, it is as though I were looking into the face of a loved wife asleep, and my sense of love for the beauty I see nearly makes me cry. That is what I would fight for if I had to go and war came. And when I say that even if we won a war we should survive into another world that would be hard to love, it is because I feel that that world would inevitably be destroyed, not perhaps the physical fields, but the spirit behind them.

Although CW's many accounts of hunting have been largely omitted, an account of a very local day – the last for CW that year – is worth including.

December 15th The meet was at Mickleton and it was a grey dull day and foggy on the hills. We found in Norton Hall coverts and ran quite fast over bad market garden country to Baker's Hill and lost. Later we had a short hunt with another fox from Norton but he was headed just as he was making for the vale and got into a haystack and was not bolted. We went away over Meon Hill and a fox was pushed out of an old lime tree behind Clopton House. We went away over Meon and ran the side of it before going down towards Quinton. We hunted along the hill and had some jumping and then out on the Coombes side and back over the hill again and down by Slatter's and out into the vale at last. Hounds ran fast in the vale towards the railway, swung right-handed, crossed the Stratford road again short of Wilicote and raced away, leaving Quinton on the right, to Preston Bushes. There they may have changed foxes, for they slipped away fast back for Sheepleys till scent became catchy. By the time they reached and crossed the Stratford road by Sheepleys again, almost in the dark, they were hunting with difficulty. They were stopped by the railway in the dusk, pointing for Rumer Hill. A long hack home after 2½ hours galloping. Muggins went very well and hardly seemed tired at all. I got home at five in the dark. The hunt was 13 miles as hounds ran.

~ 1939 ~

CW begins the year by reviewing the matrimonial field, including for the first time his future bride, Audrey Chandler of Hidcote House.

January 1st The chief among them is Mary Wilson *(of Aston Somerville, a fairly recent attachment of CW's, 24 years old, met on the hunting field.)* She has all the things I seek in a wife, including money of her own. If only I felt that I loved her as well as liked her I should try to marry her. Next to her may well be Audrey Chandler who I hear is coming back from Ceylon, not having married Philip Johnson, to whom she was half engaged when he was at Mickleton, and to marry whom she set out to Ceylon some time ago. She presumably has some money of her own, has a sweet nature like her mother, and is a comfortable and familiar person, with whom one would always feel at ease. Anne Osborne would grow into a nice plump little woman with a superficial mind and fond of bridge, but would never do for me. Jane [Lane] is charming but too neurotic and anyway does not attract me sexually....So it goes on. I shall probably go on dithering till it is too late. As for Winifrid, I feel I have lost her completely. We have nothing to talk about somehow, and it is sad that it is not even sad to me now.

As for money I am better off now and the works are still busy. I have £8374 invested, including my shares in the works at 20/- and the income from that is about £420, allowing for 7½% from the works. My life there is so much easier now, with only four days a week and a long holiday, that I can go on, though I will not face being tied there indefinitely. If there is no war I shall go on but doing less, and shall go abroad in the summer and then perhaps decide. Last year I spent: House £155. Car £56. Clothes £46. Self £116. Various £95. Hunting £112.

In writing, my Country Life book [*A World of One's Own*] has been fairly well reviewed and has sold fairly well, but I don't know yet whether they'll take the other lot of essays or the characters. 'Cora' is to come out from the Cockerel this year. My book of short stories is not yet settled. I do not now regard writing as a possible <u>profession</u> but what I want is a country life with all it implies of shooting, hunting, books, friends, good food and wines, and writing added to those things as an absorbing occupation which need not make money but does at times.

A socially active winter followed, with some hunting as usual, and a cocktail party for 110 guests at the King's Arms hotel in Chipping Campden. CW acquired a new car (a Morris 12 coupé) and a new horse, the gift of a friend of a friend who was seeking a good home for one of his stable. During these months, the idea of buying the Tithe Yard opposite the church in Chipping Campden came to CW. The on-off affair with Grizel Wood came to life again, and events in Europe begin to intrude with increasing urgency.

March 17th This latest coup of Hitler's [the annexation of Czechoslovakia] makes war look almost inevitable, if not this year, then in another two or three years, I am afraid. I am thinking of joining the Territorials. No letter from Grizel. I fear she has started on her old cycle again. Am going to the Whitworths for dinner and to a dance in the Town Hall with them after.

March 31st Qualms about marriage, and particularly children, the thought of which I can hardly face. It all goes back every time possibility forces me up to facing it – fear of being tied to the works, of being tied by a family. Can I face it? I am getting on with my essays and my brain is working better. When the book is done there will come the problem of a publisher, which will not be easy in these days of crisis and bad trade for such things.

April 2nd Last night to the Chandlers at Hidcote to ask Ben if he'd sell me the Tithe Yard to build on and I rather think he will. I have the key and have looked it over this morning and think it will make a very delightful site. If he'll sell I'll buy it, though I may not build at once.

April 11th My 37th birthday, my 249th day's hunting.

April 13th Last night I dined at the Kennards at Mickleton and Audrey Chandler was there. She says Ben will sell the Tithe Yard, she thinks. The only thing is to go on normally and get out plans and so on, despite these perpetual alarms and crises. Audrey is very charming and sweet and familiar. I feel at home with her always, though I do not really know her well, and if it were not for Grizel, and if she showed any signs of wanting me, I am not sure that she would not be a person I should get very fond of.

April 15th Have had Ben Chandler to tea and we've looked at the Tithe Yard. I think he will sell it, though he is still non-committal about it. He wants £400

---

if he does, and I think the stone left from the ruins of the old tithe barn should be worth about £200 towards the cost of the house.

April 17th   Ben is willing to sell the Tithe Yard for £450 on condition that Norman Jewson does the house. I have written to Norman today to ask him to come over. So, if there is no war, I shall be living there in a year. It is exciting, quite suddenly and unexpectedly and my mind is full of plans for the house, which I want to keep down to £1000 if I can. That I could pay for out of this year's savings, and Aunt Lilian will give me the site, if she keeps her promise.

April 25th   Norman Jewson is coming to-day to discuss the house. Yesterday I sent *Lady from Yesterday* [formerly 'Cora'] to Sandford and they are to start printing now. [Later] Norman does not think I shall do what I want for £1000, but is going to let me know what can be done.

May 1st   Aunt Lilian is going to give me the Tithe Yard and I have phoned Ben and our solicitors are going to get going. Norman comes to dinner on Thursday to discuss the plans. I am very excited about it all and can see myself living there.

May 3rd   Have been to see the Vicar[174] about his wife's dogs, which run in the garden next to the Tithe Yard, and also about pulling down a long corrugated iron roof there that he has promised Ben he would take down. He was as pig-headed as a dolt about it, and denied flatly that he had ever made such a promise. He is one of the stupidest and most tactless men, even for a vicar, that I have ever met.

May 4th   Norman [Jewson] to dinner with plans for the house, which I like. By the time I am in it, it will have cost me £1500 to £2000 I think, but I shall go on if there is no war.

A few days later, CW set off on horseback (on the gift horse, which had proved unsatisfactory) to ride to the Sandfords at Eye, where it was going to live. He travelled via Upton-on-Severn and the journey took him two days.

Towards the end of the month, when CW was planning a holiday in France, a chance meeting with Mary Poncia, sister of CW's old painter friend Hudson, who lived at

---

174   Canon Brian O'Loughlin.

Southam near Leamington, resulted in their deciding to go there together. They went via Paris, to Avignon, Orange, and La Ciotat near Cassis, where the painter Hudson was living.

June 6th   Hudson was in a deplorable condition yesterday, sitting in a café over a glass of beer, bleary-eyed, unshaved, his top false teeth broken and not in, and very fuddled. He looked at us without recognising us at first, then began crying. We spent till 5.30 with him and slowly got him to pull himself together and talk to us. He cried a lot, was full of maudlin self-pity, which alternated with a blind anger and persecution mania. He talked seriously of the people of Cassis having tried to poison him and suspected us of having come to take him to an asylum. He has apparently been drinking very hard for weeks, and has got into the hands of an unscrupulous café-proprietor to whom he owes money, although café-debts are illegal in France. He has made himself very unpopular in the place and has been fighting and sick – it is the old tale of his Campden days magnified.

CW and Mary managed during the next few days to get Hudson paid up, tidied up and sobered up enough for him to board a train for Paris and home. Both CW and Mary developed bad colds and themselves set off for Dijon and Autun in cold, rainy weather, reaching Paris on June 15th and Campden soon after. Hudson had got back to London, but once there disappeared, to be found days later wandering in a drunken state in Fulham. He was briefly institutionalised, but was back at Southam with his mother by the end of June, well recovered and remembering to send CW a long, grateful letter and a cheque for £2 towards expenses in France

Meanwhile, despite three weeks together that had proved remarkably happy in most ways, and some inevitable talk of marriage, the relationship between CW and Mary became one of occasional days (or nights) together. The story of the building of the Tithe House begins to occupy the diary more and more, as does the slow march towards war.

June 29th   This evening round to the Tithe Yard to look round. It is the loveliest site in Campden: in the town, yet of the fields. There are beautiful buildings on every side, both as you look from it and as you go to it, and there are pleasant views of the hills and fields over the rooftops of the old town. It is quiet and if peace stays with us and I get my house there and retire and live in it I know I shall be happy. It is exactly what I have wanted all my life.

June 30th A quiet day at home. This war seems to be almost inevitable now, and it makes me personally selfishly sad, because I am just beginning to see before me the next ten years of my life, the fruit of all my struggling and work in the last sixteen; my retirement; my peace; my hours with my books and garden; everything I have longed and worked for destroyed before it is born. I am getting great pleasure from reading Anatole France's *On Life and Letters,* essays all written before 1914, and so full of truly balanced culture, the Greek spirit, that they fill one with envy for those years that are so near and yet so far.

July 4th The tension hangs over Europe and one grows used to it and almost callous. I think I shall go on with the house. The purchase of the field is settled and I long to be able to live there and create it all – and yet it may never be if war does come. I am very busy on air raid work at the works, in case war comes suddenly, and we are very busy there still.

July 11th Last night I was settling down to write when young Temple from Upton Wold came for me and took me off to Blockley with Tom Barnes, Jack Bridge, Charlie Ladbrook and Pritchard, Jane Lane's groom. We had a most riotous evening of laughter and drinking and fooling at the Wake there. We all of us got on the electric cars called 'Dodge-Ums' and made a sort of game taking each other's hats. Soon everyone joined in and in half an hour no one was wearing his or her own hat at all. Charlie Ladbrook had on a chauffeur's cap, I a beret, Bridge a woman's hat, and we laughed until we ached, at each other's antics, till twelve. Then we went to Upton Wold and ate cake and cheese and drank more beer and I got home late. To-day I have been hard at work on A.R.P. [Air Raid Precautions] at the works and have got everything nearly ready.

Bill Jefferies, the running huntsman, on Sunday night. 'I've put it in my will, but I don't expect as they'll do it, as I wants to be taken to the kennels when I'm dead and boiled up for the hounds. If I knew as that was going to happen I should die 'appy, because I should feel as though the very last bit of me 'ould go hunting, and that's what I want to feel.'

July 14th *(After two days in London, going to the ballet and to the Cézanne and Rowlandson exhibitions.)* In the evening I went to see Nina and found Gordon Russell there, just back from Sweden, which seems, with Denmark, the dream of the bourgeois socialist; very fine if it were not so <u>dull</u>.

July 14ᵗʰ Two estimates for the house. Espleys for £1750 and Ward of Shipston £1950. I am now trying Keitley, for I want it for £1500.

July 27ᵗʰ Have had the builder Keitley in. His price is £1900. He is going to try to bring it down.

August 2ⁿᵈ In the evening Keitley came in with his new price for the house, £1760, which I have accepted. A blow yesterday. Mrs Cook (my housekeeper for years) has had troubles with her old mother-in-law and has decided to go back to Birmingham where she came from, and she and Bert are leaving Campden in a week and I shall be without a housekeeper, if I don't find one soon, and it is not at all easy, especially for evenings.

August 5ᵗʰ Have been and marked out the position of the house with Keitley and he is going to start the walling round the site next week, so it is beginning. The more I live in it on paper, planning the garden and furnishing the rooms and so on, the more I know I shall like it. It pours with rain and has been the wettest, coldest summer I can remember. I have not been hot since I left Paris.

August 12ᵗʰ Have settled everything about the house with Norman and Keitley. It is to cost £1650, which will include the walling and gravelling the forecourt. I shall have to spend £200 on the garden and on furniture, then I shall have a home for the rest of my life and a home I shall never tire of living in.

August 16ᵗʰ I have decided to go to France again for 10 days next week. I go to St Malô by boat on the 24ᵗʰ and come back on the 3ʳᵈ September. I shall go down to Tours I think.

August 17ᵗʰ Have decided to go to Dinard by air as it only costs £2 more and takes 2 hours instead of 9. Have nearly got my stories finished and hope to do them by Wednesday. If there's no war I shall publish them next year.

August 19ᵗʰ The war seems to become more and more inevitable every day. Things have gone too far now for Germany to turn back and, as I see it, she, or her leaders, would rather lose a war than lose face. I cannot see how it can be avoided any longer. It may even come next week. The strange thing is that the sense of despair and paralysed gloom, which the Munich crisis created in me last year, has given way to a calm acceptance, so that I face war now as one faces a coming storm.

August 20th The situation looks worse and worse. I begin to doubt whether I shall get to France at all, after all. I am going to hear the news at Nina's, for even the threat of war has not made me get a wireless.

I feel sure that war will come and yet I am very calm within myself and quite ready to face it without any effort to do so, just ready to accept another and a terrible aspect to life, quite different from all that I have hitherto known. I say I look at the prospect calmly, and so I do, but I know that all I have striven for in life, and all I have hoped and worked for and am on the point of attaining will almost certainly never be mine now. Well – that is life; something on which one cannot rely, no matter how careful one may be, and yet a thing one must love as a whole, or go mad. I would prefer not to live through what is coming, and that I will end my life if it comes, but I don't think I shall. At other times I have the illusory hopes of every human being that I shall survive and be better off, in a year, in six months, whatever may happen to others, I shall be back enjoying my life again as I have meant it to be. Yet one will never be the same, and one will probably not survive the constant bombing that will be the fate of towns such as Birmingham, where I shall have to go and live. Yet so be it.

August 25th I have fallen, for I have bought a portable wireless set[175]. I have also bought a deed box in which to deposit all my diaries and manuscripts at the bank if war comes. And I have to go to Birmingham. The news still looks bad and I can't see how war can now be stopped, except by a miracle – and miracles don't happen to nations, only, and very rarely, to individuals.

August 26th Have arranged for the bank to take my MSS and papers, have repaired the locks on my front door, and am ready to act as I am needed to do now. It is rather like a sentence of death with no time stated for the execution. This morning, I picked all the plums in the Tithe Yard and Mrs Harris[176] is going to bottle them. I suppose I shall be able to get down here sometimes, whatever comes.

---

175 Presumably for use in Birmingham, see November 20th 1940 and p.255.
176 CW's new housekeeper, who lived in Vicarage Cottages opposite Stanley Cottage in Leysbourne.

August 27th In the papers a faint possibility of war being averted, but so faint. It is a perfect day, brilliant sun, a little wind, and lovely views all round. War seems utterly impossible, something that cannot happen. It seems quite impossible that such a madman as Hitler can exist on such a day and in a world that can be so lovely. Yet I think it is only a matter of a few days now, during which abortive negotiations will go on.

August 28th We wait, we listen to the news, we become accustomed to the thought of our whole world falling about our ears and to the peculiarly persistent belief that oneself will survive, whatever may happen to others. I am working very hard at the works and everyone is telephoning for beds for emergency use. We have only about 250 left now. I am going to walk up to Broad Campden to see the Osbornes after dinner. They have just come back from a yachting cruise in the Channel and have seen nothing but warships and aeroplanes, and all the outgoing merchant ships armed. I fear there is no hope now, except of a few days respite.

August 29th We know no more, except that Europe has never been nearer to war without being at war. We wait, hopelessly hoping that at the last moment some sense may be put into Hitler's head.

August 30th Replies and counter replies and long waits. A sort of numbed sense of being already accustomed to it all, and a fatigue resulting from work and the apparently hopeless future for humanity – and for oneself.

September 1st Germany attacked Poland yesterday and I expect by Monday we shall be at war with her. There seems to be just a chance that Italy may stay neutral, but I doubt whether she will if France goes to war with Germany as well. There is still the tenuous possibility that a final miracle may make Germany withdraw and negotiate. What our future is, what the future of English life is, God alone knows. If the war lasts long there will be enormous changes, tending towards Socialism and Communism, and maybe the future happiness of man, although I doubt it. But unless it is very short, perhaps six months or so, we shall never see life the same again. I mean English middle-class life, my own life, the life now just within my grasp. As I see it now my duty lies at the works with the men there. I go there even tomorrow in case there is bombing. Next week I may even have to go and live there. One's time scale has to be changed from one of weeks and months to one of days, hours; this morning, this afternoon, tomorrow. Quite possibly one may survive and live into a new world. Very possibly one may be killed. Life has been good and generous to me; it has given me love; it has hurt me; it has given me the power to feel, to create, to suffer, to be wise, to laugh, to weep; now is the testing time in which all I may have learnt from it will be tried. I am perfectly serene within and can face, and have faced in my imagination all that may happen.

September 3rd It is like *Alice through the Looking Glass* gone bad and wicked. Germany announces that she is not at war and is attacking Poland; Italy seems to be going to stay neutral. Germany has agreed not to bomb open towns and has already done so. And we wait to see what will happen to us. I have no doubt that we shall declare war on Germany in a day or so, when London has been evacuated perhaps. It seems to me that the real initiative in Germany has gone to Goebbels and Ribbentrop and has gone out of Hitler's hands. The Germans have alienated Italy and except for their uneasy pact with Russia, they are isolated and Russia will devour them in the end. By that pact they have alienated the Catholic Church which, before, supported fascism because it hoped for a new world-religious domination under the wing of a new world-political one. It is all chaos and madness, and all because the commandment to love one another has never yet had truth or force beyond the small circle of the family or the group, and by no means always there.

Campden, as the whole of England, is calm and peaceful, except for the bombers, which fly over all day. The reception of the children from London here last night was a masterpiece of old maids' fussy co-operative common sense and went off well. I took three to Spring Hill cottages, three poor cheeky little Cockneys who were terrified of being separated and afraid of the isolation of the countryside after the streets of Poplar. I have to go to the works tomorrow, Sunday, because the men are working the week-end and my works manager must get a day off in the week at least.

September 4th Now we and France are at war with Germany and this morning a German submarine has sunk a liner[177] off Scotland, full of Americans going home. So far no air raids, but I suppose they will come soon. Everything very quiet. Campden in perfect weather is like a dream town, a symbol of

---

177   The S.S. *Athenia*, with 1418 on board, sunk by U-boat U-30.

---

utter peace. Every village, the whole countryside, after grim sandbagged Birmingham, has suddenly become possessed of a charm which had faded during those last comfortable years. I am furnishing a bedroom at the works and shall have to sleep here during the week soon I expect. *Adam Bede* is a consolation, and my beloved *Don Quixote* in Shelton's translation too.

September 5th Birmingham is going to be rather trying, I am afraid. There are only two trains, one in and one out, and the one out is the late one which does not get me home till seven. Soon it may be too dark to get out by that, if we have to drive with side-lamps only, even if I get enough petrol. I am furnishing my room at the works though, and shall at least try to get long week-ends here.

There is no news of any fighting in France so far and there have been no air raids here. The oddest thing about life is that everything is so normal. In the September sunshine civilian life goes on exactly as it was before, and one did not expect that. Then suddenly one finds the station closed, the bank sandbagged, or that one cannot dine comfortably at night, or that one must rush and put up shutters in one's windows, and that brings one up against the fact of the great madness that has come over life. Yet in a week or two everyone will be taking it all for granted, gas masks, tin hats, blackout, as though it had been normal for years, and will think of peace as a thing that may have gone for ever.

September 6th The war in its fourth day seems a year old, and nothing happens yet that we hear of. German planes came over the East coast this morning but were driven back. Nothing has happened in France. It is all stupid and wicked and vile, and yet it is necessary if we are to survive free from German domination. I begin to feel that it will last for years and that life will never be the same, or be taken up by us in the same way again. I go to work with my tin hat and gas mask every day and even so soon begin to regard it as the normal thing to do. Petrol rationing starts at the end of next week and if I can't get more than the private allowance I shall only just have enough to get home for weekends with.

September 8th I have 70 gallons of petrol in store, enough to last me until Christmas even if I don't get any allowance. Somehow the war, because there is no news, and because for us it has not really begun yet, has retreated out of one's mind and already ordinary life is taking up its old importance again. But I fear it will be a long and bloody business, and we have yet to face the reality of it.

Last night Robin Whitworth lent me Middleton Murry's[178] notes for the Armistice broadcast which he was to have done – very interesting, but his old thesis again; that mechanised humanity is doomed to self-destruction unless it experiences a Christian change of heart which results in action and the creation of a new world. That may be true, but such a thing will never happen. Man is gifted to see the possibility of such things, but hardly to make them real, except subjectively and alone.

September 10th There are fourteen evacuee children at Campden House and a schoolmaster and [they] are very good to them. Little news of the war, which has not begun for us yet. Hitler is hoping still to make peace when he has conquered Poland, I think, and therefore refrains from attacking us. When we refuse to listen to him unless he withdraws, the time will come and we shall not have a pleasant experience – unless the French do by a miracle break through the Siegfried Line before he can move men from Poland to stop them.

September 11th I go on, weary of my long days in Birmingham and still cooking my own dinner which, though it is nothing to do with the war, seems to be caused by it. It is tiring when I only get home at seven, but I take a little pride in being self supporting. No raids and everything strangely and uncannily quiet so far. If Germany does not completely conquer Poland in four weeks she will have lost the war, though it may take years to teach her and many lives and much pain. It won't end without desperate efforts to break our morale and many raids, if they have the petrol for them.

September 14th The war seems very remote now as one becomes accustomed to the changes in life that it has brought about so suddenly, but I fear the worst is yet to come before we win, which we shall inevitably do – yet what is going to happen if Russia comes in on Germany's side, I wonder?

September 15th I have been allowed, to my pleasure and surprise, 38 gallons of extra petrol for October and November. So, provided I can manage the driving in the winter nights, I can go on living here all the time – a great relief.

---

178   John Middleton Murry. 1889-1957. Prolific critic and essayist, and second husband of Katherine Mansfield.

September 17th A man at the Whitworths who travels all over Europe selling wood pulp has just returned from Germany and says that even the Germans themselves say that Germany cannot win a war that does not bring them complete victory quickly. Now Russia has come in and has occupied Eastern Poland what do we do? Go on fighting till Germany gives way? Or make a peace? It is my belief that Russia will in the end step into Germany, having carried on propaganda beforehand, and create a revolution there and set up a Communist government before we can get there. Yet we should have the Saar and the Ruhr, the very vitals of German industry. One can only speculate, as about the weather. And here, everywhere, in England we have perfect autumn weather and peace, which makes one utterly forget that there is rape and murder and starvation only a few hundred miles away to the East.

September 20th Each day I sit and listen to the news and I wonder how long it will go on and how bad it will get in the way of air raids, and I feel a distant and watered hatred of Germany. But so far it is too far off for one to feel it as part of one's own experience. I have an increasing determination not to kill directly, whatever I may be called on to do.

September 27th To Manchester with another manufacturer and saw our man, who is in a position to place orders for 500,000 beds for Polish soldiers who are being formed into an army in France. We are going to see him in London in a week. If it comes off we shall make a considerable sum of money out of it, which the Government will no doubt take from us to a large extent. The new Budget this afternoon, which will be a pretty hard shock I expect.

To plunge into the peace of Campden after Manchester and Birmingham is like diving slowly and gently into deep water surrounded by green banks.

September 28th I find that my whole orientation is changed by the war. Before it my whole energy was concentrated on getting my house built, retiring, and establishing my life at Campden as I had looked forward to it over years and years. Now the possibility of that till the war is over has gone, and although I still hold it before me as an aim and hope, it depends on so many things that are absolutely out of my control that I am not living for it as a reasonable thing, but only as a dream that still <u>may</u> come true. And in the mean time I find myself giving more and more time to the works and I find too that I look on the place as a valuable basic element of my life now, as regards survival through the economic difficulties of the present and the future.

The sense of anticlimax since the war begun is extraordinary. Everyone was so keyed up to face constant air raids for the first month or two, confusion, death, and destruction of the country's normal life – and nothing has happened at all. Probably more will happen soon, but maybe not. At the moment one feels that life goes on as it was before, yet it is not the same. All the things one was about to do are stopped because there is a war, and yet the war leaves everything as it was so far – except for the blackout at night and the petrol rationing.

September 30th The war looks as though it will settle down to be a long business and as though it will spread to other parts of the world. The future, even the future of next week, is always half-hidden by a cloud of fog and doubt and one will have to live in the present all the time. And yet, going about Campden this morning, paying accounts, seeing to this and that, chatting to people, a touch of autumn in the air and the street lovely in the sunshine, one could feel no break in the continuity of one's association with beauty and quiet things.

October 2nd Here I sit on this evening a month after the war began, in my room with all my things about me, my dinner jacket on, my silk shirt, my fire burning, and nothing really changed in my life at all. And one expected to be crawling about in a ruined Birmingham, rescuing people from bombed houses. It may still come, but so far nothing has changed except that I have less petrol, have to catch an earlier train, have no hunting, and have been unable to start my house. That and appallingly heavy taxation and a probably reduced income and capital, and the chance of retirement further off instead of nearer, is all that has happened to me. But I shall not be surprised or bewildered if more does happen soon, when Hitler realises that he has got to fight a long war. The megalomaniac at bay we have yet to see, and with the power of destruction of modern science it will not be a noble sight. However, one more month of life has been given me, and that is a lot.

October 6th My first week-end at home for weeks, pottering in the garden which I must get tidy for the winter, picking apples and training my roses on the walls in perfect October sunshine. Campden, with fewer cars, has regained something of its old remote atmosphere. I begin to long to have my house built and think of going on with it after all, though I'm not sure it isn't best to put the money in the bank and wait.

October 8th Yesterday gardening in the still sunshine, only disturbed by bombers from Rissington [near Burford]. Robin [Whitworth] very full of his Peace Pledge Union[179] and talk of a Federated Europe, but they are all tilting at windmills, for everyone agrees in principle with their aims. It is how they can be achieved at all is the question.

October 9th Very good cheese fritters for dinner, which Mrs Harris, who now cooks for me at night, makes well, also part of a rabbit that I ran over on Saturday. Mrs Harris is very good and kind and thoughtful and better than Mrs Cook. She lives opposite and comes and gets my breakfast, then comes and lights my fire at 5.30 and gets dinner, a very satisfactory arrangement.

October 14th I walked up to the Naumans at Campden House and had tea there. A young man there who had been in the Kiel raid[180], said that the defences were very good and that twenty planes were lost, but a lot of damage was done. His plane was completely overturned at 15,000 feet by gunfire and the crew were thrown all over it. He just managed to get back and right before it was too late and get home undamaged. Flying over Germany on reconnaissance flights the batteries did not fire on them and the men waved. We have apparently decided not to bomb towns at all. When our men go on pamphlet raids they carry no bombs and when they go on bombing raids on military objectives if they drop bombs on towns they get into trouble when they get home. When they were over some islands on the German coast they saw a man shrimping and power dived on him to see what he would do. He went on shrimping, so they took his photograph. Charles Nauman thinks that Germany will go communist and that we shall end up fighting with the German army against Russia.

October 15th An odd party last night [at a Mrs Colbourne's in Westington], the sort of people one sees in the Piccadilly Grill, and rather like the gathering at Sir Harry Scattercash's when Mr Sponge and Lucy Glitter met[181].

---

179 Founded in 1934 (and still in existence) following a letter to the Manchester Guardian by Canon Dick Sheppard, an army chaplain during the First World War.
180 On powerful elements of the German fleet at Wilhelmshafen, in very bad weather, on September 4th.
181 Characters in *Mr Sponge's Sporting Tour* by Surtees (1853).

October 17th It pours with rain still. With the lack of petrol and the blackout and rain one feels marooned. Hudson has been away having some cure, but is now back at Southam [near Stratford upon Avon] again, drinking. I am trying to get timber to go on with my house. If I can, I think I shall start building, for I want to be in it by next summer and want it more than anything else. I want to walk out to Saintbury but it rains too hard. I am very fond of the Whitworths and am so glad that they have bought a house near enough to walk to, and not further off as I had feared[182].

October 18th Ward of Shipston seems to be able to get the timber for the house as the Shipston timber merchant Mayo is his brother-in-law, and he is willing to build at the price he quoted me in August, so I shall give him the contract. If I can get it done for £1800 including the move I shall pay for it by this time next year and shall have my home for the rest of my life.

October 20th Caught the 7.29 train to London and travelled up with a nice little Austrian refugee who is cook at the Society of Friends settlement at Offchurch [near Coventry]; a sad, cold, pale man who was yet wonderful in his inner cheerfulness and his determination to begin life again. Full of happiness to be in this country, even though he is more or less interned. I went to see my contact about the 500,000 beds for the Polish forces and found only his assistant there, but found out later that the whole thing was fading out.

I have ordered a gallon of olive oil from Fortnums, tinned curried chicken, tinned ham. A dull day and London very empty and depressing and full of sandbags and grim faces. The country is a revelation of peace to come back to. I don't know how people can remain sane in cities. They don't, and that is the trouble, for men in cities govern the rest of men.

October 28th On Thursday to see *The Corn is Green* [by Emlyn Williams] at Stratford, depressingly dull and the house only half full. I took the Osbornes and a young Lieut. Green of the Green Howards, who are billeted here, a nice young man who has written a novel. Last night to a party to meet the officers of the Green Howards at Jane Roberts' and to see Nina [Griggs] afterwards.

---

182   The Whitworths had recently moved in to the Old School House in Saintbury.

November 3rd I am going on with the house and Ward and Norman [Jewson] are coming to see me tomorrow. Soon I shall have the contract settled and I hope to get in by June.

November 5th A lot of my malaise about my life is, I think, due to my age in connection with the last war *(CW was twelve in 1914).* Then, in the years through which I grew to adolescence, the form of manhood was that of a soldier for me. All my life that has probably been in my mind unconsciously, to make me feel now that somehow I am leading a false life in going on at the works and building my house and going on as I have always done. It is added to by the fact that all my local hunting friends have, having no jobs and nothing to keep them, gone already. Yet at my age and with my job I am quite clear logically that I am better as I am, and am doing my duty better than I should as a soldier. That there is no self-sacrifice in it is perhaps the root of the trouble.

November 7th H.E. Bates[183] writes and says he will do all he can for *Lady from Yesterday* if I will send it to him.

November 9th I have signed the contract and feel very excited at the prospect of building at last and fill my hours with thoughts of living there after the war and making it into the house I long for, with lovely things around me.

November 13th Very busy at the works and arranging to make another 1000 beds a week for the army. The war hangs on like a threatening thunderstorm, heavy clouds from which a few drops fall now and then. I wonder if it will break now or not, and what will be the result if it does. I begin to feel that it may drag on like this and then crumble away with internal rotting in Germany, but there may have to be a holocaust first. Yesterday I went out to Hidcote to the Chandlers for tea and showed Ben my plans.

November 19th Still this war goes on in its latent fashion, so that one accepts the comparative peace and yet waits for the German threats to be put into force. In a way, just as it was almost a relief when it began, after the long suspense, it will be a relief now that it begins in earnest. One will have some sort of definition of what has to be faced. Yesterday I went round to the house

---

183   Herbert Ernest Bates C.B.E., 1905-1974. Prolific writer known for *The Darling Buds of May* and for his short stories, many commissioned by the Air Ministry during the war.

---

and was excited and pleased to see the foundations got out and to stand in the mud and to think that in a few months I shall be living there.

November 25ᵗʰ Yesterday to the house, a mess of mud and concrete, but beginning to take shape after a fashion. Roberts, very full of his new dignity of Deputy Director of Stores and Equipment at the Ministry of Supply. He sees all the letters between Daladier[184] and Chamberlain about supplies etc and is very gloomy about the war, so far as duration is concerned. But he is amazed at the productive capacity of the country and the Empire.

Lady from Yesterday *had been reviewed favourably, if briefly, by the Times Literary Supplement, the Scotsman and the Tatler magazine; the latter asked for a photograph and CW submitted one of him on horseback, whose appearance caused much amused teasing but tickled his vanity (see Illustrations). Shortly before Christmas he spent two days in London, the diary entry for which shows what was still possible for the provincial visitor during the 'phony war'.*

December 20ᵗʰ A pleasant though tiring two days in London. I dined with Roberts at the Union Club and we had a very good dinner: oysters, Pouilly wine, partridge en casserole, a pear, then 1912 port and brandy and coffee. We talked or rather he did, for hours, and then we went to the Bon Viveur night club, a peculiarly dingy place, where we ate ham on toast and drank lager beer. I got to bed about 1.30. Yesterday I went and ordered another pair of shoes, bought a hat and cap, went to the National Gallery concert, saw Roberts at the Ministry of Supply and saw Sam [manager of the London office], took my Griggs and Palmer prints to be re-framed at Stewart and Browns, and at five met Mary [Poncia].

The evening continued at Quaglino's and the Coconut Grove night club (in which Philip Chandler was an investor) where they met the Whitworths and the Bournes from Snowshill.

Christmas was spent in Campden, each meal for several days being taken at a different friend's house. There were two days of hunting on a borrowed horse.

---

184   French prime minister, leader of the *Front Populaire*; tried in 1942 by the Vichy regime and imprisoned by the Germans.

*Woodcut illustration for
'Lady from Yesterday' by
Lettice Sandford, 1939.*

~ 1940 ~

January 1st Last year one was able to believe that life might go on, taking the direction that one hoped it would take, and lead towards sanity and peace. Now we sit, our hopes refrigerated by the ice of war, and everything uncertain and futureless. I find I don't look on the new year as a waste with no path though, but as a wilderness to be entered and lived in as best may be. When it is over life may be struggling back to a crippled normality, or it may still be striving towards that, wounded by fresh outbursts of brutality and pain. No one knows. My house grows and is as certain as things are now, for all the material is bought. I look forward to living in it though I don't like the idea of the extra cost. Yet I need such a place to settle in for the rest of my life in this town that I now belong to.

On Thursday [28th December] I went with Roberts through a considerable snowstorm to lunch at the Bay Tree hotel at Burford and Miss Gray[185] there gave me a pound of butter. In the evening I took Nina [Griggs] to the Chandlers, and Audrey was there, looking very nice. She is such a sweet person that I sometimes wonder why we have not got to know each other better.

January 2nd It is freezing and a cold wind and the snow lies. The war has broken all sense of continuity. I have no emotional life, absolutely none, for the first time in years. One goes on from day to day, not knowing what great disaster may not engulf one in a month, and one occupies oneself fussily in such things as securing butter from Ireland, getting wine, and mechanical labour such as typing; with business visits, and chatter that leads nowhere. Yet I am not depressed. I am merely vacant and lazy, sometimes bored, middle-aged[186], and beginning to face the prospect of, at best, a safe and ineffective old age in Campden, the old age of a man of taste, who has written a little, who hunts a little, who works in his garden, who has been a man of business too. That is the best. At the worst starvation, or destruction in a cellar by a bomb.

January 7th A very pleasant children's-adults' party [at Nina Griggs']; charades; Hunt the Slipper; singing by the Guineys; and so on. Home at twelve.

---

185 Sylvia Gray had owned the Bay Tree at Burford since 1935. She insisted on young 'ladies' as staff, and later owned the Manor House hotel at Moreton in Marsh. She was Chairman of the Women's Institute 1969-74.
186 He was not yet 38.

January 3rd Life, that so mysteriously disappears from us and returns to us, has returned to me once more. I can find words; I can see things. Have bought a boiler and carpets to-day for the house.

January 10th I stayed the night at Berkswell [after a performance of *Dear Octopus*[187] at Coventry with Marie Tempest [born 1864] – '*her age not in the least noticeable*']. Bill Huggins is a Colonel of Artillery and is training men with such success that he is being visited by Generals and is in danger, as he puts it, of not being sent on active service at all. The men adore him and he is exultantly happy. The war has saved him and has freed him from work he was never fitted for. The frost continues. The house is of course at a standstill. I bought a sitting room suite and a carpet at Hamptons' sale in London.

January 18th Not quite so cold, but last night there were 27 degrees of frost and it has been freezing all day. The Avon at Stratford is frozen over and people have walked across it, for the first time in my memory. To-morrow a sort of Hunt Ball in aid of the Red Cross and I am glad to hear that we are to wear pink coats, for it may be the last time. I gather that the Green Howards are soon going and the Gordons [Highlanders] coming in their place.

January 27th Snow, rain, sleet and the temperature still only just above freezing, the house still frozen. I have run out of typing paper. To the Blakemans for tea. Fifteen years ago I went into rooms there. Cecily and Bin [Blunt, her sister] and Robin [Whitworth] came in about 9.30 and we laughed and talked glorious nonsense for an hour till we ached all over.

January 28th It rained and sleeted and froze all last night and has gone on doing so all day to-day. The roads, walls and footpaths are one sheet of ice 2in thick. I managed to get the car out and drive down to Wood Stanway however, though I hardly know how I got there and back. I had to have the screen open all the way and was skidding all over the road. Even a gust of wind blew the car sideways on the ice. I got up Aston Hill safely, and home. Every grass is a rod of glass; every bough and twig a bar of crystal enclosing living wood. It is the most extraordinary sight. There are miles and miles of telephone wire down, lying festooned over the hedges. I only met two other cars.

---

187   A comedy of manners by Dodie Smith, 1938.

February 1st *(In London CW met a Colonel Paul Rodzianko at the Café Royal[188]).* He has been riding instructor to the Irish Free State Cavalry and many other things. A great talker and none too accurate I should think. He thinks the Finns can't possibly last beyond the spring and was full of talk of secret diplomatic missions between us and Germany, so we can make peace with Germany and turn on Russia with her help. He said he knew for certain that such talks were going on, but I doubt it.

Yesterday an odd bit of news; the oysters were not very good and the waiter told us that a magnetic mine had been dropped in the oyster beds near Colchester and that the fishers had been prevented from going to the best beds. I went to William Morris[189] and bought a few remnants and have ordered a lot of patterns to be sent down to choose curtains and covers from. The snow still lies deep here and there will be no building yet. In Birmingham the snow has been 2ft deep on the roofs of the works, and one of them has collapsed. We are very busy there still and should do well this year, but I gather that taxation will be worse, and restrictions more and more severe. What this world will be like after another year or two of war one can hardly think.

February 3rd It is still freezing and the snow lies, with ice under it, over everything. The house looks like some 18th century gentleman's ruin, constructed to remind him genteelly of mortality and decay.

February 11th The war so far is still a remote thing that only affects one's daily life in ways that one has already got used to: taxation, rationing, petrol, difficult business conditions, and so on. I doubt very much whether peace will be possible till it has really become war and the German armies are destroyed – which means two or three years of it, I am afraid.

A bad visitation of 'flu, convalescence and business intervene.

March 2nd All morning at the house, arranging for Charles Blakeman to cut the name and date on the keystone, and for trees to be cut down etc. I have begun to see how the garden is to be planned and have got it clear on paper now. I am going to plan it myself, I think, and do a good deal of the making of it myself too.

---

188 The famous haunt of artists and bohemians at 68 Regent Street, 1865-2008.
189 These were the last days of the original Morris & Co, founded in 1861.

March 9th Mrs Creswell: 'I don't like the new curate; he bawls like a bull.' Cressy (deaf): 'Has he now? How do you know, Effie?'

Miss Piper's Troubles, a collection of short stories, was published later in March by John Lane The Bodley Head. The house was making steady progress.

April 6th The other day Norman Jewson was expected up at the house. The foreman had to go up to the quarry and when he came back, asked if he had been. 'Ah,' one of the men said. ''E came in and 'e walked round and 'e never spoke a word to a bugger on us, then 'e buggered off'.

April 7th An awful party at Mrs Heaton's, all the old maids of Campden. She is a queer old thing, rather a menace with her views on intellectual enlightenment and so on, and yet one can't help admiring her for her vitality of spirit. She had [a copy of] *Miss Piper* and made me sign it – and is having a party of old maids next week specially to read some of the stories to them! Four lines in the Observer for it, and a whole paragraph in the Times.

April 8th The war, which, in one's day-to-day life, one seems almost to forget now, looks like waking up soon. I am sure that 'technically' we have already beaten Germany, yet it may take a long time to bring that defeat into the consciousness of the Germans, the only possible end.

April 9th The invasion of Denmark and Norway by Germany and everyone talking and listening to the news. Yet I find myself, on a day like this, instinctively withdrawing, leaving the paper unread for half an hour, not buying an evening paper and so on, and rather consciously reading about times and places that have nothing to do with me now, and taking delight in simple homely things like a glass of wine, some bread and butter, or the softness of my bed. I draw myself up like a hedgehog into a ball, I read the papers with a deliberate effort to make myself look at the news with detachment, as one looks at history, or reads Gibbon on the barbarian invasions, or Trevelyan on Marlborough's wars. It keeps one sane and one misses nothing and gains the ability to see the thing whole. As a result people think I am not interested, yet I am, intensely. I only want to see it whole and without emotion, even in its possible effects on my own life.

April 11th My 38th birthday and I feel that age now, or more. Today and in the immediate future events as important as Trafalgar or Waterloo may take place. The news, though full of rumours, is vague and uncertain at present. We seem to have sunk a great part of Germany's fleet though and to have cut off her communications with Norway.[190] Even my detachment is shaken as I wait for news to come.

April 14th Yesterday pottering, carpentering, cutting the lawn, and a walk out to the Cresswell's [at Charingworth] to dinner. The Wilsons from Broad Campden were there and Connie Guerrier, the vicar's daughter from Ebrington. A lift back in the Wilsons' car. I go to the Mackail's[191] this evening to meet their daughter Angela Thirkell[192], the novelist, whose appalling novels sell for some reason I don't understand. The roof timbers are going up at the house and all the stonework will be finished in a fortnight. I am longing to be in it and I creep about it and look out of the windows and think what it will be like to live in.

April 15th This evening I have been to see the Rathbones, who are living in the Sharpleys' old house [The Martins], a nice old couple devoted to the arts in a Victorian way.

April 21st In the evening I had Daisy and Ted Lyon to dinner and Margaret Smith, a good mixture. We had soup, a cold guinea fowl and trifle and potted Stilton, and drank Manzanilla sherry, Macon, and Cockburn 1917 port. The house grows fast. The first cuckoo to-day, and a swallow.

April 18th No news. The war drags on. At one moment one thinks Germany is really near defeat and internal rupture, and at another that she may yet succeed in drawing other countries in, so that the destruction will spread and last, giving her the illusory hope of finally getting something out of it. The house goes on well and the actual building will soon be done.

---

190   The heavy cruiser *Blücher* was sunk on 9th April; the light cruiser *Königsberg* the next day.
191   John William Mackail O.M. 1859-1945. Scottish man of letters and former Professor of Poetry at Oxford. He was a friend and biographer of William Morris and married Margaret Burne-Jones.
192   Angela Margaret Thirkell, 1890-1961. A prolific and successful novelist, she set many of her books in Trollope's fictional Barsetshire, but wrote also on social themes. Although she was not (nor did she claim to be) a great writer, CW's criticism is rather harsh, and perhaps tinged with envy.

May 2ⁿᵈ I have been to Nina's to hear the news: bad. We seem to lack co-ordinating and directing verve. We shall, no doubt, muddle through to a victory of exhaustion, which will exhaust us too, but it does seem that we ought to have been able to forestall this invasion of Norway. It was a matter of hours and we took days, despite all the gallantry that has been spent. It is time Chamberlain gave way to a more vigorous man.

On May 5ᵗʰ, accompanied by Charles Blakeman, who wanted to go to Edinburgh, CW drove North towards Glasgow on business. On the way, in Yorkshire they visited Rievaulx Abbey and the Ionic Temple on the terrace above, built by Sir Thomas Duncombe in 1753 and were enchanted by the landscaped gardens and the temple, 'a perfect 18ᵗʰ century room with ceilings painted by Brunelli in 1750, and all the chairs and tables and stools, and even the statue above it just as they had been when it was a country gentleman's tasteful toy.'

May 7ᵗʰ To-day a long day of calls on 12 shipyards with our agent Johnson, a busy, pleasant little North Countryman. At one yard there were three new destroyers under construction; at another a cruiser all camouflaged, being repaired, with a hole literally big enough to drive two lorries through, side by side. All the people were very pleasant in a dour North Country way. Jarrow is an appalling blot of slums and the cumulative effects of unemployment; pale faces; ill looking children; and older men with that puffed, almost fat-looking bloom of weakness and long indolence. The idleness still in the hopeless air of some of them was an awful sight. The monastery[193] an extraordinary black ruin among fallen houses, forlorn waste spaces, and streets where half staved urchins played in the roadway.

May 8ᵗʰ [At Newcastle-on-Tyne] At one shipyard the managing director was cousin of a colonel who, with part of his force, went right into Lillehammer, and were then surrounded by the Germans who had let them pass and had watched them all the time, and taken prisoner. The rest of the force, now home, was in the woods. Wherever they went the Germans knew of it before they got there through local espionage.

This evening I went for a long walk round the old part of the town. Indescribable squalor and dirt and dreariness with, here and there, a lovely 18ᵗʰ century

---

193   Founded in 674 A.D. and home to the Venerable Bede, author of *The Ecclesiastical History of the English People.*

---

house, or even a 17th century one, a surviving relic of the days when commerce and the beauty of a town had not yet clashed.

May 10th [At Carlisle] I heard the news of the invasion of Belgium and Holland this morning on the train [to Glasgow], and this evening that Chamberlain had given way to Churchill, which is good, for I have always thought him a great man. Poor Chamberlain. He is worn out; a good man, but too small for these times.

May 12th The news seems indeterminate, but I think this final break out on the Western Front may be the beginning of the end. We can't help holding the Germans and they can't hope to win if they can't this summer. Yet the end may be a long way off yet. It is awful to think of peaceful Holland and Belgium being bombed and torn apart. One can hardly credit it here, in this remote fell country on a day like this with no sound but the curlews calling to each other, and a chaffinch singing. It is extraordinary that so far no bombing of England has happened. I suppose it will, but petrol is the key of this war, and the German supplies can't last many months at the rate they are using them now.

On his return journey south, CW stayed with his old friends Brian and Audrey Parker at Ainstable in Cumberland; they took him to Askham Hall, 'marvellous furniture' and to Haweswater, where Brian caught 23 trout in 3 hours, some of which were later cooked for lunch at the Punch Bowl Inn at Askham by Mrs Peel, 'a descendant of the famous John Peel' as CW records with satisfaction.

May 15th [In Campden again] A lovely day and quite incredible that war should be so near, yet why mere good weather should make one feel that war is 'impossible' I don't know. The news looks very grave. One begins to see that it is possible that we <u>may</u> not win the war, yet the thought of it is absurd, somehow. The house has grown fast while I have been away and the roof is felted and partially tiled. Now work again, and the routine of one's life wrapping itself round one like a strait jacket.

May 16th For the moment the battle seems poised. The Germans may be held; they may break through; or they may be allowed to come on and get surrounded. The next four months will decide the fate of the world for centuries. At least, at the end of them if we have held, we shall know what we shall win. Soon I fear Italy will come in against us; London will be bombed; Switzerland will be invaded as were Holland and Denmark. It is still possible that Italy may stay out though. No one can tell. One can only wait and accept what comes. I can't write somehow. Everything seems so unreal because one knows that at any moment either the sunlight, the lovely green of the May countryside, the new house, really a fair and beautiful thing, or oneself, may be destroyed. And yet, for the same reason, everything too seems possessed of a reality which it has never had before, and the sayings of Christ seem to have a truth that has been concealed until this hour.

May 18th The war situation seems to grow more and more grave. It is not what the Germans have accomplished in a week that is so serious as their capacity to take us by surprise and the enormous forces they seem prepared to gamble with to try to get through this summer. Our only chance seems to be to try to destroy their lines of communication. I still think we shall stop them myself, but it will be a terrible fight. I can't feel much interest in the house or even pleasure in the perfect May weather. Everything, being so near to possible destruction at any moment, seems like a display of food seen through a shop window by a man who knows that he may well be starving by next week. I have spent the day trying to enjoy the freshness of this perfect young summer. Have been rook-shooting at Campden House this evening and had a drink there and heard the news. If we can hold on for a month without actual defeat we shall have won.

May 19th Aeroplanes overhead all day. Winston Churchill's speech[194] to-night. We shall have a very hard fight for it, yet we shall win if only we can hold on for another few weeks.

May 24th This new Enabling Bill and the threat of 100% Excess Profit Tax make me wonder whether I shall be allowed to finish the house without selling shares at a loss. But I think I shall manage it and with luck get into it. I may get it filled with evacuees of course, or soldiers, but that can't be helped. Everything still looks very black, but we may still see ourselves round the corner sooner than we think.

---

194   Following formation of the War Cabinet: ending with the promise of 'blood, tears, toil and sweat.'

May 25th A corncrake over in the field by the Mill; an owl calling; perfect stillness; the scent of honeysuckle in my room; and death, rape, destruction, agony, all over Northern France; thousands dying; everything in deadly peril; Boulogne taken. Lord, what a world. The worse it gets the more do I find myself tending to adopt the attitude of a sort of visitor from another planet. The difficulty is one's love of one's own possessions; yet I think I have been able to succeed enough in the last 6 months to be fairly proof against most things now. One can never tell till the test comes though.

May 28th Now the treachery of the Belgian King and the surrender of his army at his orders[195]. A terrible task faces our army in Northern France and the news will be enough to appal the stoutest hearts I fear. One can do little but be patient and resigned and have faith. I have joined the new Local Defence Volunteers[196]. A rather ineffective meeting to-night, as though it were to collect recruits for a local cricket club that had got into difficulties.

May 29th Floors in two bedrooms and the bathroom. My bedroom and all the upstairs will be done to-morrow and the one small bedroom plastered. It can't be more than a month till I move in. And what if they commandeer it? I shall struggle and then, if I fail, try to say *'c'est la guerre'* without bitterness.

June 3rd On Friday night I heard that there was some danger of the house being taken over for troops and on Saturday I went and saw the officer in command here and he assured me that it would be all right. However, as the small bedroom is done I have decided to move into it and sleep there. I did so for the first time on Sunday night and E. came to see me and we christened the house very charmingly. An odd feeling, sleeping in a house with neither windows nor stairs, nor doors, but I enjoyed it, and there is furniture there now, so they cannot take it over, I am told.

On Saturday night I had my first spell on [L.D.V.] duty on the hill above Broad Campden. We sat in an old station bus or servants' coach from Northwick

---

195   Unlike the Dutch, Danish and Norwegian monarchs, King Leopold stayed with his troops and surrendered rather than establish a government-in-exile in London; a position bitterly criticised by Churchill.

196   The L.D.V., affectionately known as the 'Look, Duck, Vanish'. Formed following Anthony Eden's order on May 14th, the name was changed to 'Home Guard' in July on Churchill's order, to be known affectionately as 'Dad's Army'.

Park, and it was odd to think of its hundreds of journeys to village cricket matches, dances and parties along the dusty white lanes of that other world that existed before 1914. I did from nine to twelve and three till 5.30 with Teddy Pearce and a very nice man staying here, a Major General Hobart[197], retired from Egypt, who, while waiting for a job, has joined as a private. We are a great nation because of our flexibility. Campden is full of men back from Dunkirk. They look brown and well and their faces do not show anything of the appalling time they must have had. The way we have turned defeat into something like victory is again an example of how we survive and win. What other nation in such circumstances would feel, as one can feel England feels now, the quiet deep confidence, that is the very spirit of victory?

June 8th Still this amazing weather holds, as it has done ever since May. The French seem to be holding, and on whether they do or not for the next month depends much of the fate of European civilisation. The house goes on and the outside, except for the pointing, is finished and the inside nearly so. It looks lovely, but all one's anxieties about it and the danger of the army taking it over take all my pleasure away. I am to have it in about five weeks, but I shall get the bedrooms sooner. I seem to be about to start musketry classes for the L.D.V. and shall quite enjoy that.

June 9th Very close and hot. The news still bad. If the French can't keep their defences this week the war will become a far worse and interminable thing. If, as I hope they do, the turning point will have been reached. This week is one of the most critical in European history. One waits and fears and hopes. The only philosophy is one somewhat akin to Marcus Aurelius. For myself, I say: A wise man lives without fear and without hope; he treats despair as a stranger.

June 10th Now Italy has entered the war against us. It will prolong it and cause suffering to millions more, but it will not make the situation any better for her. For the time being it will place further strain on us, but in the long run, if only we can hold out now, it can only weaken Germany. If only, if only,

---

197   Major General Sir Percy Cleghorn Stanley Hobart, K.B.E., D.S.O., M.C., 1885-1957. A proponent of mobile tank warfare, he commanded 7th Division, the 'Desert Rats', but was dismissed by General (later Field Marshal Sir) Archibald Wavell, joining the L.D.V. in the ranks. Churchill had him re-enlisted in 1941 and he was assigned to training successively 11th and 79th Armoured Divisions. Here, he developed the famous 'Hobart's Funnies', such as the amphibious Sherman tank used at D-Day. His brother-in-law was Field Marshal Montgomery.

we can hold out. Italy I feel we can deal with at sea and in the Near East. My first map-reading class for the L.D.V.

June 15th Now Paris has been given over to the German armies and left, half-deserted, like it is off the main streets, lovely still in the June sunshine, waiting for the German hordes to come, the hordes who unconsciously hunger for the culture it stands for, and yet destroy the very roots of that culture as they seek to devour it and so possess it. Yet the end is not yet, surely. There will come a time when the enormous oily bubble of German power will strain its size and be ready to burst at a pinprick. May we be only ready and strong enough when that time does come.

The house gets nearer and nearer to completion yet is some weeks off yet. It is such a worry, such a source of pinpricking anxiety neurosis that I almost wish I had not begun it. Yet I suppose I shall get into it and live in it one day. Each day I see how delightful it is going to be. Now, for instance, my bedroom windows are in and the room looks charming. When it is all done and my furniture is in it, it will be almost too much my ideal, for life that is now so threatening, to be pleasant. Writing is impossible with every day at the works and three nights a week of L.D.V. and two nights on guard as well.

June 16th In the evening Roberts called. He wants me to be prepared to take over another business for the Ministry of Supply. I said I would if he wanted me to. After dinner I went out to see Ben and Fanny [Chandler] at Hidcote. Ben, after a fortnight, has got his permit to use his car again. After living in England for 40 years he suddenly found that he was technically an alien, being an American citizen still.

The news is very bad. I feel it is very doubtful indeed if the French will hold out till autumn. If they can, if they can hold even a part of France, and keep their forces together as a living, controlled army till then we shall beat Germany this winter I think, for we would be ready to go in again by then. But the prospects are not good. America will be too late with her aid, and there will be too little of it at first. We may find ourselves isolated, subject to attempted invasion and to bombing, and carrying on the war almost alone. I think we shall fight to the bitter end, till we are either victorious or destroyed.

June 17th And now France has asked for an Armistice and we stand alone and must fight on. And yet sometimes I wonder whether it would not be better to evade it and swallow our pride for peace. But if we do fight on as I think we shall do and must, I am prepared to face it. What will happen now no-one can say; nor where the French fleet is; nor what will become of our forces in France; nor what the French air force will do. I suppose we shall soon have bombing on a fearful scale and attempts at invasion, and even invasion itself. One goes on with one's life more and more deliberately and calmly the worse it gets. The house is now to be habitable by the end of the month and I may yet get into it, though I may be simultaneously cut off from it except at week-ends, or even more finally by death. I go on with it as though peace were round the corner.

At one time I could find no consolation in the immediate beauties and joys of life because the war seems to blot out all joy. But lately, the worse it has grown, the more I have found peace and pleasure in the beauty of this perfect summer. Last night at four at the Observation Post the birds, a young plover, the grey land I love taking form out of the dusk; this evening too, when I rode up to the Water Tower, watching some L.D.V. manoeuvres on Charlie Ladbrook's pony, the view from Westington Hill was more lovely than I have ever seen it look, and it gave me great peace to be part of it.

June 18th Winston Churchill's brilliant, realistic, witty, and yet grave and again confident speech to-night[198] has made me again assured that I can face life. All the last few days I have been fluctuating and wavering between depression and over confidence. Now again I am clear. But it is also odd how one fluctuates between a high altruism and petty selfishness at these times. To be honest it is to me just as important that I should get the house finished and live in it as it is that Christian Civilisation should go on. For me it is even more important that the house should be finished. I am not very interested in what may happen fifty years hence, but I am very interested in what happens to myself, now. And I think that the majority of people, if they were honest, would have to say the same thing. The plasterers, whom I saw last night, say they will be three weeks more. The house should be habitable in a month. Shall I do it, before the men are taken away, or before I get cut off from here?

---

198 Ending with the imperishable sentence 'Let us therefore brace ourselves to our duties, and so bear ourselves that, if the British Empire and its Commonwealth last for a thousand years, men will still say, "This was their finest hour."'

June 19ᵗʰ L.D.V. from seven till nine then Teddy Pearce [a Blockley L.D.V. colleague] to a cold supper. I had a squad to teach rifle drill and I hardly knew how to use one myself, but got on quite well. I was amused at myself ordering them to shoulder arms and left wheel and so on.

I feel more confident about the war now. The chances of serious invasion seem to be remote; the danger of air raids has been with us all along; and parachutists can do very little. We have a great Navy and 1½ million men and a magnificent and growing Air Force. It looks as though the French Navy and Air Force are coming over to us, and there is a large French army in the colonies too[199]. We shall wear Hitler down in a year or two. He has only the mirage of victory in his grasp.

June 20ᵗʰ There were air raids on the East coast and South Wales last night. There will be famine in Europe by this Christmas, the Times says. It seems terrible that to beat this devil we have to starve the French and the Dutch and Belgians, who have done nothing wrong. Life is mad. My cynicism about it grows more and more thin-lipped, I fear.

June 23ʳᵈ All day yesterday trying to put some life into the L.D.V., and some sense of reality. The whole thing is being appallingly mishandled by a man called Fitzhugh, a so-called captain from the last war, and a master at the Grammar school, where he squeezes girls behind doors. He was appointed by Spencer-Churchill[200], who may have been a very brave man in the last war, but who is an old doddering fool now. General Hobart, who is now in command of Berkshire, Oxfordshire and Gloucestershire, gave me authority to go ahead and get something done, even to the extent of offending Spencer-Churchill and Fitzhugh. I asked Eldred and Fitzhugh and Major Lecordier the local R.A.S.C [Royal Army Service Corps] C.O. and Basil Fairclough to have a drink and we spent two hours talking and arguing. The result was fairly good and we arranged to meet every Saturday evening and I think things will move with more vigour. I have been busy all day getting the barricades built up the

---

199   An optimistic view: much of the French Navy went over to Vichy, and was later sunk by the Royal Navy at Mers el Kébir (Dakar); other ships were scuttled by their crews at Toulon, although some in allied harbours joined the Free French cause. Air Force losses were heavy in France and much of the remaining strength was dispersed between North Africa and the Near East.
200   Captain George Edward Spencer-Churchill, M.C., 1876-1964, of Northwick Park. A cousin of Winston Churchill.

Aston Road and in Dyer's Lane and up Conduit Hill. So far, far from offending anyone, I seem to have made better friends of them, and they do not seem to mind if someone else does their work for them as long as they get the credit, and that does not matter.

It is the generals and politicians who have ruined France, and the great French People, once proud and irresistible, have accepted their betrayal as a nation without even an attempt at revolution or protest. The France that the Revolution and Napoleon created is dead; its spirit is dead. Does the spirit of England, of Cromwell, of Pitt, of Wellington, of Nelson, survive? I think it does, in my heart and in those of hundreds I know.

L.D.V. all afternoon and again to-morrow. Soon we shall be quite organised and fit to put up at least some resistance.

June 26th My week-end activities with the L.D.V. have resulted in a note from Fitzhugh saying that if I like to join a horse patrol being formed at Broadway he will be pleased to release me. He is getting anxious because he is being shown up. He is utterly incompetent, and as vain as the devil. I have answered that I feel I can be of more use here at present as things are in such a muddle.

June 28th Another letter from little Fitzhugh finding reasons for asking me to resign and actually asking me to do so. I have hurt his pride, which he still cherishes more than his duty as the man officially in charge here. He has done nothing, literally nothing, and all that has been done has been done by myself, Fairclough and Eldred. I have answered and referred him to General Hobart. Anyway I shall probably be in command of my own company in a week or two in Birmingham. I was up till 5.30 last night. There were German planes over and they say that the telephone wires were cut to Rissington Aerodrome [near Burford] and two men taken and arrested.

In response to a letter from CW, General Hobart asked to see him.

July 1st I would never have believed that a man who prides himself on being a gentleman and a man of honour as Spencer-Churchill does so obviously would have done such a caddish thing; he has shown my letters to him, private letters, about little Fitzhugh to Fitzhugh himself, which makes it impossible for me to go on working with either of them. I have resigned and told him what I think of his behaviour. I think that my action during the last five weeks has done some good though. I have now five factories to organise in Birmingham, ours and four others.

July 3rd My L.D.V. meeting at the works with five other firms' men. We are 150 strong and I am to be in command, with a good ex-officer under me. I shall have to be on duty in Birmingham at least once a week now I am afraid.

July 15th I got a pound of butter from Miss Gray at the Bay Tree hotel the other day, so at odd moments, by spreading it thickly on my toast and putting a lot of marmalade on too, I live as if there were no war. I see that Hitler has said he will be in London by July 27th. It sounds madder and madder and as though he is finding it hard to face the prospect of another winter and still keep up his people's morale.

Towards the end of July CW had moved in to the Tithe House, although he was taking his meals at the Cotswold House hotel.

July 24th This house is more and more delightful to me every day I spend in it. The evening sun streams in at my sitting room window, so that I have to draw the curtain as I write. It is one of the happiest, most easy and pleasant rooms I have seen. How I wish Fred [Griggs] were alive to see it.

July 28th In the evening to Nina's and the Shanks there and Sir Sydney Cockerell[201]. A story told by Shanks about J.B. Priestley who was being pestered by one of his admirers as to his preferences on modern writers and books. Asked what he thought of David Garnett's *Lady into Fox*, he answered that it was the best story about a lady being turned into a fox that had ever been written.

August 7th Last night I spent in Birmingham after a successful drill in the Gas Works yard. All day working at it [Home Guard], but it is getting clearer now and will be organised in a week or so. I feel tired, and yet stimulated as I have never been before. There is a certain happiness in corporative effort and I have a sense of having sought and found and carried out a duty. It is exhausting

---

201   Sir Sydney Carlyle Cockerell, 1867-1962. A disciple of Ruskin, he had worked as secretary to William Morris, and was later Director of the Fitzwilliam Museum, Cambridge from 1908 to 1937.

and late work in about the least congenial place imaginable, yet it gives me an almost mystical pleasure. I feel fit, mentally and physically through self-discipline and happy because I have created something literally from nothing, something which no one would have created if I had not. And I find in my heart a warm and humorous and ironical love of the people I am dealing with, rough Birmingham working men.

August 16th The last two nights in Birmingham and I have now got things fairly straight with my Home Guard (L.D.V.) company. We have uniforms for all; 25 rifles; and 1000 rounds of ammunition; and I have a good revolver, which I carry with me in my hip pocket. We start patrols on Saturday night. I have enjoyed the work very much and do not grudge an hour of the time. They are all such decent men and so keen and quietly determined to do their job. But is it a real joy to get back here and I love this house more and more.

August 21st I stayed last night at the works and went on at 6.30 and supervised the patrols, stayed till 12 and had my dinner with the men, slept at the works, and got up at six to see the men dismissed. No raids and a quiet night. My dinner: stew on an enamel plate; bread and cheese; and tea made with sticky condensed milk.

I wonder why I am so much happier. Chiefly it is because I have given myself up again, I think, have cut my threads, which I had bound round myself, and with which I had put myself into my ivory tower, and accepted rootlessness in a measure, and answered my sense of duty. I have submerged myself in the needs of my job, a purely voluntary one, and it is a good thing, a period of spiritual exercise. Also there is another reason: I <u>can</u> manage and influence and get the good out of men, and I am doing it on a bigger scale and to use an Americanism, it makes me feel good. One of the men at the works came to me the other day and said would I excuse him, but he wanted to tell me how proud they all were of me. It is very nice to hear such things. The canal banks, the gasworks, the empty streets at midnight last night were queer and almost beautiful, deserted, except for us and the rats and cats.

August 25th I had just got to bed on Friday at the works and had had a short sleep when there was a lot of gunfire, and some bombs dropped, then the alarm was sounded. I got up and went round to the Guard Room to the men and found them out, under cover of the Gas Works wall. The rest of the night I spent going round with the patrols in the streets, and in the Air Raid Shelter under the works, occupied by the public. I did not feel the least nervousness, and of course the raid was not on our area, though quite near. The police are splendid; so kind and gentle with the children in the shelters, so liked by all the people. It was a fine experience, and I felt that by being there one can really do something.

August 27th A very bad raid on Birmingham last night, the worst so far. From four till ten the planes were coming over in ones and twos. Most of the bombs were dropped in the area where the works is, and there were two within 150 yards of it, and a lot of incendiaries, but the Home Guard put those out very well, half an hour before the Fire Brigade arrived. Two of the men on patrol were blown up on entry but were unhurt. From the train many charred buildings, but it is extraordinary how local the damage is. You walk along a street which is a heap of ruins and turn the corner, and in the next street the houses stand in all their ugly solidity, just as if they had never been touched since the Boer War, when they were probably built. All the men on duty seem to have behaved very well, but I am getting rather a lot of resignations on account of air raid difficulties at home. Robin Whitworth saw the whole of the raid from the roof of the B.B.C. building, where he was working. It is very odd, this life, and it is amazing how one grows used to the insecurity of it, daily demonstrated. Another few yards and the works would have been a mass of ruins; myself on duty and I might now be in hospital, or dead. And yet I have driven out here [Campden] in the August sun, a touch of autumn in the air, and have spent the evening in this house, which is symbolic of peace and the arts of peace, reading David Garnett's *Go She Must*.

Peace, beauty, the lovely red of my Morris curtains; the quiet harmony of my rooms; my books and prints; the light on the polished furniture; these things are all round me, and, though I can hardly believe it, are not any more of a dream than the death and destruction and fire last night in Birmingham, nor are those things any more real than the peace that I have created here. Life must be lived as a whole; to live well and to love well one must love good and evil as a whole.

September 1st A year ago I sat in my office listening to the news, waiting for the declaration of war, and expecting sudden mass bombing attacks which we could not have resisted effectively then, and watching life crumble all round me, the life I had grown up in since the last war. Now, a year later, I am sitting in my new house, not even begun then, in conditions which are only a little different from those then. By now one can accept the continuation of the external world of ordinary pleasures and comforts because one has accepted the closer reality of death and destruction. For a time that closer reality seemed to make anything which belonged to the pre-war world seem like a dream, because it was under a withheld sentence of death all the time. The sentence was more real than the reality of the world; now they have drawn level and life goes on, its values adjusted.

September 3ʳᵈ Yesterday Mrs Cresswell, Dr and Mrs Birch, Catherine Clark, Dorothy [Chatwin], Mrs Stracey-Clitheroe and her daughter, came for drinks in the morning. Nina and the Guineys came in the evening and the two Miss Hargreaves later. Nina came back to a cold supper and we had a pleasant hour or two together. I owe Ward £350 still and shall just get through this year I think. I have put on my old dinner suit again, as I always do in September, and my velvet jacket. Last year it seemed incongruous, but this year it seems only a pleasant reminder that war is only a temporary condition.

A man in Birmingham had his coffee house completely wrecked by a bomb. He borrowed and scraped together some chairs and some china and set up the pavement next day with a placard 'Open Air Café.' So we take life in this wonderful country.

September 7ᵗʰ A difficult but fairly uneventful night at the works, difficult because only 10 out of 22 men turned up and only one N.C.O. out of four. We managed all right but the slackness is getting very bad already and there is no power.

September 8ᵗʰ I have been looking round the nettle-covered wilderness that is to be the garden, and feel that my estimated £75 will be far exceeded. A call from Sir Percy Harris[202] and Sir Sydney Cockerell who admired the house very much.

---

202   Liberal politician, d. 1952

September 9th This air war seems to have begun on a bigger scale now and will no doubt rise to a crescendo we have not yet imagined, particularly in London and the South. Whether the Germans will decide that they have done enough to attempt an invasion remains to be seen. Lovely and peaceful here. Alarms of parachutists about, but that is more than doubtful I think. I have just read Coleridge's 'Fears in Solitude', written at the time of the expected invasion by Napoleon in 1798, and the fear went on till 1808 I suppose.

A girl in the town here was going to get married. The best man was in the army and asked for leave. He got it, but for the week after that in which the wedding had been arranged. The wedding was put off – but the bridegroom could only get the week's holiday he had arranged, so they went for their honeymoon first and came back on the day of the wedding and got married. England deserves to survive.

September 10th I begin to think that Hitler may yet try this invasion, and maybe towards the end of the month. A few parachute spies have already been caught, one on Saturday near Northampton.

September 14th To-day is supposed to be invasion day again, but I doubt if he will try it, but almost hope he does, for I feel sure we should defeat an attempt disastrously.

September 17th A great length of my boundary wall by the Almshouses has fallen down, the part that Keitley did last year. He ought to rebuild it free of charge but I doubt if he will. A letter from the vicar saying that he is ready to discuss his yapping dogs, so something has been achieved.

September 22nd The Vicar [Canon Brian O'Loughlin] came in last evening and we became superficially friendly again. He looked over the house and said he like it and we discussed the dogs and he said he would keep them away as much as possible. We parted apparently friends, but I don't want to have anything to do with him. He is a stupid and irritable individual and a liar and no more a Christian than I am myself, far less in my opinion.

I have old Harry Griffin starting to-morrow on the garden. He is a retired roadman with an old age pension and does as many hours as he can. He lives next door in the almshouses so it suits him. He says he can 'make a tidy mess on it in a month or two.' Keitley also starts my paving next week round the house. I have cut up all the felled apple trees and stacked the logs, a nice pile. It is a satisfying job, log sawing, and wood chopping. It is destructive and yet at the same time in a manner creative. A quiet night in Birmingham last night. I got home at two. I called at the Whitworths in my new uniform on my way in in the evening and Robin laughed himself sick to see me in uniform at all.

I have Fred Bennett the water diviner yesterday to see if I'd got a spring in the garden. He used to live in Campden but now lives at Upper Swell. He brought his little hazel forks and walked about, one branch of the fork held tightly, the other loose, so that it could turn in his fist. Suddenly it began, and the fork went round and round in his hand till the bark on the end he held tightly was twisted and torn. He said there was water at 12 to 18 feet between the house and the walnut tree. One day I may make a pool. (*He did not.*)

The starlings are chattering in the pear tree; the walnuts are falling; my fruit is picked; the lime tree in Leysbourne has gone golden in the last few days. Autumn is here. We have lived another year and I never thought we should a year ago.

September 28th Last night till two in Birmingham and then out by car. A quietish night, some bombs dropped, but none near. To-day paying bills and pottering. To the Naumans for a drink this evening and to see Nina after dinner. Sir Frank Brangwyn[203] has bought the house [New Dover's House] to store his collection of pictures and other treasures in, and is going to furnish part of it and let Nina stay on in the other part and look after it, which is good. From all one hears London is pretty badly knocked about now. I must go up soon. I am tempted to dare myself to stay there the night and see what a real raid is like.

September 29th The Robertses in this morning for a drink; Roberts, [his son] Hugh, Mrs Roberts, and Hugh's very attractive wife. Roberts has asked me if I will be a director of Super Oil Seals, a company I already have shares in, and of which he is Chairman. I said I would and hope it will come off. It

---

203 Sir Frank Brangwyn, R.A., R.B.A., R.W.S., 1867-1956. Largely self-taught, self-confident and cosmopolitan, he produced a huge number of works in many media, including powerful images during the First World War.

---

will mean another £250 a year to me and as they are on very important work, privileges as to petrol.

October 3ʳᵈ Last night during a warning period I went round eight public shelters with a warden to see what sort of task it would be to run a mobile canteen. It was an amazing sight. They were all in one of the slummiest parts of Birmingham. One, a huge series of trenches to hold 1300 people, had about 400 in. (There had not been any bombs dropped in the area lately; when there have it fills up for the next few nights.) There were narrow benches along the walls, long corridors about 8 feet wide and 10 feet high, with 6 feet of earth above. It was a maze, a catacomb. People of all sorts were there, old, young, sick, lame, blind, deaf; children sleeping with their faces unwashed, looking oddly innocent in the candlelight; old men and women whose wrinkles were lined with dirt and whose clothes were in rags; and suddenly the face, here and there, of a girl or a young mother who had remained lovely, or of an older woman whose eyes told that she had known love. Smell, darkness, foetidity, an air of despair and depression. Then suddenly, like the lovely face, that immortal, sublimely ordinary, astonishing, commonplace, spiritual, material, defiant, yielding thing, English humour, came out of the sordid grey deadness of the place and lit up one's thoughts, and made one remember that where our people are still alive there is hope and courage and irresistible strength. It was a sombre journey though. After the big shelter I went to others, one holding 500, one 100, and others 50 or so. If I write again it will be with eyes that have seen these things.

October 19ᵗʰ On Tuesday I went up to London by the 7.18 train and went to the Board of Trade and the Ministry of Home Security and in the afternoon I went to the Home Guard H.Q. and was very pleasantly received by a Major Westmacott who raised his eyebrows at my request to spend a night with a company and see what an air raid was really like, but he at once arranged for me to go out with a company in Westminster and telephoned to Sir Alexander Napier at battalion H.Q. in Upper Grosvenor Street. I went and saw him and he got hold of a Major Monney who took me round to company H.Q and introduced me to everyone and eventually left me at Buckingham Gate the H.Q. of No 1 Company, A Zone. I arranged to go back there at seven and went to Brown's where I was staying, and had some dinner. Soon after seven I walked down and reported. The warning went a little later and the barrage began and the bombs began to drop. The company commander's name was Cowan and he had a lot to do, so I sat on a bed in his office till he had finished and then went down into the bar with him and had some drinks. All the time the bombs were falling and the barrage was going. It seemed to be the convention to ignore the war completely, and I adopted the convention and found it good.

About 11 we went out to inspect posts, Cowan and myself and a Mr Cooper, a sergeant, a solicitor. What can I say of my first experience of a really bad air raid? I was not frightened. I felt a certain sense of humour develops rapidly as a sort of shield. I was very impressed by the beauty of London by moonlight with no street or house lights, a beauty of peace and age, and it was increased by the contrast of the destruction going on all round. The buildings were dyed pink by the light of the fires. It was unearthly and lovely. We went round the streets, visited the posts, spent a lot of our time going down on our bellies as the long wailing whistle of the falling bombs came towards us, and we survived. The noise was terrific, and yet there were spells of silence which made the streets suddenly seem like Campden.

A huge fire had started down the river at a furniture warehouse, and it lit up the tall buildings with an extraordinary pink glow and made me think of Wordsworth's sonnet as though I were upside down. We went up on the roof of Rochester St Police Station, where there were spotters, and saw the scene below, a scene of lovely sleeping roofs; of trees; of the river winding away; and of flashes, explosions, and descending flares that brilliantly lit up the roofs. There was the crackle of machine-gun fire; there were bursts of gunfire; cars and fire engines rushed past in the street below; and the planes zoomed down overhead as they dived to bomb the fires.

At about 8 Cowan said, 'I'm afraid it's not a very good show for you, old man.' At 9, 'Ah, they're putting up a better show for you now.' And at 11, when we went out, 'Quite a good show for you to-night.' At one, 'One of the best shows I've seen.' At two, 'A real blitz for you, old man.' After that we were too busy. Broken glass littered the streets by then, so that one walked on it like walking through autumn leaves, and bits of shell cases fell all round, pattering through the other noises like the sound of acorns on a still day in October. We inspected a block of flats that had had a near miss and found the walls inside plastered with splinters of glass, and in other rooms all the glass sucked out into the street. There were extraordinary effects to be seen: an undamaged building with all its windows intact between two completely shattered ones; a curtain sucked out through the joints of two sheets of plate glass, and the glass unbroken; a sentry blown into his sandbagged post and not hurt.

The general impression is difficult to give. One of destruction completely wanton; of calm bravery from people of every class, from civilians, soldiers, wardens, police, firemen; of entering a world where new conditions prevail, so that one adapts oneself to them at once, catching the manner from those around one. It was a strange experience and I should think I am one of the few who have been and sought it deliberately. I am glad that I did, for having done it I feel I can face almost anything.

I went on with Cowan and Cooper till 4.30. We visited the St James's tube station and saw the hundreds of people sleeping on the platforms. The smell of the people and the tube air was not pleasant but it was nice to get away from the bombs for a bit. The humour of the cockney wardens and police was marvellous. We went to the Y.M.C.A. canteen at the old Westminster Hospital and had some tea. It was full of drivers taking cover till morning, their buses in the streets outside. In the streets there were no civilians. Coming out again was not pleasant. I had a strong desire to go back and stay there, for I was very tired. It was 4.15. We went back to Buckingham Gate, going down on our stomachs a lot. At one point my tin hat fell off and rolled away into a gutter by the Army and Navy Stores and I felt as if I had no clothes on at all. The bomb fell in the next street, not down my neck as I felt it was going to do. Office windows crashed into the roadway. We got up and went on.

By five the raid was coming to an end. There were long silences. Once or twice more bombs were dropped, and the gun fire began again, and died down. Then, after a long silence, the all clear went. It was as though the nerve from an aching tooth had been killed. One relaxed at once and stretched, felt as though, from a confined space, one had entered a large room. Cowan had to go out again to post guards on shops to prevent looting. At 5.45 I walked back to Brown's through the grey dawn, having said good-bye to Cowan. He was dead beat if ever man was. I got to bed at 6 and ordered them to call me at 10. The safety of my bedroom was really wonderful, increased by the Edwardian air of the hotel and its conservative country quiet. In the morning I had an appointment at the Ministry of Health.

October 20th This afternoon Frank Nobes and Jigger James came with a tractor and a circular saw and cut up all the old beams from the tithe barn for me. They were good oak and ash, and as hard as nails, but they were no good for building work as they were full of nails. I now have a good ton or more of logs for the winter. Tea and Pope's 'Rape of the Lock' and afterwards to dinner at Wood Stanway. German planes over and a lot of gunfire Gloucester way.

November 18th Last night I slept for ten and a half hours, until 9.30 and I am spending the day indoors as it is raining, pressing my clothes, pottering and reading, and letting myself take refuge in my ivory tower. I have just realised that I must be one of the few who, 1. Do not possess a wireless. 2. Have never read a detective novel. 3. Have never done a crossword puzzle, and have never wanted to do any of those things.

November 20th A delightful day on Tuesday working in the garden with old Griffin till teatime. Then a smug, warm time by the fire as happy as if I had been sitting beside a woman I loved. Then came the German planes. From seven they came over continuously for hours and even dropped bombs here, up at Springhill, where there is a new camp, and hit, of all places, an isolated lodge quite a mile from any other house, and wounded some people in it. Birmingham suffered very badly and it was one of the worst raids we've had. A bomb fell in the street outside the works and broke a lot of glass, but so far no direct hit, though I expect one.

It was not to be long before CW's misgivings were fulfilled.

November 23rd This morning I have rung up the works, as I always do on a day when I do not go in now, and have got no reply. I fear the worst and have put in a call to the police station to find out.

November 24th While I was waiting for my call to the police Adams, the works manager, and Nicholls the secretary came in the works car, Adams, who had been on duty, grimy and white. The works was hit at 10.30 by a very powerful bomb and blown to bits and set on fire. I went in after giving Adams

---

and Nicholls lunch and Adams a bath, and saw it all. It is a heap of bricks and charred beams and twisted girders, except for two shops at one end, and part of the dispatch wing at the other end. There were no casualties either to the Home Guard or civilians, though the Home Guard room, the cellar, was cut off from outside and they had to use the narrow emergency exit. Quite a lot of stuff can be saved, and there will be quite a lot that was covered by insurance, but the building is a hopeless wreck. I think we may be able, if it is not hit again, to start up again in a limited way in a month or two, but it is a terrible scene of desolation and where to start quite baffles me – and also arouses my obstinacy. There is no office left, no phone, no light, no power, no typewriters, no records, nothing, not even a pencil. The most valuable papers are in the safes, which have not yet been opened, but they may not be usable. I have some stores of stationery here and copies of all our invoices. I face the task to-morrow. I came home via Berkswell in the hope of seeing Bill Huggins, who is home on leave, but he had gone to Eton to see his boys. Betty was there, and a lot of refugees, and the Bishop of Coventry, whom I like and told me about the terrible raid there on the awful Thursday night.[204]

November 26th Two days of hard work and I begin to see the situation more clearly. At first despair filled me, then an obstinate determination to go on, then alternations of one and the other, till the determination triumphed. It is going to be a hard task though, yet I <u>will</u> do it. I will not be beaten. The men, when I spoke to them and told them so cheered and clapped. They are, most of them, magnificent. Most of the important papers are safe and we have rescued the safes from the smouldering ruins and opened them and found their contents all legible. The loss will be at least £25,000, some of which we shall get back soon and some not till after the war – if and when we win it. I feel stimulated by the challenge and I know I can meet it if I make the effort. It is a good feeling, to accept such a challenge and face difficulty. If they hit us again though we shall be knocked out I am afraid.

November 27th Things are getting clearer. We have started some of the men on production in the undamaged shops and hope to borrow power in a few days and to get roofing materials in a week. The rest of the men, in gangs, are shovelling and wheeling away the debris and are working well, although they

---

204   Much of the historic centre of Coventry, including the Cathedral, had been destroyed on 14th November.

---

stray off to the pubs sometimes and I have to go and fetch them. My mind is made up: all my energy is directed on the object I wish to attain, and I feel confident in attaining it; therefore I am happy, though I am doing things I do not like doing and living a life I have tried to get free from for years.

November 28th Another day of struggles to bring order out of chaos, burnt papers, heaps of rubble, rusting machinery, with some success. We look like getting roofing done soon with the aid of the Reconstruction Panel and I hope to get the place fairly well at work in a month if we don't get hit again. My phone has arrived. I must settle down to work now for, having no office except a room in a nearby cottage for the whole staff, who work elbow to elbow, I have a lot to do here. I am now having a rough temporary office made under a sound bit of roof from old boards from the ruins and it will be done by Monday.

December 7th I have been all round Broadway and Shipston and Chipping Norton and Stow buying corrugated iron sheets for the roofs at the works and have got about 500, to be picked up.

December 8th It is extraordinary how much quiet, conscious pleasure I get from this house and from living in it with all my things. It is a better sort of pleasure perhaps, than that which comes from personal relationships. A house, a book, a garden, a print of beauty and refined restraint, cannot give one pain. The only way in which they can fail one is by being destroyed, and the loss of a loved possession is at least not the possession's fault.

December 12th Last night I went over to dine with Roberts at the Bay Tree Hotel at Burford and had a good dinner and lovely wines. A bad air raid going on all the time. They dropped some bombs on Gordon Russell's at Broadway and others on Cheltenham and Honeybourne and six in the fields here. Birmingham was badly hit again and an oil bomb burst in the air over the works and covered everything in a black film. We are getting on well and shall be going fairly into production by the New Year if we don't get hit again.

While I was dining with Roberts a telephone message came for him so say that the King [George VI] was visiting Fisher and Ludlow, the big motor body firm, of which he is chairman, near us, today. I went down with him after lunch at the Union Club and a small crowd of about 100 had gathered, and the King came, very simply, in a car, escorted by policemen, and went round the ruined factory. I was as near him as I shall ever be, a yard off at most, and saw him well. A nice, simple face, grave, tired, but in good health. He was in uniform, with a British Warm [greatcoat] on and very simply dressed. The Lord Mayor with his chains all round him looked very foolish. He talked to a few of the men; was shown round by Roberts; and in a few minutes went back to his car and drove off to a loud cheer from the little crowd, into the grey murky weather, along the streets of bombed buildings.

December 15th Charles Blakeman called yesterday with his young wife[205]. He has known her for five years and has lately got a week's leave to get married. She comes from Edinburgh and is an artist and almost a lady, and will suit him very well, I should think. He made her become a Catholic before he married her. They seem very happy and he is improved I think, at least in manners. I hope she won't make him into a prig however.

I have bought three Calvert[206] [woodcuts] to serve as a remembrance of the bombing of the works, for it is a good thing to celebrate a disaster: The Bride, The Chamber Idyll and The Sheep of his Pasture (£4 each). I got them from Colnaghi's through Nina, who heard that they had them, and I have always wanted them ever since Griggs introduced me to them twenty years ago.

During the last big raid some bombs were dropped near Saintbury, in Weston Park, and Cecily [Whitworth's] old spaniel bitch, Pig, hearing the explosions, got up and rushed round the house barking and snuffling about under all the chairs and beds, thinking that someone had shot a rabbit.

December 24th I went to a shop yesterday to buy a present and came away with three tins of Norwegian trout, two of prunes, two pots of French mustard, and two jars of honey. The shops are getting very empty. No raids to-night and dead silence. The invasion scare seems to be about again, but I do not credit it. I don't think the Germans have a ghost of a chance of winning, but I do begin to feel as though the war may drag on till it becomes a weary stalemate.

---

205   May Cassie, 1917-2000.
206   Edward Calvert, 1799-1883. One of the disciples of William Blake called 'The Ancients', he worked as an engraver of pastoral subjects on a small scale, turning to oil painting later in life.

CW spent Christmas with the Whitworths at Saintbury among a house-party of eight and 'talked a lot and danced about and kissed under mistletoe and were generally frivolous and dirty-minded.' The party went to Taunton Races on 26th December, where the Blunt (Cecily's) family were there in strength. They came back via Bristol 'far worse damaged than Birmingham' and the party came to the Tithe House on the 29th after CW had spent the day shooting at Hartwell, near Bibury, with the Parker Jervises. But his mood was sombre as the New Year approached.

December 30th Have paid all my bills and now I face the New Year with cut down expenses but a very much reduced income, despite my addition from Super Oil Seals. It may not be as bad as I think however. It is a grim year to face and I do it with a tired body and mind, but I <u>will</u> overcome my obstacles and go on, whatever comes. How empty my life has become, what a waste, emotionally; a desert, which I am crossing, still striving for the mirage I saw in my youth, but tired now and doubtful of its ever becoming reality. Writing is lower in me too that it ever has been before, the hope of really achieving anything by it, I mean. I am at a drear pitch and I go on.

~ 1941 ~

January 1ˢᵗ I now have this house [The Tithe House] all paid for and shall manage this year easily. My investments £8000 and the income from them £450, say about the same as last year, though their capital value is of course very much down. I have spent during the year, apart from the house: Housekeeping £172. Car £64. Clothes £48. Self £60 (I get a bigger expenses allowance from the works now). Various £106. Hunting £23.

An enjoyable party at the Cresswells last night; a sort of young people's party and dance for [their children] Phoebe and Estcourt at which I felt neither young nor old. All the girls I knew out hunting before the war as mere children have shot up about a foot, put their hair up and become dignified young women. A lot of rather oafish young men. I got home at two, rather on the verge of getting tight, for Cressy was very generous with his whisky.

January 6ᵗʰ Cold, wet and depressing all day and yet I am not very depressed, for the activity and occupation of getting things going again at the works keeps me from introspection – and even when I do burrow into myself I find myself happy, though I have many causes for being full of anxieties.

A letter from Bob Jeune[207] who used to take a furnished cottage here for hunting. He is married and living at the Dower House at Stratford and is in the Intelligence waiting to cross-examine German prisoners. He has a son a year old. What things I may do yet. He seemed as well confirmed an old bachelor as ever I have known in the old days.

From 7ᵗʰ January until the end of the month CW was ill with what began as exhaustion, but was eventually diagnosed as jaundice by Dr Birch, the Campden doctor, in whom CW had little confidence. This illness left CW weakened and obliged him to resign from the Home Guard. Confined to the Tithe House for several weeks, he read widely and wrote idyllically from there:

January 13ᵗʰ Have spent a day of blissful, rather tired and lazy enjoyment, ecstasy almost, in and about the house. I went upstairs to look out at the

---

207   Robert Dyne Jeune, 1892-1985 of Whaddon Manor, Glos. Served in the First World War reaching the rank of Captain. Seconded from Reserves to Intelligence Corps in July 1940. His son was Hugo.

church. It was lovely, severe, unusual, clear-cut, and the tombs and grass before it, and the pollarded limes were bathed in light and shadow of the same unearthly quality. From the other window, out over Campden, the little town lay asleep in the mist and its own smoke, and the smoke, lit by the sun here and there, curled away on the still air. There was a sense almost of spring in the air. A bird twittered an evening note or two; a blackbird called as it flew off; and all around, visible from my window, lay the hills, a great arc from Blockley Hill round to the Hoo, the rim of the familiar and lovely cup of land that I know and love so well. Beneath, Campden furled itself in sleep once more, for the thousandth time in its history, as yet unharmed by war.

Often at times like this I feel that I am part of a continuous chain of love from Blake, through Samuel Palmer and Griggs, love of the same beauty and perfection, and knowledge of the same hidden, quiet, ineffable peace, that is beyond human distortion or pain. Please whatever God there may be that Campden may stay unhurt, and that I may live, and be able to afford to live, and to be able to afford to give my days to loving it and the beauty in it for the rest of my life.

Slowly, thanks to a stream of visitors, reading and rest, a bland diet and Sanatogen, CW was better by the end of the month.

January 29th I went to the works this morning and found all going fairly well, though this weather has held them up a lot. I also saw A.P. Thompson [a specialist] and he gave me a very thorough sounding. He says I have had a very bad attack and he describes me as a worn man and says that I was probably in a very run down state before. He says the greatest danger is a recurrence and I have got to go very quietly for two or three months. In ordinary times, he said, he would have ordered anyone in my position abroad for a month. It is a pity they are not ordinary times, for there is nothing I should like more.

Nothing could suit me better however than his prescription for the next few months. I get free from the Home Guard now it is no longer vitally necessary, with a clear conscience; I go to the works three days a week and for short days only; and I spend the rest of my time here, in the place where, all my life, I have longed to spend the whole of it. I am going to take all the advantage I can of the situation, and have no doubt that the works will carry on as well as if I went every day. It is just the kind of illness I have longed for over and over again for the last few years. My only regret is that it is not peace-time and I cannot go abroad.

January 31ˢᵗ A day in Birmingham and none the worse for it. I got home at 5.30 after going to the works and Super Oil Seals. The thoughts that I think in my proper Campden world are, when I have been to Birmingham, like flowers that have been picked and put in water; the thoughts that I think when I have been at home all day are like flowers that still belong to their roots.

February 9ᵗʰ Christopher [Sandford] came to lunch and we went for a walk in the afternoon and to see Nina [Griggs] in the evening. To-day we went to see Ben and Fanny Chandler for tea, and to the Whitworths after. Audrey Chandler was at home and had a friend, Peg Lindsay, staying with her. Audrey very charming. She has improved very much in the last few years, has become a complete woman much more, maybe as a result of her rather sad excursion to Ceylon, *(see entry for 1ˢᵗ January 1939)* and her return unmarried, for such things mature one very much.

February 10ᵗʰ To-day I have agreed with our agents the amount of our claim on the Government for the damage; £33,000 odd. If we get that, even after the war, we shall be safe, even if we lose money now. I think though we shall be able to make profits again this year, if we are not hit again.

February 14ᵗʰ This evening quiet at home, reading and wondering why I can't or don't write any more. Where is that other world? When I think of it, it is as though it were something so intangible, so great that I cannot believe that I do not enter it now. Yet I do not. It is like air; like mist; sunlight; yet it <u>is</u> another world, a world apart, or I apart from it. Now it is as though I only knew it as one knows an unvisited foreign land, from photographs and books. Yet I do know it, know all about it; know its geography, its climate, its remotest valleys – but with my memory only. Sad it is – yet that I do not feel sadder is the saddest thing of all.

February 20ᵗʰ A cold day and a white blanket of snow on the hills, but I have been able to get out a bit and have dug another yard of my new path. I get huge lumps of stone out, the foundations of the old Tithe Barn, as I go along, and roots of nettles as thick as my fingers.

February 26th I am probably going to buy a pig from [Charlie] Ladbrook and get him to kill it on the quiet, and get the bacon and ham cured. About tea time Hudson and Mary [Poncia] came, in Mary's car. They stayed till 6.30 and I gave them a gallon of petrol to get home with. Hudson seems very well and quite normal again, and is painting. Mary nice, but thank God I didn't marry her.

March 1st Last night to a party at the Lindsays at Wormington with Audrey Chandler, with whom I have never yet warmed, as Keats put it. But she seemed ready to, and when we came back about one, came in for tea. Then we forgot the tea and had a lovely hour on the sofa. She is rather a darling and I hope that this first going out together may lead to our seeing more of each other. I shall leave it though and see if she comes again, as it is so difficult to tell whether one is wanted or not, at any rate for more than an evening like that.

March 6th A side of bacon and a ham lie, wrapped in newspaper, in the back of the car. Charlie Ladbrook came, winked, said would I go down in the car about eight. I went, and he brought these out. When I came to pay him he reminded me that I had lent him £10 years ago, which I had forgotten, and wouldn't take my money. I take it to be cured by a butcher in Birmingham to-morrow. The total weight is 63 lbs.

March 11th A very delightful week-end [with the Sandfords] at Eye, enjoying their lovely house and the quiet freedom they allow their guests. On Saturday we went to tea at Berrington[208] with Lord and Lady Cawley, the second generation of a cotton family, very pleasant. The house belonged to the Rodneys and Lord Rodney sold it to the family of the present Lord Cawley, lock, stock and barrel, with its Empire furniture, Rodney[209] battle pictures and all. They seem never to have touched it since, but have never become quite part of it. A Lancashire accent in such an atmosphere is odd at first. They are nice, simple people though.

March 15th My pleasure in this house goes on growing and gets greater, not less. I am in love with it and do not care to go far away from it. Everything,

---

208   Berrington Hall, Herefordshire, designed by Henry Holland, *circa* 1778-81. Now National Trust.
209   Admiral George Brydges Rodney, 1718-92. Victorious at the battles of Cape St Vincent, 1780 and Les Saintes, 1782; renowned for his pursuit of prize-money.

furniture, rooms, garden, proportions, colours, associations, pictures, books, sun at the windows, the little world I see from them, gives me joy. And to-night, sitting by the fire reading the life of [Andrew] Marvell[210], the room softly lit, the fire burning gaily, I feel as much in communion with what is good and desirable in life as I could be in any church in the world.

March 22nd To London yesterday. The West End, at least, is very little more damaged than it was in October. The shops are still full of things but very dear. Cigarettes, chocolates, silk pyjamas, ties, socks, things not to be had in the provinces, are plentiful, and in the restaurants there is every sort of dish, dear, but perfectly cooked and no hint of substitutes, except very good synthetic cream.

April 6th With a few plants from Evesham this morning and a basketful of oddments from Stanley Cottage garden my main bed is complete. Dr Birch tells me that there is a danger of another attack of jaundice for a year and insists that I have the X-ray. I alternate between wanting to ignore the whole thing and wanting to keep it up as a means of spending more of my time here and escaping from life if it gets too difficult. On the whole though I think I can escape neurotic escapism, though one can tell little about oneself, however critical one may be.

April 10th A very bad raid on Birmingham last night and a basket of incendiaries dropped on the works, but most of them fell on open ground and were put out. A lot of damage in the city and all the main streets badly hit and many fires. I walked up to [the centre] lunch and it was a scene of desolation; the streets roped off and buildings still burning and hoses being played on them. The stations were all right however, and the trains were running regularly. Everyone looked very tired, but all are calmer than last winter, not reacting with laughter too much, but dully set and bearing it. The sirens have just gone again here [Campden] and the planes are going over and a bomb has been dropped a few miles off. It looks like another bad night.

The cigarette shortage has been very bad and I have been smoking a pipe, which I don't like. I have found a firm in London now, though, who are going to send me 500 a month, which will partly keep me going. There is a bigger stream of planes than last night and I dread lest they should hit the works again.

---

210   Andrew Marvell, 1621 - 1678. Metaphysical poet and parliamentarian.

April 15th I feel very depressed about the war and am occupied by a kind of suspicion that the Germans may be too clever or too powerful for us in the end. Military genius and boldness of initiative they seem to have to a degree we do not allow for, and that, with their political unscrupulousness may overcome us in the end I fear. If that happens life will not be worth living.

April 16th Margaret Smith and Edith Lawrence and Claude Flight[211] have just called. He has been living for years in a cave [at Chantemerle] on the Seine between Paris and Rouen, which he bought for £2 freehold. He now lives with Edith Lawrence [at Donhead St Andrew] near Shaftesbury.

April 21st A perfect spring day, warm and fine, and everything coming to life. The cuckoo once, uncertainly, yesterday, and two or three times to-day. How tired one gets of him before he goes, yet how full of all the hope and promise and beauty of spring is in his call during the first weeks after he comes.

The news seems a little better, and I feel that we may yet hold on in Egypt till we can turn the scale[212]. If only we can, if only we can. I dare not hope for it yet, but it begins to seem possible. I start fire watching at the works again on Thursday and do not look forward to it.

CW had spent much of the time since recovering from jaundice creating the garden at the Tithe House. This included making a vegetable garden, planting apple trees, levelling the ground for a lawn, and creating an herbaceous border, for which 200 plants had been ordered from Suttons. The work was largely complete, including terracing, by the end of April.

April 23rd How much do we need our patron Saint to-day, his day. I feel very serious about our ability really to reach a victorious decision over Germany.

April 27th The Barbarians have entered Athens.

May 16th Have been working all day gravelling my path in the bottom garden, and have begun to arrange for the building of a summer-house there. I am

---

211   Claude Flight, 1881-1955. A follower of the Italian Futurists, he worked in linocut, a technique learned from Edith Lawrence, who was his second wife.

212   Rommel's Afrika Korps had taken much of Libya in his advance on Egypt, and Tobruk was under siege.

going to do it myself, using some of the beams from the old Tithe Barn and some timber I have got from a bombed house, and elm boards. The lawn is just beginning to show green, if you look at it lying down.

So far as food is concerned I seem to be well-off. I get eggs easily; I have my side of bacon; I get chocolates from Fortnum's, and tins of meat and fruit; synthetic cream sweetened with honey from Cornwall; cigarettes regularly from London; and I still have cheese left from my last lot from Ireland.

May 29th Yesterday to Luton and on to London; at Luton to see the Churchill tank, for which we [Super Oil Seals] are making seals. In London the damage seems much worse than when I was last there, yet the impression one gets is still of the vastness of the surviving city, with all its life going on smoothly. All round our office in Dane Street [Holborn] the damage is great and Red Lion Square and Theobalds Road are almost wiped out. A quiet night at Brown's. This morning to Fortnum's to buy stores, then to the Board of Trade, where I was partly successful in getting steel for export. I saw Danielle Darrieux in *Mademoiselle ma Mère*[213], not bad, but one is annoyed with the French, and somehow, though it shouldn't, that takes away from one's appreciation of French art for the moment.

June 2nd Yesterday Robin and Cecily [Whitworth] and Sanchia, Robin's sister who is so charming, to tea and I went back there [Saintbury] and Ted Lyon and Léon Goossens[214] the oboe player were there. Later I went in to the works to fire watch. Nothing happened and I got 7 hours sleep, but feel tired to-night.

June 13th This evening Russell Alexander, Norman Jewson, and Nina [Griggs] in for drinks. Russell looks old and worn and bears traces of his love affair [with Elizabeth Fairclough] in his face. It must have been a searing experience for a man like him. I have bought some sherry in Birmingham. Sheldons [of Shipston-on-Stour] have nothing but brown at 100/- a dozen left now. Am sending in my plans for the summer house to the local Council for approval to be passed. On Monday I go to Newcastle for a week.

---

213   Film made in 1938
214   1897-1988. The leading oboist of his day.

June 26ᵗʰ Sir Arthur Robinson, retired Parliamentary Secretary to the Ministry of Health, who has become a director of Super Oil Seals, to stay for the night. A delightful old man, full of sensitive appreciation of Campden, Shakespeare, Fred's work, Middleton Murry, and a hundred things that I appreciate too. I like him and shall enjoy working with him, I am sure.

June 29ᵗʰ I have been out to the Chandlers with Nina. To-morrow I am going to see Robin [Whitworth] at the F.A.U.[215] training unit at Northfield with Cecily. I was very struck by Audrey Chandler's attractiveness this evening. She has been at home with measles.

The following analysis of the war situation is interesting, in that it is written long before either El Alamein or Stalingrad, which are generally taken as the turning point of the war, but were not to happen for over a year. It also contains the only allusion in the Diary to the Battle of Britain, unusual in someone who seems to have followed the progress of the war with close interest.

It is early to say yet, but I feel we shall see the turning point of this war in our favour as last year, when Hitler, having taken France, failed to exploit his conquest by the immediate invasion of this country. His conquest of France, as it did not lead to that, has been of no direct service to him in his main object of beating us. Having failed then he has seen us grow stronger, has been beaten in the air, and now has to gamble on this mad invasion of Russia. His armies are sprawled out over the whole of Europe and he now faces a war of indefinite duration, with ever increasing attacks on his own country. I do not think Russia will fall as France did, if the will of her people to defend their soil is as strong: if, in other words, the Communist system has given the majority enough faith in the future to be worth fighting for – and that I feel is so. If it is, even with the military victories, Hitler will exhaust Germany, while we destroy her cities from the air. His oil reserves will be exhausted, the Roumanian oil fields bombed, and the Russian oil fields, if he gets them, destroyed before he does so. He cannot win now.

CW's somewhat rose-tinted view of communism was perhaps not so unusual at the time, when 'Uncle Joe' Stalin was seen as our staunch ally, rather than a murderous autocrat.

---

215   The Friends Ambulance Unit had been founded by the Quakers in 1914 and was staffed largely by conscientious objectors (of whom Robin Whitworth was one.)   Manor Farm at Northfield, Birmingham, was the home of Dame Elizabeth Cadbury.

The dilemma of the Catholics amuses me. I would prefer or even welcome Communism here before Catholicism. The Catholics see in our fighting alliance with Russia a menace to their fossilised but great religion. I see in it hope, hope that a true system of social reform will come to England, wrought out of foreign dreaming and English practical resource.

June 30th Yesterday to see Robin Whitworth in his training camp, rather depressed, poor dear, at being suddenly cut off from all his life and set, a rather delicate plant, among all the male discomforts of a camp: no baths; a rough bed; companions who do not wash; bare scrubbed tables. (He has had a bath every day of his life, and often two.) It will do him good I think and if it roughens him and does not break him will be the best thing for him. Eton, Oxford, a rich wife, all the comforts he could want – then this. He will feel it, but he ought to, for his own growth.

July 6th After a board meeting I asked Roberts if he would get me one or two more directorships, if such power came his way, and he said he would. If, as I suppose now, I shall have to go on earning an income after the war, I would rather do it that way than any other. He tells me that he knows I have qualities of detachment and judgement that are very rare, and I am glad he realises it, for I think I have. One can at least be immodest in one's diary.

After tea I got 24 eggs, and on to [the Woods at] Wood Stanway to dinner. There they all seem well. Winifrid seems well and happy. She has a more active life to lead now and it does her good. The garden is a sort of suburban-arcadian idyll, full to bursting of onions, lettuce, cabbages, beehives, hens, everything, and the whole family works at it in spasms. It was good to see Winifrid, but we have allowed so much dead time to get between us that we cannot talk intimately about ourselves now.

July 12th I went down to the garage to get the car seen to, and walked back and called to see Kilkelly the estate agent about selling my shop property [the former Live and Let Live.] I have told him to sell at anything over £2000. When I got back Hartwell had arrived with a load of gravel for the concrete foundations of the summer house, and I stayed and saw it unloaded and went round to the Eight Bells and had a drink with him. A large card was on the door saying that the pub was closed as there was no beer[216], but we went round the back and found Tom Barnes, Harry Griffin, old Gabb, the postman, Arthur Margetts, Lawrence Ladbrook and three Gordon Highlanders all drinking there and I spent a pleasant half hour with them and had three half pints of cider.

July 22nd   Struggles at the works to get the financial chaos straight; work in the garden making steps; reading in the evenings at Toynbee[217]; bed about twelve; all with my joy in this house and garden woven through, like a silver and gold thread in a dun fabric.

July 24th   Fire watching last night at the works, dinner with Robin at the Queen's [Hotel] first. Toynbee is good to read now. He gives one a broader view of life as it is happening round one with such apparently appalling speed. It seems to me that both this and the last war (they are one) is a struggle between the country which seeks to impose on the world a political world order equivalent to the economic world order of Western civilisation by force (Germany) and those who want to let the results of economic development impose themselves in peace on men. It is an attempt to be Western civilisation's 'Roman Empire'.   One thing is certain: either the widespread economic net of western civilisation must be followed by a world political order that corresponds to it in extent, or the whole world must be subject to a long misery of wars. It is for the privilege of leading the world freely to create its own political order, a flexible, living thing, rather than to have it forced, a dead framework, on it, that we are fighting now. The real task is the elimination of parochial nationalism – by force and the substitution of foreign overlord-ship, or by free action and union.

July 26th   Today I had the good fortune to hear that Dr Kennard at Mickleton was retiring and had sold his practice and house and wanted to sell his (new) Atco lawn mower. I rang him up and went to tea and wrote a cheque for £28 and brought it back in the trailer. Now I can cut my lawn quickly and without exhaustion.

---

216   In those days, the Eight Bells was a beer and cider house only.
217   Arnold Joseph Toynbee, C.H. 1889-1975. Influential author of *A Study of History*, the first six volumes of which, published between 1934 and 1939, would have been available to CW; a further four were published after the war.

July 29ᵗʰ   Only a year and three days ago I came to live in this house, and now I feel as though I had been there all my life. At the end of July last year also I went to a London that had suffered no air raids and spent a very pleasant evening there. There had not been a bomb dropped on Birmingham and there was little thought of the works ever being the ruin it is now.

July 31ˢᵗ   Back from London by the 6.05, a crowded train with the corridors full. I went to see the Board of Trade about getting payment for the money we have spent on machinery. When one compares London now with London a year ago, what a vast and melancholy difference there is. And yet how wonderfully it stands and goes on with its life; how it persists in being itself. I stayed at Brown's and dined at the Aperitif in Jermyn Street quite well, though expensively. My bill was 17/-, for smoked salmon, chicken, raspberry tart, anchovies on toast, and a carafe of white wine. This morning I went shopping and bought sultanas, crystallised lemon, shortbread, passion fruit cordial, saccharine, orange juice, oatmeal, vermouth, and sherry, at Fortnum's, to be sent on.

I went up with an Irishman from Wexford, who told me that they had no petrol for January to March at all; they have lots of butter, beef and potatoes, but no coal or paraffin; that Ireland is full of Germans and Italians; and that a lot of the younger Irish are leaving the country to work here or join up.

August 3ʳᵈ   Twenty-seven years ago to-morrow the convulsion which has gone on and on, dismembering the world and throwing up incalculable new forces, and which has produced two gigantic wars, began. The whole of my adult life has been lived under its direct or muffled threat. Will it go on as long as I live, till the world I was born into ceases to be recognisable, even by its traces, or will it end soon, and a new world with kinship with the old begin to emerge?

A lovely day. I have been working on the summer house. To supper at the Campagnacs and the Mackails here when I got back. They come and perch on a seat in the garden like two birds, and twitter and then often go off without one seeing them. They are a couple who belong entirely to the world that is dying, and they know it, and watch this world's struggles as though already they had ceased to belong to it.

August 5th   Yesterday to the Horse Gymkhana in aid of the Red Cross at Court Piece Farm. Like a pre-war dream, even to the rain that fell nearly all afternoon. A huge number of entries, mostly children, and some very good ponies. A big crowd and hundreds of cars; all the North Cotswold [Hunt] people, dressed as they were two years ago, and their minds little altered. It is significant for the future, and not in the best sense, that even this form of the old life goes on, both outwardly and inwardly here, while in Germany and Russia the fate of Europe is being fought out. I feel that they will be the countries that will lead civilisation in the more distant future, even if we come out of this war comparatively unscathed and victorious, because they will have had the challenge of actual war in their midst, while we, even with our bombing, have only the effects of war. Yet to see that gathering of country people, with all their old virtues and faults; the horses; the white-painted jumps; the judges; the cars; the children; the farmers, landowners, people; all gathered together as if nothing were happening but that Gymkhana, created in me a delicious nostalgia.

August 11th   I met [Sir Frank] Brangwyn on Saturday. I had always thought from his name and his work that he was a big broad man, but he is a little pink and white fellow, more like Chaucer's December than anyone I have seen, with a little thin forked white beard and the mildest face imaginable. He is not going to stay long, but goes back to Ditchling. Nina stays on there[218] indefinitely.

August 16th   Kilkelly, the land agent, has just rung up to say that he has an offer for my shop property [the Live and Let Live] of £2000 and I have decided to take it. I shall invest the money in good industrial shares and get as much or a little more income and none of the bother. I am delighted.

CW spent the next fortnight in Scotland visiting shipyards on the Clyde, at Leith and Burntisland, and at Aberdeen. He noted: 'More confirmation of our success in the Battle of the Atlantic; a convoy of over 100 ships through safely recently and the escorting vessels destroyed 14 submarines.' *In Glasgow he stayed in a* 'large and very expensive hotel, swarming with Americans and Canadians who have just arrived. They have filled the lounge and the dining room with their voices and laughter and persons.'

---

218   At New Dover's House, which Brangwyn had acquired to store his pictures, allowing Nina Griggs to go on living there.

August 24th A pleasant day settling back again into the thoughts and habits that belong to me here, cutting the lawn, reading the Observer, having tea with the Whitworths, and going to hear Churchill's speech[219], very fine. Whenever I hear him I feel a greater man than I know I am. Gordon Russell there, and Bernard Newdigate[220].

August 30th Bernard Newdigate has called and we spent an hour looking up references to Dover's Hill and the games for his notes to his Drayton's *Polyolbion*. He is a pleasant, dry old man, of great refinement, but it is very difficult to get beyond the wooden and polished exterior he presents to the world. He is mad about Drayton and it has been his life's hobby to edit and study him.

It may have been this conversation that eventually led to CW writing his study Robert Dover and the Cotswold Games, *published in 1962.*

September 1st I took Winifrid to Bath and Bristol with me, where I had business and drove 160 miles, quite an experience these days. A successful visit to Bristol, where I was lucky enough to get an introduction to the Petrol people and got my allowance increased to 20 gallons a month, which I have been trying to get for the last two years. On to Bath[221], which looked lovely, and a visit to the Admiralty and a marvellous tea at Fortt's, then back over the hills.

September 8th A long letter from Christopher Sandford who, it turns out, is now a staff captain in the Home Guard intelligence. He lives at home, has cars and dispatch riders and clerks, and covers three counties. He has asked me to be a director of the Chiswick Press but I have asked for more information. He holds over half the shares but seems to get no profits.

September 23rd It is odd how no one can understand how I can live here alone and not be miserable and bored. They all say: 'Why don't you marry? What do you do? Don't you long for someone to talk to? Aren't you miserable sleeping alone?' and so on. And I can't tell them that I do not hope for love to

---

219   Following his meeting with President Roosevelt on board H.M.S. *Prince of Wales* at Placentia Bay, Newfoundland.
220   Bernard Henry Newdigate, 1869 - 1944. Type and book designer with the Shakespeare Head Press.
221   The so-called Baedeker Raids on the city were to come in April 1942. Part of Admiralty Headquarters had been evacuated there in 1939.

come into my life again. I can only say that I am quite happy; that I like solitude and privacy; that I am never bored; that I read and talk to myself if there is no one else to talk to. To see anyone living a life that would be misery to them makes other people exasperated and puzzled I suppose.

October 1st   I came down from London with Philip Chandler, Audrey's brother, and we drank gin and tonic water and had dinner together and a bottle of claret and had quite an enjoyable journey. He and Audrey came in this evening for a drink – Audrey very attractive to me, and I am going to meet her in Evesham (where she is nursing) [for the Voluntary Aid Department] for dinner one night next week.

October 6th   This evening to see Robin and Cecily [Whitworth], Robin back from the week-end and going to take charge in Liverpool of a new F.A.U. unit there. Stephen Fry[222], back from America, was there. He came over in a bomber at 30,000 feet and had to wear his oxygen mask a lot, and landed in Scotland. He goes back on the 20th. He feels sure they will repeal the Neutrality Act soon and declare war eventually, but says the average American sees the war as a thing far off and not affecting his ordinary life at all. Yet all, even the isolationists, want to see us win. It is difficult to generalise about so vast a country, but I feel from what he said that America will not let us down.

October 13th   Yesterday Audrey Chandler came to supper here. Somehow I had known, ever since I took her to the Lindsay's dance at Wormington, that there was something between us that might come to life. I have always liked her and been attracted by her, but I have been put off by her never having made any noticeable effort to put herself in my way. Last night we kissed and talked and drank sherry and ate as naturally as could be, and then we came back into this room and kissed again, and it became obvious that we should make love.

Later...... as film captions used to say:

She said, very subtly and quietly, 'I am so terribly fond of you.' When I know I am loved I love; so it has been, and so it was again. At once, after these words, she became the most loveable and desirable person in the world, and we lay

---

222   1900-1979, son of C.B. Fry, the famous cricketer, and a cricketer himself. He worked for the B.B.C.

there talking till twelve, and I was extraordinarily happy, and it seemed as though I had at last found the way out of my deadness of spirit. Then she had to go, and I saw her off into the dark night, as she drove down to Fladbury, where she is nursing now, and went back to bed with a strange exaltation in my heart, as though something were revealed to me that I had not dreamt of before.

I had never imagined that she felt like that, and of course I realised that with her, and with her feeling so, and with myself as I am, to go on would lead us to marriage. I knew it at once, instinctively, and as we lay there, told her some of my history, as it is related in this diary, so that she should not be under any illusions about me. I told her too that I saw that if we were to love each other it meant marriage, and that I had made up my mind that I would not marry unless I found myself so much in love that I could not help myself. I did not commit myself, neither did I close the door, either on her or myself.

The remaining pages of the diary are, not surprisingly, given over to the rapid growth of the love between CW and Audrey Chandler, analysed with his usual acuteness, but leading a mere two weeks later to the realisation that he was, at the age of nearly 40, to throw aside his old, self-sufficient bachelor life and all that was implied by that. On the last day of October the understanding that they had both reached was, typically, put into writing by CW, who carried the letter in his pocket for two days before entrusting it into the hands of Charlie Ladbrook, who was working as a postman.

There followed all the excitement and frustration of arranging for a wedding in wartime. The engagement ring was bought at Asprey's (£66), furniture and other necessities for the Tithe House at Harrod's and John Lewis, a piano from Broadwood's in Birmingham (Audrey was an accomplished pianist) and, a telling symbol of the change in CW's life, a radiogram, which owing to wartime scarcity, cost £79 – more than the engagement ring – and some string-pulling. A committee of English bed manufacturers, of which CW was chairman, raised a subscription of £45, which went to buying prints by Graham Sutherland and Henry Rushbury. The diary comes to an end on 30th December and the couple were married at Mickleton Church on 17th January 1942; the honeymoon was spent at Brown's Hotel in London.

~ Afterword ~

I was born in December 1942 and my sister Judith in July 1945. It was clear that the Tithe House, built as a bachelor's home as it had been (it has been enlarged since), was becoming too small for a family of four, and in January 1947, in the depths of that harsh winter, we moved to The Malt House, Broad Campden. My father continued to manage the works, and with his directorships of Super Oil Seals and of Nu-Way, heating engineers in Droitwich, was busy until the mid 1950s. The works, S.B. Whitfield & Co Ltd, was sold to a larger company then, and no longer exists. There was no more hunting, although the family sometimes followed hounds by car. The Malt House had a large garden and vegetable garden, field and mature cherry orchard and was run for a few years as a market garden, worked by Ernest 'Peony' Buckland, assisted for a time by the genial Ernst, a German prisoner of war, and producing a modest quantity of bacon each year, as well as the crop of cherries, for which a buyer was found in good years.

As my father acknowledges in the diary, the creative streak in him for writing had dwindled before his marriage, but this was replaced by a deep interest in local history, which, combined with his love of Campden, resulted first in *A History of Chipping Campden*, published in 1958, then *Robert Dover and the Cotswold Games* in 1962. His researches led him to the local ramifications of Shakespeare's friends and family, resulting in a number of pamphlets and articles for the *Notes and Queries* of the Bristol and Gloucester Archaeological Society. He was elected a Fellow of the Society of Antiquaries. He continued his habit of writing poetry, but nothing for publication, and left several collections of short poems in typescript. My father did revive a sporadic diary habit in the 1950s, but these later volumes have sadly not survived.

By the early 1960s my mother had begun to suffer from Multiple Sclerosis, a condition whose ineluctable progress and effect on my mother gradually drove my father into a melancholic state where pity, anger and helplessness, combined with his heavy smoking habit, resulted in a series of strokes, from which he died in March 1967, just short of his 65th birthday. Some years later, when the Tithe House came on to the market again, my mother bought it back and had it enlarged by one bay to the south, as by then she was confined to a wheel-chair and life on the ground floor. She died there in December 1993.

Most of the work of transcription has taken place within the sound, every fifteen minutes, and the full ring on Tuesday evenings and Sunday mornings, of the bells of Mickleton Church, where my parents were married.

Paul Whitfield

~ Campden Windows ~

Written in October 1926 for F.L. Griggs's proposed work on Campden, which was published posthumously in 1940 but without poems. CW sent the poem out as a Christmas card in 1934.

From my front window I can see
The quiet street, green with grass and tree,
And houses, watching timelessly
Peace surely found;
And people passing nod to me,
On errands bound.

The cuckoo passes overhead,
As though the empty roadway led
From copse to copse, where bushes shed
May flowers like snow;
And sleeping dogs seem feigning dead,
The whole day through.

At evening, from my other window,
Gold-bright the hills and woods all grow,
And like a tide the green hills flow
Round orchard walls,
And kindly gardens that all know
The blackbirds' calls.

Tranquil there the cattle graze,
And there a foal, my friend three days,
Sets me off chuckling as I gaze,
When, all of a sudden,
He leaps and throws his legs all ways,
So small and wooden.

Each year I live here still I find
Grave Nature, with her grey eyes, kind,
And, in my tedious self confined,
No sooner meet her,
Than all the shy thoughts in my mind
Run off to greet her.

~ Christopher Whitfield ~
~ A Bibliography ~

Five Poems, *privately printed for the author by Chamberlain & Sons, Campden, 1925, edition of 500 copies, 150 copies sold at 1s 2d, the remainder mostly burnt.*

The Village and Other Poems, *The Alcuin Press, Chipping Campden, 1928, 100 signed and numbered copies; 55 sold at 10s. (The first publication by the Alcuin Press.)*

The Wood Gatherer and Other Poems, *printed by the Crypt House Press Ltd., Gloucester and London, 1931, 100 numbered copies.*

A Child's Day and Other Poems, *printed by the Newarke Printing Co Ltd., Leicester and London, 1935, for private circulation, 50 copies.*

A Winter Morning, *25 copies printed for private circulation, 1941.*

Mr Chambers and Persephone, *with wood engravings by Dorothea Braby, the Golden Cockerel Press, 1937. Limited edition of 150 copies, unlimited edition of about 1000 copies, some destroyed in the Blitz.*

A World of One's Own, Twenty-Four Essays, *woodcut engravings by Geoffrey Miller, Country Life Ltd, 1938, over 1,000 copies sold.*

Lady from Yesterday, *with 5 wood engravings by Lettice Sandford, The Golden Cockerel Press, 1939.*

Miss Piper's Trouble, *John Lane The Bodley Head, 1940.*

Together and Alone, two short novels, *with engravings by John O'Connor, the Golden Cockerel Press 1945, 500 copies, of which 100 quarter- bound in white morocco.*

A History of Chipping Campden, *Shakespeare Head Press, Eton, 1958.*

Captain Robert Dover and the Cotswold Games. Annalia Dubrensia *edited by Christopher Whitfield, Henry Sotheran Ltd, 1962.*

A Guide to Chipping Campden Parish Church, *1961.*

Articles, 1961-1967, see CADHAS Notes & Queries, Vol. VI No I, 2008, article by John Taplin, for references:

The Kinship of Thomas Combe II, William Reynolds and William Shakespeare.

Lionel Cranfield and the rectory of Campden.

The parentage and connexions of William Combe of Warwick.

Some aspects of the Aston-Sambache case, 1600-1602.

Shakespeare's Gloucestershire contemporaries and the Essex Rising.

Sir Lewis Lewknor and The Merchant of Venice: a suggested connexion.

Four town-clerks of Stratford-upon-Avon, 1603-1635.

Thomas Greene: Shakespeare's Cousin.

Sir Edward Greville of Milcote and Clifford Chambers, the Muses' Quiet Port.

Some of Shakespeare's contemporaries at the Middle Temple.

Anthony and John Nash; Shakespeare's legatees.

Several volumes of poems and stories and 'A Calendar of Characters' remain unpublished in typescript.

~ Family Tree ~

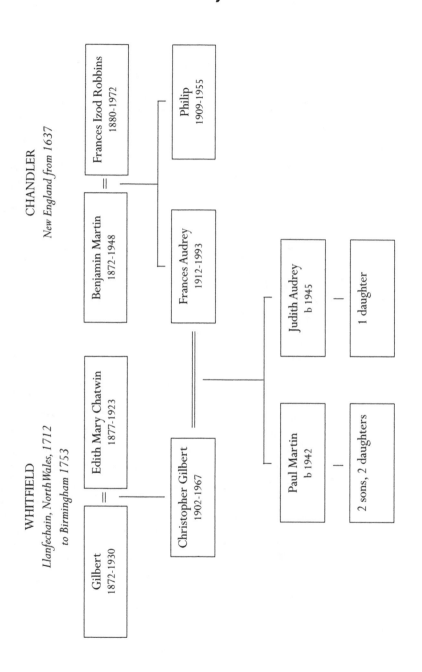

CHANDLER
New England from 1637

Frances Izod Robbins
1880-1972

=

Benjamin Martin
1872-1948

Philip
1909-1955

Frances Audrey
1912-1993

WHITFIELD
Llanfechain, North Wales, 1712
to Birmingham 1753

Edith Mary Chatwin
1877-1923

=

Gilbert
1872-1930

Christopher Gilbert
1902-1967

Judith Audrey
b 1945

1 daughter

Paul Martin
b 1942

2 sons, 2 daughters

Index